Women's rights

MANCHESTER
1824

Manchester University Press

DOCUMENTS IN MODERN HISTORY

Series editor:
Dr G. H. Bennett (University of Plymouth)

Series advisor:
Dr Kevin Jefferys (University of Plymouth)

The *Documents in Modern History* series offers collections of documents on the most widely debated and studied topics in modern British and international history. The volumes place fresh primary material alongside more familiar texts, and provide thought-provoking introductions to place the documents in their wider historical context.

All volumes in the series are comprehensive and broad-ranging. They provide the ideal course textbook for sixth-form students, first-year undergraduates and beyond.

Also available:

Anglo-American relations since 1939
John Baylis

Roosevelt's peacetime administrations, 1933–41: a documentary history of the New Deal years
Harry Bennett

The Labour party: 'socialism' and society since 1951
Steven Fielding

From Beveridge to Blair: the first fifty years of Britain's welfare state 1948–98
Margaret Jones and Rodney Lowe

Television and the press since 1945
Ralph Negrine

The impact of immigration in post-war Britain
Panikos Panayi

The Vietnam wars
Kevin Ruane

Britain in the Second World War: a social history
Harold L. Smith

British trade unions 1945–95
Chris Wrigley

Documents in Modern History

Women's rights
Struggles and feminism in Britain c.1770–1970

Fiona A. Montgomery

Manchester University Press
Manchester and New York
distributed exclusively in the USA by Palgrave

Published by Manchester University Press
Oxford Road, Manchester M13 9NR, UK
and Room 400, 175 Fifth Avenue, New York, NY 10010, USA
www.manchesteruniversitypress.co.uk

Distributed exclusively in the USA by
Palgrave, 175 Fifth Avenue, New York,
NY 10010, USA

Distributed exclusively in Canada by
UBC Press, University of British Columbia, 2029 West Mall,
Vancouver, BC, Canada V6T 1Z2

British Library Cataloguing-in-Publication Data
A catalogue record for this book is available from the British Library

Library of Congress Cataloging-in-Publication Data applied for

ISBN   0 7190 6954 8   *hardback*
EAN   978 0 7190 6954 3
ISBN   0 7190 6955 6   *paperback*
EAN   978 0 7190 6955 0

First published 2006

15 14 13 12 11 10 09 08 07 06   10 9 8 7 6 5 4 3 2 1

Typeset
by SNP Best-set Typesetter Ltd., Hong Kong

Printed in Great Britain
by Bell & Bain Ltd, Glasgow

Contents

Acknowledgements

Thanks are due to: Jill Palmer who battled with good humour both with my writing and putting the book into house style and provided much general support; Carol Slade, Rosemary Senior and Jane Jones who did preparatory typing; Bath Spa University Library and especially Maggie Collins and Anne Dowle of the inter-library loans department who managed to secure copies of many obscure works and Ann Siswell who advised on copyright; University of Glasgow library, the Mitchell Library Glasgow and the British Library. Many colleagues provided encouragement, particularly Elaine Chalus (who gave ideas for a change of title), Catherine Robinson and Denise Cush. The staff at Manchester University Press were extremely helpful, especially in answering queries. Lastly, but by no means least, my family who put up with the writing and to whom the work is dedicated.

Every effort has been made to keep within the 'fair dealing' copyright agreement. If any proper acknowledgement has not been made, copyright holders are invited to inform us of the oversight.

Introduction

Women in the 1780s had few rights, especially if married: they could not vote, make a contract, sue or be sued in their own names and their earnings or incomes belonged to their husbands. By the 1970s, the situation had changed: full enfranchisement had been secured in 1928 and equal pay and an end to sexual discrimination in theory, if not always in fact, had been secured. Women had struggled over two centuries with progress not being linear. Not all of women's rights were secured solely by the activity of women themselves. The equality legislation of the 1970s, for example, owed a debt to the European Union.

Furthermore, one of the greatest boons for women was the advent of effective contraception which both gave women improved health and released them from the burden of raising and nursing children almost constantly throughout their adult lives. Prior to this, between the ages of twenty-five and forty a woman was almost always either pregnant or nursing a child. Smaller families with two children born closer together freed women to go into employment. However, this was not as simple as it might seem. Having fewer children meant that women were now expected to devote more time to parenting, and any defects in children's behaviour such as juvenile delinquency were laid at the mother's door. Women were still responsible for the majority of domestic tasks and when men helped with childcare, they tended to do the more rewarding aspects (the ones which women enjoyed!) such as playing with their children rather than nappy changing.

Opportunities by the 1970s had been widened therefore, but equality was still not achieved. Within the labour force, women remain underrepresented in many areas and even now are paid less. Women continue to suffer domestic violence to a greater extent than men and many are still sexually exploited. And, it was not until the 1990s that working-class women benefited from the educational reforms to the same extent as the middle classes.

For convenience this collection of documents is divided into seven themes: law, marriage and family, education, work, politics, health and sexuality. These chapters are not, however, exclusive with many documents at home in more than one section. Thus the struggle to gain the right for a woman to choose whether or not to have an abortion would be equally valid in both chapters on health and sexuality.

The book begins with law since it was law which created contemporary understanding of what constituted 'a woman' and the behaviour she should follow. Over the period, women gained rights over their children, their own bodies as well as a political presence. Care must be taken, however, with the use of the category 'woman'. All women did not have the same work experience: class and later ethnicity affected women's lives.

The chapter on marriage, motherhood and the family details changes in family structure and size which also reflected class difference. In the 1780s, the end of marriage was usually occasioned by death, by the 1970s divorce was common and more couples were making a definite decision to cohabit. Feminists in the late nineteenth century highlighted the lack of financial independence for women within marriage and campaigned for this to enable women to be in a position to make a genuine choice as to whether to marry and not simply be forced into marriage since there was no viable alternative to it. Instead of being a commercial contract, marriage would then move towards a relationship of equality. This would be furthered by granting women custody rights over their children, making divorce available to them and containing domestic violence – all of which required legal action, again demonstrating the cross-over between themes.

Education and work are similarly intertwined. Writers such as Mary Wollstonecraft were aware of the need to provide careers for women to ensure financial independence and this is turn required an education moving beyond mere 'accomplishments'. For a time, working-class girls enjoyed a superior education to that of their middle-class sisters. Women were reckoned to possess a form of 'moral superiority' which gave them a unique understanding of the needs of mothers, children, the sick and the weak and allowed middle-class women to take part in activities related to these areas. Women's war work revealed that women could do men's jobs whether it be in engineering, on the land, transport or in the civil services. Such gains in educational opportunities were to be short-lived as far as World War I was concerned and it was only labour shortages in the 1950s which occasioned more part-time work for women. World War II however led to the creation of a 'cradle to the grave' welfare state which with the foundation of the National Heath Service improved women's health.

In whatever area women were concerned, they always had to overcome the conviction that a woman's place was in the home to enable them to speak out and campaign. This was particularly true in relation to politics and sexuality thus there was a tendency initially to keep sex campaigns separate to avoid negative publicity. Women were aware of such constraints. Paradoxically too, while it may have been more difficult in one sense for middle-class women to protest in public, in another they had all the advantages of time, connections and money given by their class. The sexual revolution however highlighted the position of the unmarried. Having been despised as an old maid, she was also of value due to the help she provided within the family unit, now, however, the unmarried began to be considered sexually abnormal.

Interdependence therefore is evident throughout the chapters: women's position in the work-force simply reflected their subordinate place within the family. And, many of the areas where women took political action were influenced by this concept of this role as a wife and mother. Thus, some Chartist women analysed the need for political action in terms of safeguarding the working-class family and its values.

Each chapter begins with a general introduction within which references to the extracts are given in bold. Thus, in Chapter 1 Law, p. 9, 'Her earnings belonged to her husband which meant that he could even claim her benefits from a Friendly Society **(1.2)**, the **(1.2)** refers to document 1.2. This enables the reader to follow the argument through the sources. Each extract has been given a title to give an idea of its content.

Any selection of documents is bound to disappoint some. For reasons of space, each chapter cannot deal in depth with all aspects of the topic. It is intended to introduce the reader to the wealth of primary material. The collection deals primarily with England with little on the Celtic fringe. As far as the black history is concerned, an attempt has been made to include reference to experiences in work, health and politics, but a separate book could be written on these topics.

The extracts are chosen from a wide variety of sources. As always, the authenticity of each source must be examined. Nothing must be taken at face value. As well as considering the authorship of the document, it is important to establish whether the person setting down the account is near enough in time and close enough geographically to provide an accurate rendition; did the author have a vested interest in setting down a biased account?; what was the purpose of it?; what was the document's intended audience? As E. P. Thompson wrote, sources must 'be interrogated by minds trained in a discipline of attentive disbelief'.[1] Equally modern meanings must not be read into the past.

Sheila Rowbotham's *Hidden from history*,[2] written in 1973 under the influence of the women's lib movement, the second war of feminism and the general broadening of social history to include topics such as the family and sexuality, explained how women had been hidden not simply by the survival of, or the ways in which, evidence had been recorded, but also because male historians had not asked questions of these sources in such a way as to uncover women's experience.[3]

In line with such thinking, Davidoff & Hall's study *Family fortunes* (1987) revealed that middle-class men working in the business world relied, to an extent previously unknown, on networks of familial support – such support was often crucial to a man's successful rise in the public sphere.[4]

Davidoff & Westover commented in 1986 that, in regard to women's history,

> documentary sources are often partial and inadequate. Not only is the experience of women filtered through the eyes of social commentators, most of who (sic) were men, but there are substantial gaps in the documentary evidence about what women were doing. Women's lives have been considered trivial and unchanging and thus unworthy of serious historical study, particularly in their domestic role.[5]

They therefore advocated the use of oral history to fill in the gaps.

There is no doubt that women were seen as someone's wife, daughter, mother or sister and that official sources do have many deficiencies. However evidence from Acts of Parliament, parliamentary commissions, and Hansard can throw light on official attitudes. Such evidence is buttressed by material from *inter alia* the unstamped press, suffrage pamphlets, the Women's Labour League, surveys on housing, living conditions, sexuality. Where possible the extracts are by women themselves: what did they hope to achieve and why? They illustrate not merely what women did, but also provide examples of both the processes which enabled women to act as they did and the boundaries that retarded their activities. Great use is also made of *The Times* which not only provides information on what was happening on a daily basis but also gives an example of contemporary attitudes. Even here however, the question of the audience must still be considered. In the actual extracts the imperial system of measurement is retained.

Over the last thirty years, 'women's history' has moved from a position of recording achievements and returning women to history books, to a situation where feminist historians studied women on their own terms. Instead of being viewed as victims, women are now agents of the historical process. This collection of documents chronicles these changes.

Notes

1 E. P. Thompson, *The poverty of theory*, London: Merlin Press (1978), pp. 220–1.

2 S. Rowbotham, *Hidden from history*, London: Pluto Press (1973).

3 For a review of developments in women's history, see F. A. Montgomery, 'Historiography: Feminist and women's history' in *Readers guide to British history*, London: Fitzroy Dearborn (2003), pp. 640–2.

4 L. Davidoff & C. Hall, *Family fortunes*, London: Hutchinson (1987).

5 L. Davidoff & B. Westover, *Our work, our lives, our words*, London: Macmillan (1986), p. ix.

1

Women and the law

Timeline

1753   Hardwicke's Marriage Act.

1801   Addison/Campbell Divorce Act.

1839   Custody of Infants Act: mother given custody of children under seven years old.

1857   Matrimonial Causes Act: men could divorce women for adultery. Women had to prove cruelty, incest, sodomy etc in order to divorce men.

1870   Married Women's Property Act.

1873   Custody of Infants Act.

1878   Matrimonial Causes Act: separation with maintenance to wife.

1882   Married Women's Property Act: married women had right to separate ownership of property from husband.

1884   Married Women's Property Act.

1884   Matrimonial Causes Act: aggravated assault grounds for judicial separation.

1885   Criminal Law Amendment Act: age of consent raised to sixteen.

1886   Guardianship of Infants Act: women could be sole guardian if the husband died.

1918   The Representation of the People Act: gave vote to all men over twenty one and women over thirty years old.

1918   Maternity and Child Welfare Act: local authorities appointed committees to oversee the welfare of mothers and children.

1919   Sex Disqualification (Removal) Act: opened upper ranks of Civil Service and Law to women.

1922   Married Women's Maintenance Act: some maintenance under separation orders.

1922   Irish women receive vote with creation of Irish state.

1923 Matrimonial Causes Act: women have right to sue for divorce on grounds of adultery.

1923 Bastardy Act: increased the payments by fathers to their illegitimate children

1923 Guardianship of Infants Act: gave divorced women the right to the custody of children.

1928 Equal Franchise Act: women received vote on same basis as men.

1937 Divorce Act: desertion and insanity grounds for divorce.

1944 Equal Citizenship Act.

1945 Family Allowances Act: gave benefit of 5s for first child.

1946 National Insurance Act.

1964 Married Women's Property Act.

1967 Medical Termination of Pregnancy Act: legalised abortion on medical grounds.

1967 Family Planning Act: enabled local authorities to provide advisory birth control services.

1969 Divorce Reform Act: divorce could be granted after two-year separation if both partners wanted it or after five-year separation if one wanted it.

1970 Matrimonial Property Act: gave wife an equal share in family assets.

1970 Equal Pay Act: established the principle of equal pay. Gave private companies five years to bring in equal rates of pay for men and women.

1971 Attachment of Earnings Act.

1971 Industrial Relations Act: restricted workers' rights.

1973 Guardianship Act.

1975 Sex Discrimination Act: discrimination on grounds of gender made illegal.

1976 Domestic Violence and Matrimonial Proceedings Act: made injunctions against, and arrests of, violent abusers easier.

A woman's legal position illustrates most clearly her role within society. In the eighteenth century, the law excluded women from all professions, deprived them of political rights and subjected them to men. The law therefore created the legal category 'woman' and determined what behaviour should be considered normal. A woman who broke the law was not simply committing a crime but was also violating society's expectations of her sex.

While marriage was the desired goal and purpose of life for women of all classes, in legal reality it meant the end of an independent existence. As Blackstone, the celebrated eighteenth-century jurist, noted (1.1), 'the very being, or legal existence of the woman is suspended during the marriage'. This had far-reaching consequences. She lost the rights she had enjoyed as a feme sole (a single woman). She could not sue, make a contract and she had no rights over any property she may have had (that now belonged to her husband). She could write a will but her husband could disregard it on her death. Her earnings belonged to her husband which meant that he could even claim her benefits from a Friendly Society (1.2). She could be confined to a lunatic asylum on her husband's say-so up till the Mad Houses Act 1774 which then required a medical certificate before admission though this could be easily circumvented. And, perhaps of greatest concern, she had no rights over her children.

Furthermore, if the husband turned violent or abandoned his wife, the chance of any legal redress was minimal though at times there were exceptions. (1.3) Divorce was extremely difficult to obtain even for a man, and for a woman was near impossible. There were only four petitions by women in the period before 1857. If an Ecclesiastical annulment was not possible, the husband had to obtain a decree of divorce from the Ecclesiastical Court. This had to be followed by a successful claim for damages for 'criminal conversation' ('crimcon'), by proving adultery, then the action could proceed to a bill for divorce culminating in a private Act of Parliament. Divorce in practice, then, was for wealthy males and its financial costs even for a man could be ruinous. (1.7)

The laws governing marriage were extremely slack prior to Hardwicke's Act of 1753. Marriages could be contracted by children aged as young as seven, though not consummated until puberty (fourteen in boys, twelve in girls). Hardwicke's Act, however, ended legally all kinds of clandestine marriage. Marriage had to include parental consent (if both parties were not at least twenty one) and the calling of banns and the formal ceremony had to take place in a church. (1.4) The main aim behind this Act, however, was to protect inheritance, and therefore the wealthy, by outlawing unsuitable unions – parents could prohibit any marriage they considered unsuitable. It was not designed to bring any more rights to women.[1] In 1801 the first divorce Act granted to a woman was that of Jane Campbell (Addison/Campbell Divorce Act). Campbell was granted a divorce from her husband,

Edward Addison, on the grounds of his adultery with her sister, Jessy Campbell. Very unusually she was also awarded custody of her children. (1.5) A promise of marriage was taken very seriously and thus jilting led to a breach of promise case. (1.6)

The practical consequences of a woman's position were illustrated in a high profile case concerning Caroline Norton, the granddaughter of Sheridan the playwright. Married to a brutal husband who physically abused her, she found that he had the right to forbid her to see her three young sons. Her husband took out an action for criminal conversation with the then Prime Minister, Lord Melbourne. Whatever way the action went, Caroline would lose her children despite the fact that she had not committed adultery or left her husband. She had no right to apply for a legal hearing because as a married woman she had no legal existence. Public opinion was against her because she had behaved in a way inappropriate for women. She should have been docile and passive, accepting of her lot.

Her pamphlet, *The separation of mother and child by the law of custody of infants considered*, 1837, pointed out that a father could give his child to a stranger and that it was totally unacceptable that a father should be able to deprive the mother of her children. Norton asked that mothers should have custody of children under the age of seven and that the custody of older children should be decided by the courts. This was denounced both inside and outside Parliament. John Kemble predicted dire consequences, claiming that it would lead to the breakdown of society. (1.8) As a result of Norton's efforts the Infant and Child Custody Act was passed in 1839. Children under seven could now live with their mother providing the Lord Chancellor agreed and the mother was of good character. Ironically, since Caroline's children were now in Scotland, English law did not cover her, and indeed her youngest child William died after a riding accident without her being there. Her husband then relented and let the two remaining boys live with her for part of the year.

Caroline Norton was followed by other women and the occasional man (1.9) eager to change the laws regarding divorce, married women's property, child custody and maintenance for married women. Barbara Leigh Smith (later Bodichon) and a group of like minded women who became known as the 'Langham Place Circle' petitioned Parliament that married women's property be treated the same as men's. This got nowhere but they continued to campaign for relevant clauses to be inserted into the 1857 Divorce and Matrimonial Causes

Act. (**1.10**) This Act did include some provision for married women's property, but only if the woman had been deserted. The 1857 Act set up one court in London to grant divorces which made it very difficult for the working classes to have access to it. It also enshrined the double standard: men could divorce on grounds of adultery alone but not women. A woman had to prove that her husband was guilty of rape, sodomy or bestiality; or, if she was suing on the grounds of adultery this had to be coupled with incest, bigamy or cruelty. This reflected the idea that adultery was the most serious offence a woman could commit within a marriage because it raised the possibility that children might not be legitimate and therefore inheritance could pass to a bastard. In contrast, a man's adultery was considered trivial.

The 1878 Matrimonial Causes Act largely resulted from the efforts of Frances Power Cobbe. It enabled magistrates to grant writs of separation to women whose husbands had been convicted of aggravated assault. This did not allow remarriage. Designed to protect working-class women, it made clear that husbands did not have the right to chastise their wives physically.

Married women's property continued to exercise reformers. Frances Power Cobbe wrote a stinging critique in *Fraser's Magazine* of existing practice, pointing out that it could not be justified in terms of justice, expediency or sentiment. (**1.11**) The Married Women's Property Act of 1870 gave married women the right to their own earnings. (**1.12, 1.13**) A woman could now insure her own life or that of her husband and take an action in her own name for recovery of any of her separate property. This was followed in 1882 (**1.14**) by another Act which gave wives the right to retain their own property after marriage though they still had no legal residence apart from their husbands' and courts could enforce 'conjugal rights'. Furthermore, if she had the means, she was now liable to maintain her husband and children. (**1.15**) She was also subject to bankruptcy. The 1885 Criminal Law Amendment Act raised the age of consent from twelve to sixteen and brought in new measures against disorderly houses, procuration and abduction. This was used by the NSPCC to secure prosecutions for incest with girls under sixteen. The Act also included a clause on male gross indecency (Labouchere Amendment).

While these measures were useful, women were still a long way from equal rights. Accordingly, feminists began to campaign for the vote on the grounds that this was the only real measure which would lead to improvement.[2] By the end of the nineteenth century, married women's rights had been enlarged but were by no means equal to those of men.

The First World War re-opened the franchise issue. While not all men had had the vote under the old system, or those who had had it may have disenfranchised themselves by moving away, it was no longer possible to justify denying members of the armed forces the vote. The problem as far as politicians were concerned was how to limit the number of women in the electorate since women as a whole made up a larger percentage of the population. The Representation of the People Act 1918 gave full manhood suffrage with a voting age of twenty one. Women, however, were subjected to two restrictions: an age qualification of thirty and the need to be eligible for local government franchise either on their own or their husband's behalf. This meant owning or occupying land or premises worth £5 a year. All working-class men now had the vote but many working-class women did not. However, in 1928 women's struggle for the vote was finally successful when the Conservative government passed the Equal Franchise Act granting the vote on the same terms as men.

The Sex Disqualification (Removal) Act (1919) said that 'A person shall not be disqualified by sex or marriage from the exercise of any public function, or from being appointed to or holding any civil or judicial office or post, or from entering or assuming or carrying on any civil profession or vocation, or for admission to any incorporated society . . . and a person shall not be exempted by sex or marriage from the liability to serve as a juror'. (**1.16**) This Act gave women restricted entry to the higher echelons of the Civil Service (if they were unmarried – there was still a *de facto* marriage bar) and allowed them to sit on juries, though again there was a property qualification and magistrates were often unwilling to allow women jurors on any cases which they thought would harm their sensibilities, so for example they would often cough if a sex case was coming up, to warn women off. Women could now become magistrates, join the legal profession and go to Oxbridge. It is important to note, however, that though this Act removed some disabilities there was no mention of equal pay.

The Times 14 November 1922 (**1.17**) highlighted the position women were still in, even after the end of World War I. Arguing for a change in the divorce laws not 'to encourage a disrespect for the marriage bond' but in line with the Social Purity Movement, it pointed out the injustice of insisting women stayed married to lunatics or those suffering from a hitherto undisclosed disease, which was a thinly disguised reference to venereal disease. Furthermore it took issue with the question of actions for breach of promise, pointing out that marriage was not comparable to a 'purely commercial agreement' and therefore it was completely untenable to force a couple to submit to marriage under such circumstances.

The National Council of Women also pointed out that women still needed their husbands' consent when they were to have an operation, thereby emphasising their position as men's property. (**1.18**) The Matrimonial Causes Act 1923 put women on an equal footing to men by enabling them to obtain a divorce solely on the grounds of adultery. A woman could also petition on the grounds of her husband's 'unnatural' offences, though for once, the husband did not have a reciprocal right. He had to prove that unnatural practices had injured his health, thus making a case for cruelty. The 1937 Divorce Act made desertion and insanity grounds for divorce. The Married Women's Property Act of 1964 (**1.21**) gave husbands and wives the right to 50 per cent of any money saved by the wife from the housekeeping, unless there was an agreement to the contrary. In contrast, a man did not have the right to half the savings he had made from any allowance given to him by his wife.

The Matrimonial Homes Act 1967 gave both husband and wife the right of occupation of the matrimonial home. Neither could be evicted from the marital home without a court order. Women could also make mortgage payments even if the mortgage was in the husband's name. This enabled wives to ensure that the home was not lost because of a husband defaulting on the payments. The Matrimonial Proceedings and Property Act 1970 gave courts discretion to distribute joint assets of a husband and wife on a fair and equal basis according to the contribution each had made to the marriage. In dividing family assets, judges tended to award wives one third and husbands two thirds on the grounds that they would have greater expenses since they would probably be supporting two homes. (**1.23**) By the third quarter of the twentieth century then, while women had made strides forward, they were still not equal in law to men.

1.1   Legal position of married women

By marriage the husband and wife are one person in law: that this, the
very being, or legal existence of the woman is suspended during the marriage, or at least is incorporated and consolidated into that of the husband:
under whose wing, protection and *cover* she performs everything; . . .

For this reason, a man cannot grant anything to his wife, or enter into
covenant with her, for the grant would be to suppose her separate existence: and to covenant with her, would be only to covenant with himself:
and therefore it is also generally true, that all compacts made between
husband and wife, when single, are voided by the intermarriage . . .

If the wife be injured in her person or her property, she can bring no
action for redress without her husband's concurrence, and in his name, as
well as her own: neither can she be sued, without making her husband a
defendant . . .

. . . A woman's personal property, by marriage, becomes absolutely her
husband's which at his death he may leave entirely away from her: but if
he dies without will, she is entitled to one third of his personal property,
if he has children, if not to one half . . .

By the marriage, the husband is absolutely master of the profits
of the wife's lands during the courverture; and if he has had a
living child, and survives the wife, he retains the whole of these
lands, if they are estates of inheritance during his life: but the wife is entitled to dower, or one third if she survives, out of her husband's estates of
inheritance; but this she has whether she has had a child or not.

. . . With regard to the property of women, there is taxation without
representation; for they pay taxes without having the liberty of voting for
representatives.

Sir William Blackstone, *Commentaries on the Laws of England* (1753) edited
by Wayne Morrison, London: Cavendish Publishing (2001), vol. 1, pp. 441–5.

1.2   Women's earnings belong to her husband

Of Friendly Societies
I have been led to these reflections, by investigating the situation of some
Female Benefit Clubs, which seem to be exposed to peculiar disadvantages,

in conference of the legal disability which married women labour under, of retaining the earnings of their labour in their own hands. Most of these Clubs are chiefly composed of married women; as the principal induce-ment to enter into them, is, to insure a decent subsistence during the laying-in month; a period, in which, of all others, a labourer's wife is in most need of extrinsic assistance. The laudable objects, however, of these excellent institutions, may be entirely frustrated by the exercise of that legal authority with which a husband is invested. As he is entitled to receive his wife's earnings, he can not only prevent her from paying her regular subscriptions to the Club: but if she falls sick, he is, I conceive, no less authorized by law to demand the allowance which is granted by the Society, and to appropriate it to his own use.

F. M. Eden, *The state of the poor or, an history of the labouring classes in England, from the conquest to the present period*, London: J. Davis (1797), p. 630.

1.3   Doctors Commons

A cause came on to be tried in Doctors Commons,[3] between an eminent tradesman in Piccadilly, and his wife, for repeated acts of cruelty, adul-tery, and giving her the foul disease, and other ill usage, when, after many learned arguments, (the innocence of his wife not being in the least impeached) the judge pronounced the man to have been guilty both of the cruelty and the adultery, and divorced the woman from her husband, and condemned him in full costs, to the satisfaction of the whole court.

Annual Register, 11 December 1767.

1.4   Hardwicke's Marriage Act 1753

The consent or concurrence of the parent to the marriage of his child under age, was also *directed* by our ancient law to be obtained: but now it is absolutely *necessary*; for without it the contract is void. And this also is another means which the law has put into the parent's hands, in order the better to discharge his duty; first, of protecting his children from the snares of artful and designing persons, and next, of settling them properly in life, by preventing the ill consequences of too early and precipitate marriages. The offence of *clandestine marriages*: for by the statute 26 Geo. II, c. 33 l. To solemnise marriage in any other place besides a church, or public chapel wherein banns have been usually published, except by licence from the archbishop of Canterbury; – and, 2. To solemnise marriage in such church or chapel without due publication of banns, or licence obtained from a proper authority; – do both of them not only render the marriage void, but subject the person solemnising it to felony, punished by transportation for fourteen years: as, by three former statutes, he and his assistants were subject to a pecuniary forfeiture of 100*l*. 3. To make a false entry in a marriage register; to alter it when made; to forge or counterfeit, such entry, or a marriage licence: to cause or procure, or act or assist in such forgery; to utter the same as true, knowing it be counterfeit; or to destroy or procure the destruction of any register, in order to vacate any marriage, or subject any person to the penalties of this act; all these offences, knowingly and wilfully committed, subject the party to the guilt of felony without benefit of clergy.

Sir William Blackstone, *Commentaries on the Laws of England* (1753), vol. 1, p. 453; vol. 4, para. 163.

1.5 Amendment to the Addison/Campbell divorce Bill 1801 [main papers, 13 March 1801]

'And in order to secure as far as Circumstances will admit the virtuous education of the Children of the said Jane Campbell Be it Declared and Enacted that it shall not be lawful for the said Edward Addison to remove his daughter from the Care and Custody of her Mother during her Minority and that the Son and Daughter of the said Edward Addison shall during their respective Minorities be deemed and taken to be to all Intents and Purposes Wards of the High Court of Chancery.'

Private Act, 41, Geo III c.102
HL/PO/PB/1/1801/41G3n287

1.6 Breach of promise of marriage

Chapman against Shaw
The Plaintiff Wife Elizabeth Chapman, brought this action against the Defendant, Mr Shaw who is by profession an Attorney, to recover a satisfaction in damages for a very serious injury to wit for a breach of a promise of marriage. On the part of the Plaintiff a great variety of witnesses were called most of whom were her own near relations. They provided that for near the space of two years the Defendant had visited almost every day at the house of the Plaintiff's father, that he had repeatedly promised to marry her, that preparations were made for the purpose and the time fixed when the marriage should be solemnized. That he had declared he could not be happy without her. But without the least reason on the part of the Plaintiff the Defendant had married another Lady.

A very able defence was made to this action. It was agreed on all hands that the Plaintiff is a young Lady of the strictest virtue and integrity, and belonging to a very respectable family of Holborn. There was as little doubt but that the Defendant was descended of very respectable parents in Yorkshire and the twelfth son of the family.

Lord Kenyon summed up the substance of the evidence to the Jury, accompanied by a number of excellent observations on the nature of the offence and the favourable circumstances that appeared for the Defendant.

Verdict for Plaintiff.

The Times, 24 May 1790.

1.7 Effects of divorce laws

5 May 1843
Sir, – I was very glad to see your remarks in The Times of last Friday, on the existing divorce laws of this country, of the hardship and cruelty of which I afford in my own person a striking instance.

A few years since, having then a family of three children, my wife fell a victim to the arts of a seducer. I brought my action against him and obtained a verdict for trifling damages. I was then induced to proceed in the Ecclesiastical Court for a divorce, not conceiving it possible that any opposition should be offered. The woman, however, was base enough to oppose the suit, solely for the purpose of wringing alimony out of me, who at that time had an income of 100*l.* a year only, and was left with the three children on my hands.

This claim for alimony the Court of Arches allowed to the extent of 40*l* a year, although the woman was living at the time in open adultery with her seducer.

Well, after the proceedings had been pending a year, I obtained a decree for a divorce.

The expenses of these proceedings have brought me actually to the verge of a prison, in which I shall to all appearance be incarcerated in a very few days. All this, miserable as it is, I would have submitted to cheerfully, if it would have freed me from my bonds and enabled me to marry again, but the absurd existing laws on the subject of divorce sentence me, in addition to the sufferings in mind, body, and estate which I have endured, to perpetual celibacy, and deprive my children of proper care, because I have no money to take me through the House of Lords.

I do entreat the favour of you again to devote a portion of a column to the advocacy of an alteration in this state of things.

I am, Sir, your very obedient servant, S.N.

The Times, 5 May 1843.

1.8 Opposition to Norton's law of custody

... If this last and strongest and only effectual prevention still existing against separation, (viz. the certain assurance in the mind of every wife, that, if she will desert her husband's house, the sphere of her duties, and, be it ever so remembered, the only proper home of his children, she does ipso facto lose the right of access to them,) – if this prevention be once taken away, it is as certain as anything in the whole world of direct cause and effect, that separations will increase! You cannot diminish the checks to licentiousness without increasing the chances of their occurrence! ...

... What is manifest, as to the operation of the Bill, is this; that it directly violates the great fundamental law of society, the law of paternity; it directly annuls the father's right to have *sole* command in his own house, and over his own legitimate children, whilst the same responsibility for their conduct is thrown on him as ever; and this we affirm to be grossly unjust, and therefore grossly immoral ...

... This sole and absolute power over the children, to the exclusion of everyone else, is a fundamental right vested in the man, as man and father, from the beginning. The paternal power is the oldest and most sacred right belonging to a man – the right that ought to be most religiously guarded. Such being the doctrine deducible from the authority of the Christian Scriptures, Sergeant Talfourd's Custody of Infants Bill, that proposes to destroy this right is therefore directly antichristian.

J. M. Kemble, 'Custody of Infants Bill', *British & Foreign Quarterly Review*, 7 (1838), pp. 269–411.

1.9   Of less value than poodle dogs

Mr. Fitzroy has just brought before the House of Commons the startling principle of English law that women are of less value than Poodle dogs and Skye terriers. They do not receive the same measure of protection as these nobler quadrupeds. Where punishment consists in fines, of course the amount of the fine affords us a certain measure of value as to the worth of the object injured. Any peculator who infringes against the provisions of the Dog Stealing Act may be imprisoned with hard labour for a period of six months, or be sentenced to pay a fine not exceeding £20. With regard to women, any man may, at his pleasure, kick, bruise, beat, knock down, and stamp upon them, and all that the magistrate can inflict by way of summary punishment is a fine of £5, or, in default, two months' imprisonment with hard labour. It would be a very material improvement in the position of women if a short clause were introduced into the Cruelty to Animals Act which should include them in the provisions of that beneficent statute. All that would be necessary would be, 'And be it enacted that for the purposes of this act any woman or women, shall be taken and held to be ewes, donkeys, cats, dogs, and not otherwise; and that any person or persons who shall be proved to have inflicted bodily injury upon any woman or women as aforesaid, shall undergo the same penalties and punishment as though he had inflicted bodily injury upon any of the ewes, donkeys, &c., as aforesaid.'

Now, Mr. Fitzroy wishes that women should at least be placed upon the same footing as the lower animals, and receive the same amount of protection from the law.

The Times, 12 March 1853.

1.10   Divorce and Matrimonial Causes Act 1857

The Property of Deserted Married Women
On Monday next the following provision in the Divorce and Matrimonial Causes Act (the 20th and 21st of Victoria chap. 85) will come into operation with respect to the property and earnings of deserted married women. Section 21 – 'A wife deserted by her husband may at any time after such desertion, if resident within the metropolitan district, apply to a police magistrate, or if resident in the country to justices in petty session, or in either case to the Court, for an order to protect any money or property she may acquire by her own lawful industry, and property which she may become possessed of, after such desertion, against her husband or his creditors, or any person claiming under him, and such magistrate or justices or Court, if satisfied of the fact of such desertion, and that the same was without reasonable cause, and that the wife is maintaining herself by her own industry or property, may make and give to the wife an order protecting her earnings and property acquired since the commencement of such desertion from her husband, and all creditors and persons claiming under him, and such earnings and property shall belong to the wife as if she were a *feme sole*; . . . If any such order of protection be made, the wife shall, during the continuance thereof, be and be deemed to have been, during such desertion of her, in the like position in all respects with regard to property and contracts, and suing and being sued, as she would be under this Act if she obtained a decree of judicial separation.'

The Times, 5 January 1858.

1.11   Married women's property

. . . many husbands are unable, from fault or from misfortune, to maintain their wives. Of this the law takes no note, proceeding on reasoning which may be reduced to the syllogism:

> *A man who supports his wife ought to have all her property;*
> *Most men support their wives;*
> *Therefore, all men ought to have all the property of their wives . . .*

The legal act by which a man puts his hand in his wife's pocket, or draws her money out of the savings' bank, is perfectly clear, easy, inexpensive. The corresponding process by which the wife can obtain food and clothing from her husband when he neglects to provide it – what may it be? Where is it described? . . . what is the actual fact? Simply that the woman's remedy for her husband's neglect to provide her with food, has been practically found unattainable. The law which has robbed her so straight-forwardly, has somehow forgotten altogether to secure for her the supposed compensation . . . So much for the Justice of the Common Law. What now shall we say to its Expediency? . . . the husband should manage all the larger business of the family. The law then *when the husband is really wise and good* is a dead letter. But for the opposite cases, exceptions though they be, yet alas! too numerous, where the husband is a fool, a gambler, a drunkard, and where the wife is sensible, frugal, devoted to the interests of the children, – is it indeed expedient that the whole and sole power should be lodged in the husband's hands; the power not only over all they already have in common, but the power over all she can ever earn in future? . . .

But it is the alleged *helplessness* of married women which, it is said, makes it indispensable to give all the support of the law, *not* to them, but to the stronger persons with whom they are unequally yoked. 'Woman is physically, mentally, and morally inferior to man'. Therefore it follows – what? – that the law should give to her bodily weakness, her intellectual dullness, her tottering morality, all the support and protection which it is possible to interpose between so poor a creature and the strong being always standing over her? By no means. Quite the contrary of course. The husband being already physically, mentally, and morally his wife's superior must in justice receive from law additional strength by being constituted absolute master of her property . . .

Frances Power Cobbe, 'Criminals, idiots, women & minors', *Fraser's Magazine*, 78 (1868), pp. 782–6.

1.12 An Act to amend the law relating to the property of married women (9 August 1870) 33 & 34 Vict., c. 93

1. The wages and earnings of any married woman acquired or gained by her after the passing of this Act in any employment, occupation, or trade in which she is engaged or which she carries on separately from her husband, and also any money, or property so acquired by her through the exercise of any literary, artistic, or scientific skill, and all investments of such wages, earnings, money or property, shall be deemed and be taken

to be property held and settled to her separate use, independent of any husband to whom she may be married, and her receipts alone shall be a good discharge for such wages, earnings, money, and property. . . .

7. Where any woman married after the passing of this Act shall during her marriage become entitled to any personal property as next of kin or one of the next of kin of an intestate, or to any sum of money not exceeding two hundred pounds under any deed or will, such property shall, subject and without prejudice to the trusts of any settlement affecting the same, belong to the woman for her separate use, and her receipts alone shall be a good discharge for the same.

8. Where any freehold, copyhold, or customary hold property shall descend upon any woman married after the passing of this Act as heiress or co-heiress of an intestate, the rents and profits of such property shall, subject and without prejudice to the trusts of any settlement affecting the same, belong to such woman for her separate use, and her receipts alone shall be a good discharge for the same. . . .

14. A married woman having separate property shall be subject to all such liability for the maintenance of her children as a widow is now by law subject to for the maintenance of her children; provided always, that nothing in this Act shall relieve her husband from any liability at present imposed upon him by law to maintain her children.

1.13   Court of Common Pleas, Westminster, May 27

Digges v. Godderer

This was a somewhat interesting case, being the first action which has raised a peculiar point under the Married Women's Property Act 1870 (33 and 34 Victoria, cap. 93) . . .

It appeared that the plaintiff, an actress, had been living apart from her husband, and had realised sufficient money to purchase some furniture, which was seized under an execution against her husband. She now claimed this furniture as her own under the 1ˢᵗ section of the above statute, which provides:

'That the wages and earnings of any married woman acquired or gained by her after the passing of the Act in any employment, occupation, or trade in which she is engaged, or which she carries on separately from her husband, and also any money or property so acquired by her through the exercise of any literary, artistic, or scientific skill, and all investments of such wages, &c., shall be deemed and taken to be property held and settled to her separate use, independent of any husband to whom she may be married, and her receipts alone shall be a good discharge for such wages, earnings, money and property'.

Some portion of the property of the plaintiff arose from gifts made to her by gentlemen, who it was said, admired her artistic skill, and it was contended that Section 1 did not apply to money accruing thus, the word 'gifts' not occurring in the statute; and it was argued that the plaintiff's property could be lawfully taken in execution as the property of her husband.

The learned Judge directed a verdict to be entered for the plaintiff, and gave the defendant leave to move the Court on the points of law raised.

The Times, 28 May 1872.

1.14   Married Women's Property Bill 1882

Sir C. Campbell, said he felt bound to protest against this Bill [Married Women's Property bill. 1882], which effected a complete social revolution. Not a woman in a million had the slightest idea of what the Bill proposed to do, nor had the attention of the country at large been directed to its provisions. By putting on the paper a notice of opposition to this measure he had endeavoured to obtain a small medium of justice for poor married men.

Mr. Warton thought the measure one of the utmost importance. The third clause of the Bill would in effect let in restraint of marriage. No man would marry a woman with property, knowing that she could set him at defiance so long as the marriage continued. The fact that the Bill had been hurried through the House of Lords was not in its favour, and he begged the House to pause before sanctioning a social revolution.

The Times, 12 August 1882.

1.15   An Act to consolidate and amend the Acts relating to the property of married women (18 August 1882)

Be it enacted, &c., as follows:

1. (i) A married woman shall, in accordance with the provisions of this Act, be capable of acquiring, holding (a) and disposing by Will (b) or

otherwise (c), of any real or personal property as her separate property, in the same manner as if she were a *feme sole*, without the intervention of any trustee.

2. A married woman shall be capable of entering into and rendering herself liable in respect of and to the extent of her separate property on any contract (a), and of suing and being sued, either in contract (b), or in tort (c), or otherwise, in all respects as if she were a *feme sole*, and her husband need not be joined with her as plaintiff or defendant, or be made a party to any action or other legal proceeding brought by or taken against her; and any damages or costs recovered by her in any such action or proceeding shall be her separate property; and any damages or costs recovered against her in any such action or proceeding shall be payable out of her separate property, and not otherwise.

3. Every contract entered into by a married woman shall be deemed to be a contract entered into by her with respect to and to bind her separate property, unless the contrary be shown. . . .

5. Every married woman carrying on a trade separately from her husband shall, in respect of her separate property, be subject to the bankruptcy laws in the same way as if she were a *feme sole*. . . .

13. A husband shall be liable for the debts of his wife contracted, and for all contracts entered into and wrongs committed by her, before marriage . . .

21. A married woman having separate property shall be subject to all such liability for the maintenance of her children and grandchildren as the husband is now by law subject to for the maintenance of her children and grandchildren; provided always, that nothing in this Act shall relieve her husband from any liability imposed upon him by law to maintain her children or grandchildren.

1.16   Sex Disqualification (Removal) Act 1919

. . . A person shall not be disqualified by sex or marriage from the exercise of any public function, or from being appointed to or holding any civil or judicial office or post, or from entering or assuming or carrying on any civil profession or vocation, or for admission to any incorporated society . . . and a person shall not be exempted by sex or marriage from the liability to serve as a juror.

Provided that, notwithstanding anything in this section, his majesty may by order in council authorize regulations to be made providing for and prescribing the mode of the admission of women to the civil service of his majesty . . . and giving power to reserve to men any branch of or posts in the civil service in any of his majesty's possessions overseas, or in any foreign country; and any judge, chairman of quarter sessions, recorder or other person before whom a case is or may be heard may, in his discretion, on an application made by or on behalf of the parties . . . make an order that the jury shall be composed of men only or of women only as the case may require, or may, on an application made by a woman to be exempted from service on a jury in respect of any case by reason of the nature of the evidence to be given or of the issues to be tried, grant such exemption. . . .

Nothing in the statutes or charter of any university shall be deemed to preclude the authorities of such university from making such provision as they shall think fit for the admission of women to membership thereof, or to any degree, right, or privilege therein or in connection therewith. . . .

LVII, 325 f.: 9–10 George V, c. 71.

1.17 The legal position of women

For a considerable period proceedings in the High Court of Justice have shown that there is a real need of reform in the law relating to women . . . It is hard to see what social or religious purpose can be served by refusing to sever a matrimonial bond between an insane murderer and his wife. It is equally hard to understand what benefit there can be to the community in fettering a woman to a man who by reason of disease – undisclosed at the time of marriage – is incapable of becoming the father of healthy children. This is not a question of rendering the law of divorce so lax as to encourage a disrespect for the marriage bond. There is a serious social issue which involves the well-being of the nation. If Mrs Rutherford be right in her estimate that there are 'sixty thousand men and women tied to lunatics confined in our asylums' and 'innumerable thousands of silent sufferers' it is difficult to comprehend how there can be any public-spirited opposition to an alteration of the law. Women have been given rightly a part in the governance of the country. They have been recognised, after a long struggle, as having important duties to fulfil in our social system. They deserve, therefore, to receive better treatment under the law, and they should be made aware, at the same time, of the responsibilities of their new status. But there is another side to the question – a side on which Judges have often commented. The action for breach of promise of marriage is a constant source of criticism. It cannot be said that it could be in the public interest that a couple should be married when one of them has lost all love for the other. There are cases, no doubt, in which the woman suffers by loss of the opportunity of making another match, or by expenditure in contemplation of matrimony, but, as Mr Justice McCardle said in a case yesterday, such actions raise a serious social question. A contract to marry cannot, or ought not to, be compared with a purely commercial agreement. As the Judge said, it is different from a bargain made in the counting-house, and an action based upon what amounts to 'a life-long contract' is in many ways 'a degrading one for the woman, because she was asking a jury to assess the commercial value of the man whose affection she had lost'. We do not quarrel with the verdict in the action which led to these remarks by Mr Justice McCardle. We must agree, however, with the dilemma which was put in the summing-up. Either a defendant has to marry a woman whom he has ceased to care for, or he had to face the ordeal of an action in the High Court. Of recent years the Divorce Court has been overburdened with work. Its task would be greater were men and women to marry without affection merely to avoid legal proceedings. As Mr Justice McCardle said, one must picture 'the married life which would follow when the woman had been led to the altar by a man under the threat of an action for breach of his promise of marriage'.

The Times, 14 November 1922.

1.18   Married women and the law

To the Editor of *The Times*
Sir, The decision in the Peel case that a married woman is presumed to be coerced by her husband when she commits certain crimes in his presence has brought vividly before the public one of the absurdities surviving in our law of married women. May we call attention to the fact that this is not the only such survival out of keeping with the more enlightened attitude now held towards married women? The law of coverture, although certain of its worst consequences were swept away by the Married Women's Property Acts, and by the decision of the House of Lords in the Jackson case, has never been abolished in its entirety. That doctrine is that a man and his wife are one person, and that the husband is that person. The wife's 'legal existence is incorporated and consolidated into that of her husband'. It is no more than 30 years since the Jackson case definitely

negatived a claim that a husband had the right to imprison his wife, which was based on this doctrine.

At the same time, the wife's position as her husband's property is still in practice, as for example, when she is not allowed to decide for herself, like other adults, whether or not she shall submit to a surgical operation. Her husband must first give his consent.

We submit that these doctrines, which belong to an age of servitude and serfdom, should be explicitly annulled by legislation, so that marriage may become an equally responsible partnership, which is necessary to the building up of the highest kind of family life.

I am yours faithfully

Frances Balfour, President of the National Council of Women of Great Britain and Ireland

The Times, 22 March 1922.

1.19   Married Women's (Maintenance) Act 1922

Bills Advanced
The Married Women (Maintenance) Bill was read a second time. The Lord Chancellor said that as the law now stood the weekly maximum a man could be ordered to pay for the maintenance of his wife and family, if the wife obtained a separation order under the Summary Jurisdiction (Married Women) Act 1895 was £2. In view of the general increase in the rate of wages and the diminution in the buying power of money, the Bill proposed that the husband might further be called upon to pay 10s for each child.

The Times, 30 November 1920.

1.20   Representation of the People (Equal Franchise) Act (1918)

... For the purpose of providing that the parliamentary franchise shall be the same for men and women, sub-sections 1 and 2 of section 4 of the Representation of the People Act, 1918 (in this act referred to as the principal act), shall be repealed, and the following sections shall be substituted for sections 1 and 2 of that act: –

... '1. A person shall be entitled to be registered as a parliamentary elector for a constituency (other than a university constituency) if he or she is of full age and not subject to any legal incapacity and has the requisite residence qualification, or has the requisite business premises qualification, or is the husband or wife of a person entitled to be so registered in respect of a business premises qualification. . . .'

'2. A person shall be entitled to be registered as a parliamentary elector for a university constituency if he or she is of full age and not subject to any legal incapacity and has received a degree (other than an honorary degree) at any university forming, or forming part of, the constituency. . . .'

For the purpose of providing that the local government franchise shall be the same for men and women, sub-section 3 of section 4 of the principal act shall be repealed, and the following section shall be substituted for section 3 of that act: –

'A person shall be entitled to be registered as a local government elector for a local government electoral area if he or she is of full age and not subject to any legal incapacity and is on the last day of the qualifying period occupying as owner or tenant any land or premises in that area, and has during the whole of the qualifying period so occupied any land or premises in that area . . . , or is the husband or wife of a person entitled to be so registered in respect of premises in which both the person so entitled and the husband or wife, as the case may be, reside. . . .'

1.21 Wife's share in house

Judgement

The Married Women's Property Act 1964 was passed on 25th March 1964 and provided by section 1 that 'if any question arises as to the right of a husband or wife to money derived from any allowance made by the husband for the expenses of the matrimonial home or for similar purposes, or to any property acquired out of such money, the money or property shall in the absence of any agreement between them to the contrary, be treated as belonging to the husband and the wife in equal shares'. That Act changed the substantive law but was retrospective in its operation and applied to events that had taken place before its commencement.

The Times, 30 July 1964.

1.22   Wife agreed to be hit on Saturday

The new ground for divorce, that since the respondent has behaved so that the petitioner 'cannot reasonably be expected to live with the respondent', was retained in the Divorce Reform Bill yesterday by the Commons Standing Committee on the Bill without a division . . .

Mr Abse (Pontypool, Labour) said, that a woman called on him professionally complaining about her husband. She was bruised and battered. He sent for the husband whose solution was that he would be content to knock his wife about only on Saturday night, instead of every night.

When Mr Abse told the wife of this offer, she said: 'Saturday nights only? That will do nicely'.

Sir Elwyn Jones said that the wording of the Bill in this part was little more than reformulation of the present test of cruelty.

The Times, 25 April 1968.

1.23   Share in family assets for wives in divorce cases

By our Legal Correspondent
The Court of Appeal has laid down for the first time the guidelines to be followed by lower courts in distributing the family assets after a divorce.

Lord Denning, Master of the Rolls, made it clear yesterday that the Matrimonial Proceedings and Property Act 1970, recognised that the wife who looked after the home and family contributed as much to the family assets as the wife who goes out to work. He said: 'The one contributes in kind, the other in money. If the Court comes to the conclusion that the home has been acquired and maintained by the joint efforts of both, then, when the marriage breaks down, it should be regarded as the joint property of both of them no matter in whose name it stands'.

In the case before the courts, he said, the fairest way was for the wife to have one third of the family assets as her own, and one third of the joint earnings. She would certainly in that way be as well off as if the capital assets were divided equally, which was all that a partner was entitled to.

The Times, 9 February 1973.

1.24   Sex Discrimination Act 1975

Sex Discrimination Bill falls short of targets, women say

The Government's Sex Discrimination Bill, passing through its committee stage at Westminster as the British showpiece contribution to International Women's Year, is causing some disenchantment among women's rights campaigners . . .

Last week women demonstrators chained themselves to Westminster railings, and threw a brick through the window of Transport House in apparent ingratitude. The Women's Liberation Movement has passed resolutions dissociating itself from the Bill, on the ground that it does not cover tax, pensions, social security, industrial and marital legislation.

The main doubt about the Bill, is how far it will affect the fundamental definition of women in British society as dependents and mothers. Women cannot claim sickness or unemployment benefits for dependents; they retire earlier than men; and their husbands have to fill in their tax forms. Even if employers and local authorities extend child-care facilities, women still have to interrupt their careers, with subsequent job handicaps, far more than men. Other legislation to help women is in prospect. The Government's pension proposals will give women better rights in occupational and state pension schemes. The Employment Protection Bill will give six weeks' paid maternity leave and the right of reinstatement after absence. Equal pay will be fully in force at the end of this year.

But no politician has yet proposed that men should sacrifice the continuity and rewards of their careers to share in children's upbringing. Apart from encouraging a slow shift of obsolete attitudes, the practical impact of the Bill for some women may be merely an incentive to work even harder.

The Times, 5 May 1975.

1.25   Unlawful discrimination

The area most likely to throw up legitimate, demonstrable cases on December 29 [when the Sex Discrimination Act became law] is that of employment (though the Equal Pay Act rather than the Sex Discrimination Act will deal with any arrangement over money included in a contract). The paradox here is that while cases of discrimination will possibly be easier to prove over promotion they are more likely to be reported over dismissal and redundancy. A woman in a job who is passed over for promotion may wait and hope for a more sympathetic manager, rather than jeopardize her chances with the firm.

But the following women seem to have cases that could be taken to court. The job of supervisor over a group of women assembling valves became vacant in a large factory. A number of men applied. So did a woman, from the same section, with appropriate supervisory experience from a feeder factory. The management favoured the woman's application. However the union opposed her nomination, and won the day.

In another firm, a key senior post of group personnel manager was created during reorganization of the company. A woman with 15 years' senior personnel manager experience applied. So did a couple of less qualified men. The woman's application was vetoed by a director – on the ground that it would be wrong to have a woman in a senior position talking to factories about their staff.

Both these women have strong cases. The reasons for not promoting them – that men need the money and the job more than women, who are probably married and supported anyway – will no longer be acceptable in the new year. They are the same reasons that traditionally get mentioned in redundancy cases, especially at times of economic cut back, as in the following instance.

An electronics firm was forced to make one clerical worker redundant. The choice was between an equally qualified and experienced man and woman. Both worked full time; both were married. The man had no children. The woman was paying for her children's education and supporting her son through college on her salary. Eventually she was dismissed . . .

Housing, facilities and services all come under the Act, thereby making it illegal for a television rental firm to refuse to allow a married woman to rent a television unless her husband signs the form . . .

The Times, 3 December 1975.

1.26   Nine million women workers get a new deal

On Monday, December 29, two complex, linked pieces of legislation come into force whose effect will be to revolutionise the relationship between Britain's nine million or so women workers, the men they work with and the people they work for.

These are the Equal Pay Act 1970 and the Sex Discrimination Act. They may find not only employers, but some male workers, trade unionists and even some civil servants unprepared to comply.

Both Acts, and particularly the former, are hard to understand. Once grasped, however, the Acts become legitimate game for circumvention – like avoidance of income tax liability – by employers who either wish to keep down labour costs or who object to women holding responsible jobs . . .

The penalties for evasion are already clear. A case that goes against an employer at a tribunal could involve him or her in stumping up back pay or other compensation for up to two years from December 29 next.

The Equal Pay Act is neither solely about pay and only arguably about equality. Contrary to a general impression, it is also just as much about men as about women.

It says that a woman is entitled to equal treatment to a man where the work she is doing is the same as or broadly similar to that of a man, or where different, has been given an equal value by a job evaluation exercise. A man has the same rights where the opposite situation prevails.

Secondly, discrimination will be removed from collective agreements, employers' pay structures and statutory wages orders containing provisions relating to men only or women only.

The Times, 1 December 1975.

1.27   Women's lib march on No 10

Carrying powerful torches specially imported from Denmark that they later found difficult to put out, three hundred women supporters of Mr William Hamilton's Anti-Discrimination Bill marched to the House of Commons last evening.

They found that their only audience comprised workmen building the car park. MPs had gone home several hours before. So the women continued their torchlight march to Downing Street. There, three were allowed to take a letter past the police barricade to No 10.

All the way they had chanted 'Equality now' and 'We want the Bill' and had been escorted by policemen who obviously felt that it was no time to impede women in an angry mood.

The reason for the demonstration was the earlier debate in the House of Commons when Mr William Hamilton (Lab, Fife, West) failed for the second year to get a second reading for his Anti-Discrimination Bill. This would have set up a board to hear complaints about discrimination on the ground of sex . . .

'The greatest area of pollution in this country is the discrimination against women from the nappy to the coffin', Mr Hamilton said.

The Times, 3 February 1973.

1.28 Taxing times for married women

I recently received a missive from the taxman. If you are a married woman, it said, please reply as if you were your husband. I asked the Inland Revenue for enlightenment. 'Well', explained an embarrassed official, anticipating feminist wrath, 'husbands are still legally responsible for their wives' tax affairs. Two or three years ago we would have asked you to give him the form to fill in. Now we let you answer questions on his behalf. That's progress'. I like the tale I heard recently about the widow who received the same Inland Revenue form. She replied: 'I am dead'.

The Times, 6 June 1983.

Notes

1 See Chapter 2, 'Marriage'.
2 See Chapter 5, 'Politics'.
3 Similar to Inns of Courts, a society of lawyers practising civil and canon law.

2

Marriage, motherhood, the cult of domesticity and the family

Timeline

1947   Marriage Guidance Council.
See also Chapter 1, 'Women and the law'.

The family has had a central role in women's history and while marriage may have meant the end of a woman's independent legal existence,[1] it did bring an enhanced status. A 'Mrs' always took precedence over a 'Miss'. Furthermore marriage made sense for a woman. It was extremely difficult to survive independently on the wages paid to women. For this reason unmarried women often lived together, as did nurses in the twentieth century, in accommodation provided with the job. Even as late as 1939, Margaret Cole pointed out, 'marriage, then, is, and must at present remain, for women one of the most obvious, even not necessarily the most remunerative of economic careers, in the sense of ways of making a livelihood'.[2]

In the eighteenth century a woman's family position was over-whelmingly one of dependence – as a daughter, wife, sister or unmarried female relative. Much advice was given to girls about what would be expected from a wife and what 'qualities' would put off potential husbands. John Gregory had no doubt that modesty, restraint, passivity, compliance, submissiveness, delicacy and chastity were what was needed. (2.1) As Dr Fordyce stated, 'That Providence designed women for a state of dependence, and consequently of submission, I cannot doubt . . .'.[3] Women should be content to be inferior secure in the knowledge that they were powers behind the throne. (2.17)

Female virtue was constructed in sexual terms. As a consequence any male characteristics (2.3) (even if they involved education) were to be avoided. As mentioned in Chapter 1, women had to be chaste and faithful to ensure that property went to the legal heir. William

33

Alexander, however, was aware of the inequity in this. (**2.4**) Nevertheless this argument was still being brought up in the debate over divorce reform in 1923. (**2.46**) Since where property was concerned, much was often at stake, it was important that rational choices of a marriage partner were made. Gisbourne felt that parental opinion should be taken into account. (**2.6**) The only section of society which appeared to have a free choice was that of the working classes (**2.7**) though they too needed to choose a partner who would be of financial assistance. Alexander recognised that widowhood might even have compensations! (**2.5**)

For upper-class women, the only solutions to an unhappy marriage were either to 'grin and bear it' or to have an affair. The working-class woman had rather more options: she could run away (more popular with husbands), commit bigamy, or take part in a 'wife sale'. There is controversy over how common wife sales were, but there is no doubt that they did take place. Gillis points out that the sale should happen only when both parties had agreed that the marriage had broken down. Should the wife not concur, then the 'sale' was not considered valid: 'A North Bovey man made a '"private agreement"' to transfer his wife in 1868. '"When he returned home with the purchase, the woman repudiated the transaction, and taking her two children with her, she went off at once to Exeter, and only came back to attend her husband's funeral"'.[4] The descriptions given of them illustrate society's view of women: she belonged to her husband as one of his chattels hence the common use of a halter round the woman's neck. (**2.8, 2.9**) Gillis considers that by the 1860s and 1870s the practice was dying out.

Despite the expectation that women should marry, some commentators did criticise early marriage: Mary Wollstonecraft from the point of view that a young women would not appreciate a good husband's qualities, and others on the grounds that such marriages often caused poverty. There was no doubt in contemporaries' eyes that a woman's place was in the home. Women were seen as guardians of morality and there was constant concern about the morals of the working classes. (**2.12**)

Within the family, the mother's role was crucial: 'The Victorians regarded it as axiomatic that the home was the foundation and the family the cornerstone of their civilisation and that in the family were first learned the moral, religious ethical and social precepts of good citizenship'.[5] The image of the Victorian family was that of an organism in which everyone had his/her place and was content within it. The middle-class woman managed the household, while the working-class one did the actual work. The ideology of domesticity assumed greater prominence from the middle of the nineteenth century. The 'Angel of the House' (**2.13**) – arising from Coventry Patmore's epony-mous poem which stressed women's passivity in comparison to man's assertiveness – became an aspiration not just for middle-class women but also for the wealthier artisans. In practice, however, this was simply an ideal: even the middle classes often needed to rely on their wives' help and capital, while for the working classes two incomes were vital. This middle-class ideology also laid stress on the home as a haven of domestic peace and order – a refuge from all the problems of the world. This image was promoted as a proper form for a family. Given the interest in separate spheres (domestic for women, public for men) there was growing concern over what was seen as the lack of knowledge of housewifery on the part of the working classes. Parlia-mentary commissions such as those into mining in 1842 constantly criticised working-women's domestic skills, in particular their lack of mothering. (**2.14, 2.15**) Furthermore, the reaction to married women working was held by Engels, from a socialist perspective, and Ashley, from a conservative one, to lead to a world turned upside down which would have dire consequences for society. (**2.18, 2.19**) Even radical opinion, such as that of the *Poor Man's Guardian* emphasised that the home was the woman's sphere (**2.16**) though like the Chartists, they were actually arguing for a family wage to be paid to working men which would enable them to support a family.

Women's position within marriage was subjected to critiques throughout the period. Thus William Thompson in 1825 referred to, 'Home . . . the eternal prison – house of the wife'.[6] (**2.20**) From the 1880s feminists advocated reshaping the marriage relationship. In par-ticular the idea of male strength and female fragility was rejected. Edward Carpenter pointed out that the image of the 'oak and ivy' was actually one of parasitism. (**2.21**) Women should not be considered the property of their of husbands and the economically dependent wife was on a par with a kept women. In a blistering attack, Hamilton saw marriage as practised (not the institution as such), as a trade and thus a debased ideal. (**2.22**) Women married because this was their only viable form of livelihood. She also suggested that women strike to ensure appreciation for what they did. Mona Caird (**2.25**) not only criticised marriage but also motherhood as an oppressive institution though Eliza Linton castigated 'the girl of the period' for her lack of traditional qualities. (**2.24**)

While middle-class women were calling for changes in the marriage relationship, working-class women were still subject to violence (**2.25**) and poor conditions. (**2.26**) And, though it was recognised that wife beating did occur in other classes, the general consensus was that it was predominantly a working-class phenomenon. Feminist campaigners pointed out that one of the most reprehensible aspects of it was that it had become such a common occurrence, that neighbours rarely went to help. Power Cobbe's analysis highlighted the lack of legal rights and equality suffered by women and called for the vote to empower them. She also took issue with the notion that a woman was a man's property. (**2.27**)

Even if a working-class woman was lucky enough not to suffer physical abuse, the struggle simply to survive, given the large numbers of pregnancies and the lack of money, was herculean. Enquiries by the Women's Co-operative Guild, Marjory Spring Rice and Rowntree revealed the harsh conditions in which women lived. Not only was there a never ending battle against dirt, but also constant scrimping was needed to keep the family above water. (**2.31**) The ingenuity which working-class women demonstrated in their attempts to feed a family astounded social investigators. Anna Martin pointed out that it was unjust to judge working-class women by middle-class standards. (**2.32**) This was an important realisation because many middle-class organisations such as the Charity Organisation Society and Salvation Army used middle-class ideals of 'respectability' to determine whether or not a working-class family qualified for charitable assistance. Against a background of a desire to create 'homes fit for heroes', the Labour party sent out a questionnaire asking working women what kind of house they wanted. (**2.33**) Nevertheless by the end of the 1920s many families were still living in substandard housing.

The emphasis on marital status, however, meant that women living without men either through lack of opportunity to marry, widowhood (particularly after World War I) or choice, were looked upon as objects of pity at best, or dangerous in that they were operating outwith male control. The question of 'surplus women' again came to the fore. (**2.34**) By 1921, women outnumbered men in the twenty to twenty-four age bracket by 1,176:1,000, and by 1,209:1,000 in the twenty-five to twenty-nine group. Attempts by women to show that they could function independently were ridiculed despite the fact that during World War I many women had enjoyed living an independent life and would have preferred to carry on working. Furthermore many men returned from war in a damaged psychological state which put increasing burdens on women. It was not surprising that with the easing of divorce in 1923,[7] there was an increase in the number of divorces. (**2.42**) In the interwar years, the position of the spinster became derided (**2.47**) the main fear being that having tasted independence women would no longer want to get married, thus threatening the future of the family and society.

The question of the unmarried mother was also difficult. Again, she was not conforming to accepted social mores. In the eighteenth century men had been able to confine their wives to asylums for non-compliance to social roles; in the twentieth century by virtue of the Mental Deficiency Act 1913 unmarried mothers could be put in mental hospitals often for life. (**2.38**) While there was a realisation during WWI that illegitimate births were likely to increase and that there was a need for an increase in the birthrate to replace the large numbers of men lost (**2.37**) there was still the continuing question of how to help the child without putting the unmarried mother in an advantageous position. (**2.39**) The National Council for the Unmarried Mother and her Child pointed out that the burden of supporting the child fell overwhelmingly on the mother who should not be seen simply as a 'depraved' woman. (**2.43**) In an attempt to deal with child poverty, Eleanor Rathbone campaigned tirelessly for thirty years for family allowances. In 1918 she was behind the formation of the Family Endowment Society and had some success in attracting support. After 1934, there was renewed interest as a result of the work of social investigators who revealed the physical state of the unemployed and the declining birthrate. Family allowances, which were to belong legally to mothers, were seen as a means of abolishing childhood poverty and encouraging larger families. (**2.48**)

Gradually, the myth of the angel in the house was attacked by those such as Virginia Woolfe (**2.44**) and Margery Spring Rice who pointed out that, 'For most women this is no pedestal of ease and mere moral power, for in the large majority of homes the woman is not only the most passionate upholder of the faith, but the slave without whose labour the whole structure of the family tends to collapse'.[8] Nevertheless, traditional women's magazines in the 1950s were still promoting the idea that a woman's role was to ensure that the home was a haven for men. The influence of the Women's movement, however, meant that by 1969 some men argued that they should do an equal share in the home, though this has still not been achieved.

2.1   Friendship, love and marriage

I know of nothing that renders a woman more despicable, than her thinking it essential to happiness to be married . . . if it were true, the belief that it is so, and the consequent impatience to be married, is the most effectual way to prevent it.

You must not think from this, that I do not wish you to marry: on the contrary, I am of opinion, that you may attain a superior degree of happiness, in a married state, to what you can possibly find in any other. I know the forlorn and unprotected situation of an old maid, the chagrin and peevishness which are apt to infect their tempers, and the great difficulty of making a transition, with dignity and cheerfulness, from the period of youth, beauty, admiration, and respect, into the calm, silent, unnoticed retreat of declining years.

I see some unmarried women of active, vigorous minds, and great vivacity of spirits, degrading themselves; sometimes by entering into a dissipated course of life, unsuitable for their years, and exposing themselves to the ridicule of girls, who might have been their grandchildren; sometimes by oppressing their acquaintances by impertinent intrusions into their private affairs; and sometimes by being the propagators of scandal and defamation. All this is owing to an exuberant activity of spirit which, if it had found employment at home, would have rendered them respectable and useful members of society.

I see other women, in the same situation, gentle, modest, blessed with sense, taste, delicacy, and every milder female virtue of the heart, but of weak spirits, bashful and timid: I see such women sinking into obscurity and insignificance, and gradually losing every elegant accomplishment; for this evident reason, that they are not united to a partner who has sense, and worth, and taste, to know their value: one who is able to draw forth their concealed qualities, and show them to advantage; who can give that support to their feeble spirits which they stand so much in need of; and who, by his affection and tenderness, might make such a woman happy in exerting every talent, and accomplishing herself in every elegant art that could contribute to his amusement.

In short, I am of opinion, that a married state, if entered into from proper motives of esteem and affection, will be the happiest for yourselves, make you most respectable in the eyes of the world, and the most useful members of society. But I confess I am not enough of a patriot to wish you to marry for the good of the public: I wish you to marry for no other reason but to make yourselves happier. When I am so particular in my advices about your conduct, I own my heart beats with the fond hope of making you worthy the attachment of men who will deserve you, and be sensible of your merit. But Heaven forbid you should ever relinquish the ease and independence of a single life, to become the slaves of a fool or a tyrant's caprice . . .

Before your affections come to be in the least engaged to any man, examine your tempers, your tastes, and your hearts, very severely, and settle in your own minds, what are the requisites to your happiness in a married state; and, as it is almost impossible that you should get everything you wish, come to a steady determination what you are to consider as essential, and what may be sacrificed.

From what I have said, you will easily see that I could never pretend to advise whom you should marry: but I can with great confidence advise when you should marry.

Avoid a companion that may entail any hereditary disease on your posterity, particularly (that most dreadful of all human calamities) madness. It is the height of imprudence to run into such a danger, and, in my opinion, highly criminal.

Do not marry a fool: he is the most intractable of all animals; he is led by his passions and caprices, and is incapable of hearing the voice of reason. It may probably too hurt your vanity to have husband for whom you have reason to blush and tremble every time they open their lips in company. But the worst circumstance that attends a fool, is his constant jealousy of his wife being thought to govern him. This renders it impossible to lead him, and he is continually doing absurd and disagreeable things, for no other reason but to shew he dares do them.

A rake is always a suspicious husband, because be has only known the most worthless of your sex. Its likewise entails the worst diseases on his wife and children, if he has the misfortune to have any.

If you have a sense of religion yourselves, do not, think of husbands who have none.

If they have tolerable understandings, they will be glad that you have religion, for their own sakes, and for the sake of their families; but it will sink you in their esteem. If they are weak men, they will be continually teasing and shocking you about your principles. If you have children, you will suffer the most bitter distress, in seeing all your endeavours to form their minds to virtue and piety, all your endeavours to secure their present and eternal happiness, frustrated and turned into ridicule.

As I look on your choice of a husband to be of the greatest consequence to your happiness, I hope you will make it with the utmost circumspection. Do not give away to a sudden sally of passion, and dignify it with the name of love. – Genuine love is not found in caprice; it is founded in nature, on honourable views, on virtue, on similarity of tastes, and sympathy of souls.

Dr John Gregory, *A father's legacy to his daughters* (1773), London: Brettell & Co, 1808, edn pp. 163–8.

2.2 An unfortunate mother's advice to her absent daughters

A woman can never be seen in a more ridiculous light, than when she appears to govern her husband; if, unfortunately, the superiority of understanding is on her side, the apparent consciousness of that superiority betrays a weakness that renders her contemptible in the sight of every considerate person and it may, very probably, fix in his mind a dislike never to be eradicated. In such a case, if it should ever be your own, remember that some degree of dissimulation is commendable – so far as to let your husband's defect appear unobserv'd. When he judges wrong, never flatly contradict, but lead him insensibly into another opinion, in so discreet a manner, that it may seem entirely his own – and, let the whole credit of every prudent determination rest on him, without indulging the foolish vanity of claiming any merit to yourself; – thus a person, of but an indifferent capacity, may be so assisted as, in many instances, to shine with a borrow'd lustre, scarce distinguishable from the native, and, by degrees, he may be brought into a kind of mechanical method of acting properly, in all the common occurrences of life.

Lady Sarah Pennington, *An unfortunate mother's advice to her absent daughters*, 1761, 1770, edn pp. 112–14.

2.3 Masculine women

A masculine woman must be naturally an unamiable creature. I confess myself shocked, whenever I see the sexes confounded. An effeminate fellow, that, destitute of every manly sentiment, copies with inverted ambition from your sex, is an object of contempt and aversion at once. On the other hand, any young woman of better rank, that throws off all the lovely softness of her nature, and emulates the daring intrepid temper of a man – how terrible! The transformation on either side must ever be monstrous ... But what though the dress be kept ever so distinct, if the behaviour be not; in those points, I mean, where the character peculiar to each sex seems to require a difference? ... By dint of assiduity and flattery fortune and show, a female man shall sometimes succeed strangely with the women: but to the men an amazon never fails to be forbidding.

Dr James Fordyce, *Sermons to young women*, London (1766), pp. 104–5.

2.4 Fidelity

Matrimony, in all nations, being a compact between a male and female, for the purpose of continuing the species, the first and most necessary obligation of it has been thought fidelity; but, by various people, this fidelity has been variously understood: almost all nations ... have agreed in requiring the most absolute unconditional fidelity on the party of the woman; while, on that of the man, greater latitude has been given ... and hand of severity is held so closely over the incontinence of married women, and so much latitude given to the men, because the men generally have the care of providing for the offspring; and it would be hard that a man should be obliged to provide for, and leave his estate to children which he could never with certainty call his own, were the same indulgence given to the women as to the men. A shorter way of explaining the matter would have been, to have said, that men are generally the framers and explainers of the law. Where women have shared in the legislation, they have put their own sex on a more equal footing with ours.

William Alexander, *The history of women from the earliest antiquity, to the present time; giving an account of almost every interesting particular concerning that sex, among all nations, ancient and modern*, Philadelphia (1796), New York: AMS Press (1976), vol. 2, pp. 220–1.

2.5   Benefits of widowhood

In Europe . . . widowhood, when tolerable circumstances are annexed to it, is, of all other female states, the most eligible; being free from that guardianship and controul, (sic) to which the sex are subject while virgins, and while wives.

William Alexander, *The history of women* (1796), vol. 2, p. 312.

2.6   Parental authority

Let it be remembered that, although parental authority can never be justified in constraining a daughter to marry against her will; there are many cases in which it may be justified in requiring her to pause.

Thomas Gisborne, *An enquiry into the duties of the female sex* (1797), London: T. Cadwell & W. Davies (1798), p. 254.

2.7   Choice of a partner

The poor are the only class who still retain the liberty of acting from inclination and from choice, while the rich, in proportion as they rise in opulence and rank, sink in the exertion of the natural rights of mankind, and must sacrifice their love at the shrine of interest or ambition.
   . . . courtship, at least that kind of it which proceeds from mutual inclination and affection is, among the great, nearly annihilated, and the matrimonial bargain . . . is made between the relations of the two families, with all the care and cunning that each is master of to advance its own interest by over-reaching the other.

William Alexander, *The history of women* (1779), vol. 2, p. 179.

2.8 Wife sales

'The Smithfield Bargain'
One of those scenes which occasionally disgrace even Smithfield, took place there about five o'clock on Friday evening (July 14th), namely – a man exposing his wife for sale. Hitherto we have only seen those moving in the lowest classes of society thus degrading themselves, but the present exhibition was attended with some novel circumstances. The parties, buyer and seller, were persons of property; the lady (the object of sale), young, beautiful, and elegantly dressed, was brought to market in a coach, and exposed to the view of her purchaser, with a silk halter round her shoulders, which were covered with a rich white lace veil. The price demanded for her, in the first instance, was eighty guineas, but that finally agreed upon was fifty guineas and a valuable horse upon which the purchaser was mounted. The sale and delivery being complete, the lady, with her new lord and master, mounted a handsome curricle[9] which was in waiting for them, and drove off, seemingly nothing loath to go. The purchaser in the present case is a celebrated horsedealer in town, and the seller, a grazier of cattle, residing about six miles from London.

Morning Chronicle, 15 July 1814.

2.9 Wife sale at Carlisle

On Saturday, the 7th, the inhabitants of this city witnessed the sale of a wife by her husband, Joseph Thompson, who resides in a small village about three miles from this city. He rents a farm of about 42 or 44 acres, and was married at Hexham, in the year 1829, to his present wife. She is a spruce, lively, buxom damsel, apparently not exceeding 22 years of age, and appeared to feel a pleasure at the exchange she was about to make. They had no children during their union, and that, together with some family disputes, offered them, by mutual agreement, to come to the resolution of finally parting. Accordingly, the bellman was sent round to give public notice of the sale, which was to take place at 2 o'clock. This announcement attracted the notice of thousands. She appeared above the crowd, standing on a large oak chair, surrounded by many of her friends, with a rope or halter made of straw round her neck. She was dressed in rather a fashionable country style, and appeared to some advantage. The husband, who was also standing in an elevated position near her, proceeded to put her up for sale, and spoke nearly as follows:-

'Gentlemen – I have to offer to your notice my wife, Mary Ann Thompson, otherwise Williamson, whom I mean to sell to the highest and fairest bidder. Gentlemen, it is her wish as well as mine to part forever. She has been to me only a bosom servant. I took her for my comfort, and the good of my house, but she became my tormentor, a domestic curse, a night invasion, and a daily devil. (Great laughter.) Gentlemen, I speak truth from my heart, when I say, may God deliver us from troublesome wives and frolicsome widows. (Laughter.) Avoid them the same as you would a mad dog, a roaring lion, a loaded pistol, cholera morbus, Mount Etna, or any other pestilential phenomena in nature. Now I have shown you the dark side of my wife, and told you her faults and her failings; I will now introduce the bright and sunny side of her, and explain her qualifications and goodness. She can read novels and milk cows, she can laugh and weep with the same ease that you could take a glass of ale when thirsty: indeed, gentlemen, she reminds me of what the poet says of women to general–

'Heaven gave to women the peculiar grace,
'To laugh, to weep, and cheat the human race.

The Times, 26 April 1832.
(From the *Lancaster Herald*.)

2.10 Problems of early marriages

'Matrimony'
Early marriages are, in my opinion, a stop to improvement. If we were born only 'to draw nutrition, propagate and rot', the sooner the end of creation was answered the better; but as women are here allowed to have souls, the soul ought to be attended to. In youth a woman endeavours to please the other sex, in order, generally speaking, to get married, and this endeavour calls forth all her powers. If she has had a tolerable education, the foundation only is laid, for the mind does not soon arrive at maturity, and should not be engrossed by domestic cares before any habits are fixed. The passions also have too much influence over the judgment to suffer it to direct her in this most important affair; and many women, I am persuaded, marry a man before they are twenty, whom they would have rejected some years after. Very frequently, when the education has been

neglected, the mind improves itself, if it has leisure for reflection, and experience to reflect on; but how can this happen when they are forced to act before they have had time to think, or find that they are unhappily married? Nay, should they be so fortunate as to get a good husband, they will not set a proper value on him; he will be found much inferior to the lovers described in novels, and their want of knowledge makes them frequently disgusted with the man, when the fault is human nature.

Mary Wollstonecraft, *Thoughts on the education of daughters: With reflections on female conduct, in the more important duties of life*, London: J. Johnson (1787), pp. 93–5

2.11 Improvident marriage

'While among the classes in easy circumstances the age of marriage is deferred from prudential motives, no such cause influences the labouring classes who marry early, and make no provision for their children; hence births and deaths follow each other in rapid succession, the death of one child, after existing for a few months, making way for the birth of another, each event increasing the poverty and recklessness of the parents, until at last they themselves either become the victims of epidemic fever, or swell the lists of applicants for relief from the poor's rates. The above is no fanciful picture, it is drawn from reality; and if the subject were investigated upon a large scale, it would be found as the results of the improvident marriages of the labouring classes, that the number of children born to them has been very great, and the number reared has been very small. The contrast between the labouring classes and those in easy circumstances is in no particular so strongly marked as in the relative number of the births and deaths of their children'.

Inquiry into the sanitary condition of the labouring population: Scotland (1842), HL, xxviii, p. 185.

2.12 Working-class women's lack of morality

The mother who has never felt her own moral and social rank injured by her sexual indulgences – who looks around her, and sees that all are like

45

herself – who has experienced no difficulty in settling herself as a wife – who even, if, after her marriage, she has continued her former practices, has derived positive and substantial benefits in consequence, by improving the condition of her husband, and adding to the comforts of her family, forgets – if she ever felt – that she was sinning.

Her family inherit the same lax feelings; her sons and daughters are both subjected to the same causes which prematurely evolved her own propensities; are themselves in the same state of precociousness; have the same failings, and become fathers and mothers in their turn.

Peter Gaskell, *The manufacturing population of England, its moral, social and physical conditions, and the changes which have arisen from the use of steam machinery; with an examination of infant labour*, London: Baldwin and Craddock (1833), p. 73.

2.13   The Angel in the House

Canto V

I. The Comparison

Where she succeeds with cloudless brow,
    In common and in holy course,
He fails, in spite of prayer and vow
    And agonies of faith and force;
Or, if his suit with Heaven prevails
    To righteous life, his virtuous deeds
Lack beauty, virtue's badge; she fails
    More graciously than he succeeds
Her spirit, compact of gentleness,
    If Heaven postpones or grants her pray'r,
Conceives no pride in its success,
    And in its failure no despair;
But his, enamour'd of its hurt,
    Baffled, blasphemes, or, not denied,
Crows from the dunghill of desert,
    And wags its ugly wings for pride
He's never young nor ripe; she grows
    More infantine, auroral, mild,
And still the more she lives and knows
    The lovelier she's express'd a child.

46

Coventry Patmore, *The angel in the house*, London: Rouledge and Sons (1854).

2.14   Women's lack of domestic skills

In the case of the female children the effect of their ignorance and want of instruction in needlework, knitting, &c., strikes one as the more remarkable, since, happily, these useful arts are almost universally to be found possessed by the female population throughout the land; but when we reflect upon the low state of domestic life into which the collier family is, as it were, driven by the nature and duration of their employment, and of the indifference which this unmitigated slavery begets in the mind – even of the young – to all those wholesome incitements to cleanliness and decent proprieties of person and home, which are invaluable as the means of keeping the tone of a labouring population from sinking into grossness, it excites but little wonder; nor is it surprising that tradesmen scarcely ever marry colliers' daughters where the females work below ground, as they know nothing of house-wifery. How in the name of reason should they? Are they to learn it in the pit?

First report of the Commissioners on the employment of children (1842), vol. xv, p. 399, para. 77.

2.15   Effects of women working in the pits

Michael Thomas Sadler, Esq., surgeon, Barnsley: 'I strongly disapprove of females being in pits; the female character is totally destroyed by it; their habits and feelings are altogether different; they can neither discharge the duties of wives nor mothers. I see the greatest differences in the homes of those colliers whose wives do not go into the pits in cleanliness and good management. It is a brutalizing practice for women to be in collieries; the effect on their morals is very bad; it would be advisable to prevent females from going into pits'.

First report of the Commissioners on the employment of children (1842), vol. xv, p. 31.

47

2.16 A woman's place

Mr Place's advice to the hand-loom weavers
You, as well, as many others, know well that I have always deprecated
the employment of women in every regularly conducted trade. Women
have enough to do to attend to their homes, their husbands, their
children, their relatives, and such light labour as can be done at home;
their place is home; there they must be, or there can be no order, no
satisfaction, no comfort. All is turned upside down, where the woman
is turned out of her home, – turned into a mill or a workshop. Women
who follow a regular trade like men, never can be either good wives,
good mothers, or good companions; and yet, unless these are all, the
society must degenerate, until at length it can go no lower, until deprav-
ity has reached its lowest depth, until crime and misery can be pushed no
further.

Poor Man's Guardian, 10 October 1835, p. 699.

2.17 A woman's position

I have already stated, that women, in their position in life, must be content
to be inferior to men: but as their inferiority consists chiefly in that want
of power, this deficiency is abundantly made up to them by their capabil-
ity of exercising influence; it is made up to them also in other ways,
incalculable in their number and extent, but in none so effectually as by
that order of Divine Providence which places them, in a moral and religious point of view, on the same level with man; nor can it be a subject
of regret to any right-minded woman, that they are not only exempt from
the most laborious occupations both of mind and body, but also from the
necessity of engaging in those eager pecuniary speculations, and in that
fierce conflict of worldly interests, by which men are so deeply occupied
as to be in a manner compelled to stifle their best feelings, until they
become in reality the characters they at first only assumed. Can it be a
subject of regret to any kind and feeling woman, that her sphere of action
is one adapted to the exercise of the affections, where she may love, and
trust, and hope, and serve, to the utmost of her wishes? Can it be a subject
of regret that she is not called upon, so much as man, to calculate, to
compete, to struggle, but rather to occupy a sphere in which the elements

of discord cannot with propriety be admitted – in which beauty and order are expected to denote her presence, and where the exercise of benevolence is the duty she is most frequently called upon to perform?

Sarah Ellis, *The daughters of England: Their position in society, character and responsibilities*, London: Fisher, Son & Co. (1842), pp. 10–11.

2.18   World turned upside down

... All this [industrialisation] has led to a complete reversal of normal social relationships. The working classes have had no choice but to submit to this change, which has the most evil effects. When women work in factories, the most important result is the dissolution of family ties. If a woman works for twelve or thirteen hours a day in a factory and her husband is employed either in the same establishment or in some other works, what is the fate of the children? They lack parental care and control. They are looked after by foster-parents, who charge 1s. or 1s. 6d. a week for this service. It is not difficult to imagine that they are left to run wild. This can be seen by the increase in the number of accidents to little children which occur in the factory districts. The main cause of such accidents is the lack of proper supervision ...

... It is, moreover, self-evident that the total death rate for small children is increased by the fact that their mothers go out to work ... It is often only two or three days after confinement that a woman returns to the factory, and of course, she cannot take the baby with her. When there is a break in the factory routine she has to rush home to feed the infant and get her own meal. It is obvious that this is no proper way to rear a child ...

... It is inevitable that if a married woman works in a factory family life is inevitably destroyed and in the present state of society, which is based upon family life, its dissolution has the most demoralising consequences both for parents and children. A married woman cannot really be regarded as a mother if she is unable to spare the time to look after her child; if she hardly sees the infant at all, and if she cannot satisfy her baby's elementary need for loving care. Such a mother is inevitably indifferent to the welfare of the child, which she treats without love and without proper care as if it were a stranger. Children who grow up under such conditions have no idea of what a proper family life should be. When they grow up and have families of their own they feel out of place because their own early experience has been that of a lonely life. Such parents foster the universal decadence of family life among the workers. Similar evil consequences for the family follow from child labour.

... Obviously a girl who has been an operative since the age of nine has never had a chance to acquire a skill in household duties. Consequently all the factory girls are wholly ignorant of housewifery and are quite unfitted to become wives and mothers. They do not know how to sew, knit, cook or wash. They are ignorant of the most elementary accomplishments of the housewife, and as for looking after babies, they have the vaguest notion of how to set about it.

F. Engels, *The condition of the working-class in England*, London (1845), pp. 160–1, 165–6.

2.19   Effects of women working

... this system of things must be abrogated or restrained ... It disturbs the order of nature, and the rights of the labouring men, by ejecting the males from the workshop, and filling their places by females, who are thus withdrawn from all their domestic duties, and exposed to insufferable toil at half the wages that would be assigned to males, for the support of their families. It affects – nay, more, it absolutely annihilates, all the arrangements and provisions of domestic economy – thrift and management are altogether impossible; had they twice the amount of their present wages, they would be but slightly benefited – everything runs to waste; the house and children are deserted; the wife can do nothing for her husband and family; she can neither cook, wash, repair clothes, or take charge of the infants, all must be paid for out of her scanty earnings, and, after all, most imperfectly done. Dirt, discomfort, ignorance, recklessness, are the portion of such households; the wife has no time for learning in her youth, and none for practice in her riper age; the females are most unequal to the duties of the men in the factories; and all things go to rack and ruin, because the men can discharge at home no one of the especial duties that Providence has assigned to the females ... But every consideration sinks to nothing compared with that which springs from the contemplation of the moral mischiefs this system engenders and sustains. You are poisoning the very sources of order and happiness and virtue; you are tearing up root and branch all the relations of families to each other; you are annulling, as it were, the institution of domestic life, decreed by

Providence himself, the wisest and kindest of earthly ordinances, the mainstay of social peace and virtue, and therein of national security.

Lord Ashley, *Hansard*, 15 March 1844 cc. 1099–100.

2.20 Critique of marriage

Now the conduct of the husband alone is regulated by such calculations as his own; while that of the wife is restrained by his arbitrary will, just as he restrains his children. Not only at home, to which the wife is mostly confined, does this inequality of indulgence prevail, but to a still greater degree abroad; man – in marriage – having the exclusive command of the purse and the power of imprisoning without trial or any alleged offence, his wife. While the wife is imprisoned at home (the wife of the richest as well as of the poorest man in the country, if he so think fit to direct), counting or swallowing her sorrows, or playing with bird, kitten, needle, or novel, the husband is enjoying abroad the manly pleasures of conviviality, to wit, epicurism, drunkenness, and obscene or foolish jargon of conversation; from which women are by these self-denying moralists wisely excluded, lest their habitual and unnaturally-forced reserve should check the overflowings of such manly animal gratifications. Their more appropriate business, as defined by the vile system of sexual morality, is to remain patiently at home waiting for the happy moment to welcome the sated despot, happy if the want of external excitement subsides into mere ennui, and does not vent itself on the slave in some of the endless modes of displaying the caprice of uncontrolled power . . .

The infidelity of the husband (essentially involving the happiness of the wife) to any extent, must be patiently borne by the wife; she has no redress, physical, legal or of public opinion. The infidelity of the wife (scarcely abstracting from the mass of pleasures of the husband) in a single instance, is revenged by the husband with a complication of punishment, greater than those accorded by law to many of the most atrocious crimes. This is not the occasion to show the wickedness because the immense preponderance of misery, ensuing from such inequality of enjoyment and punishment, domestic, legal and moral; but simply to show the fact that the happiness of wives is not involved in that of their husbands, is not promoted to the same extent as their own . . .

As to intellect, man, to fit his slave for the vow and the practice of blind obedience, deprives her of all means of knowledge except such crumbs as, like the sparrow, she may pick up from her master's table. As to sympathy, the power of imprisonment which man in marriage holds, cuts off his household slave from all sympathy but with himself, his children, and cats or other household animals. To some lighter public or private amusements where these associated pleasures may be enjoyed, husbands occasionally permit their wives, as they do children, to have access; but from all senses, assemblies, and incidents, that could really enlarge their minds or sympathies, they are, partly by positive law, partly by man's public opinion, backed by persecution, effectually excluded. Home, except on a few occasions, chiefly for the drillings of superstition to render her obedience more submissive, is the eternal prison-house of the wife: the husband paints it as the abode of calm bliss, but takes care to find, outside of doors, for his own use, a species of bliss not quite so calm, but of a more varied and stimulating description. These are facts of such daily occurrence and notoriety, that to the multitudinous, unreflecting, creatures, their victims, they pass by as the established order of nature . . .

In order to preserve an equal chance of happiness arising from an equal system of morals and equal civil and criminal laws, it is thus even more necessary for women than for men to maintain the check and the exercise of political rights.

W. Thompson, *Appeal of one-half the human race, women, against the pretensions of the other half, men, to retain them in political, and thence in civil and domestic slavery*, London (1825), pp. 77–9, 181.

2.21   The oak and the ivy

The long historic serfdom of woman, creeping down into the moral and intellectual natures of the two sexes, has exaggerated the naturally complementary relation of the male and the female into an absurd caricature of strength on the one hand and dependence on the other. This is well seen in the ordinary marriage-relation of the common-prayer-book type. The frail and delicate female is supposed to cling round the sturdy husband's form, or to depend from his arm in graceful incapacity; and the spectator is called upon to admire the charming effect of the union–as of the ivy with the oak–forgetful of the terrible moral, namely, that (in the case of the trees at any rate) it is really a death-struggle which is going on, in which either the oak must perish suffocated in the embraces of its partner, or in order to free the former into anything like healthy development the ivy must be sacrificed.

Too often of course of such marriages the egoism, lordship and physical satisfaction of the man are the chief motive causes. The woman is practically sacrificed to the part of the maintenance of these male virtues. It is for her to spend her days in little forgotten details of labor and anxiety for the sake of the man's superior comfort and importance, to give up her needs to his whims, to 'humour' him in all ways she can; it is for her to wipe her mind clear of all opinions in order that she may hold it up as a kind of mirror in which he may behold reflected his lordly self; and it is for her to sacrifice even her physical health and natural instincts in deference to what is called her 'duty' to her husband.

How bitterly alone many such a woman feels! She has dreamed of being folded in the arms of a strong man, and surrendering herself, her life, her mind, her all, to his service. Of course it is an unhealthy dream, an illusion, a mere luxury of love; and it is destined to be dashed. She has to learn that self-surrender may be just as great a crime as self-assertion. She finds that her very willingness to be sacrificed only fosters in the man, perhaps for his own self-defence, the egotism and coldness that so cruelly wound her.

For how often does he with keen prevision see that if he gives way from his coldness the clinging dependent creature will infallibly overgrow and smother him! – that she will cut her woman-friends, will throw aside all her own interests and pursuits in order to 'devote' herself to him, and, affording no sturdy character of her own in which he can take any interest, will hang the festoons of her affection on every ramification of his wretched life-nor leave him a corner free–till he perishes from all manhood and social or heroic uses into a mere matrimonial clothespeg, a warning and a wonderment to passers by!

E. Carpenter, *Love's coming of age* (1896), www.sacred-texts.com/lgbt/lca/ pp. 80–2.

2.22 Marriage as a trade

If it be granted that marriage is, as I have called it, essentially a trade on the part of woman – the exchange of her person for the means of subsistence – it is legitimate to inquire into the manner in which that trade is carried on, and to compare the position of the worker in the matrimonial with the position of the worker in any other market. Which brings us at once to the fact – arising from the compulsory nature of the profession – that it is carried on under disadvantages unknown and unfelt by those who earn their living by other methods. For the regulations governing compulsory service – the institution of slavery and the like – are always framed, not in the interests of the worker, but in the interests of those who impose his work upon him. The regulations governing exchange and barter in the marriage market, therefore, are necessarily framed in the interests of the employer – the male.

. . . Marriage, with its accompaniments and consequences – the ordering of a man's house, the bearing and rearing of his children – has, by the long consent of ages, been established as practically the only means whereby woman, with honesty and honour, shall earn her daily bread. Her every attempt to enter any other profession has been greeted at first with scorn and opposition; her sole outlook was to be dependence upon man. Yet the one trade to which she is destined, the one means of earning her bread to which she is confined, she may not openly profess. No other worker stands on the same footing. The man who has his bread to earn, with hands, or brains, or tools, goes out to seek for the work to which he is trained; his livelihood depending on it, he offers his skill and services without shame or thought of reproach. But with woman it is not so; she is expected to express unwillingness for the very work for which she has been taught and trained. She has been brought up in the belief that her profession is marriage and motherhood; yet though poverty may be pressing upon her – though she may be faced with actual lack of the necessities of life – she must not openly express her desire to enter that profession, and earn her bread in the only way for which she is fitted. She must stand aside and wait – indefinitely; and attain to her destined livelihood by appearing to despise it . . . she has a perfect right to seek, with frankness and with openness, the man who, in her judgement, can most fittingly provide her with the means of support.

This freedom of bargaining to the best advantage, permitted as a matter of course to every other worker, is denied to her. It is, of course, claimed and exercised by the prostitute class – a class which has pushed to its logical conclusion the principle that woman exists by virtue of a wage paid her in return for the possession of her person; but it is interesting to note that the 'unfortunate' enters the open market with the hand of the law extended threateningly above her head. The fact is curious if inquired into: since the theory that woman should live by physical attraction of the opposite sex has never been seriously denied, but rather insisted upon, by men, upon what principle is solicitation, or open offer of such attraction, made a legal offence? (Not because the woman is a danger to the community, since the male sensualist is an equal source of danger) Only, apparently, because the advance comes from the wrong side . . . So emphatic, indeed, is this unwritten law, that one cannot help suspecting that it was needful it should be emphatic, lest woman, adapting herself to her economic position, should take the initiative in a matter on which her livelihood depended, and deprive her employer not only of the pleasure of the chase, but of the illusion that their common bargain was as much a matter of romance and volition on her part as on his.

Cicely Hamilton, *Marriage as a trade*, London: Chapman & Hall (1909), pp. 36–8.

2.23 The morality of marriage

To condense the essential history of women after the introduction of patriarchal rule, into a sentence, we may say that woman originally became the property of man by right of capture; now the wife is his by right of law.

While marriage remained practically the only means of livelihood for women, there was little danger of their seeing too clearly the seamy side of the arrangement; for to see that would be to stand helpless and open-eyed between the alternatives of selling themselves for a livelihood, and starvation; or, in milder cases, between the alternatives of social failure, and a marriage which, without being altogether worldly, would yet never for a moment, have been thought of in the entire absence of the worldly motive.

'Marry, and ask no questions; who are you that you should criticise an institution which has lasted for centuries? Marriage is your natural career, your own highly-developed conscience must tell you so. If you do not adopt it, well, we fear you will find cause to regret your decision. If you can't secure a husband, we can but regard you as a failure, a supernumerary who has no proper place in the world.' . . .

'If it were not for the children, I would take a dose of chloroform to-morrow!'

These are the words of the wife of a well-to-do tradesman, who, after twelve years of marriage, finds life a burden too heavy to be borne . . .

Her husband is a 'good fellow,' with an uncertain temper. He is capricious and imprudent, and the success of the business depends on his wife, who works at it unremittingly, sending her husband and children away for a holiday now and then, while she remains to look after the customers . . .

Is it fair, she asks, that she should be claimed body and soul for a lifetime, that she should work hard and suffer severely, without earning so much as a bare subsistence? Were she not the man's wife, he would pay her a salary for far less toil, and she would be a free agent into the bargain . . .

The two essential attributes of marriage as it now stands, are the wife's dependence, economic and social, and the supposed duty to produce as many children as Fate may decide. Take away from it these two solid props, and marriage, as we have hitherto understood it, ceases to exist. It is not recognised that what makes the 'holy estate' so firm and inflexible is its atrocious injustice . . .

. . . it will be well to remind the reader, once more, that no sweeping attack upon every individual union is intended, and that a wife is not referred to as a degraded being. It is the abstract nature of the position, as legally and generally understood, to which allusion is made. An ideal marriage is possible, and indeed even now exists, in an increasing number of cases, in spite of the conditions alluded to above; and such a union appears under the name of marriage, though every trace of the old patriarchal and purchase system has vanished, and therefore it is not marriage in the sense which I am criticising . . .

What could possibly be more fatal to the wife's continued influence over her husband than the fact that she is his absolutely and for ever, quite irrespective of her wishes or of his conduct? He marries expecting exorbitantly. If the wife does not give him all he expects, he is disappointed and angry; if she does give it – well, it is only her duty, and he ceases to value it. It becomes a matter of course, and the romance and interest die out . . .

Mona Caird, *The morality of marriage and other essays on the status and destiny of women,* London: George Redway (1897), pp. 72, 98–9, 101, 131, 133, 138, 139, 144.

2.24   The girl of the period

Time was when the phrase, 'a fair young English girl,' meant the ideal of womanhood; to us, at least, of home birth and breeding.

It meant a girl who could be trusted alone if need be, because of the innate purity and dignity of her nature, but who was neither bold in bearing nor masculine in mind; a girl who, when she married, would be her husband's friend and companion, but never his rival; one who would consider his interests as identical with her own, and not hold him as just so much fair game for spoil; who would make his house a true home and place of rest, not a mere passage-place for vanity and ostentation to pass through; a tender mother, an industrious housekeeper, a judicious mistress. The Girl of the Period is a creature who dyes her hair and paints her face, as the first articles of her personal religion – a creature whose sole idea of life is fun; whose sole aim is unbounded luxury; and whose dress is the chief object of such thought and intellect as she possesses . . .

. . . and as she lives to please herself, she does not care if she displeases everyone else . . .

She cannot be made to see that modesty of appearance and virtue in deed ought to be inseparable; and that no good girl can afford to appear bad, under pain of receiving the contempt awarded to the bad . . .

It leads to slang, bold talk and general fastness; to the love of pleasure and indifference to duty; to the desire of money before either love or happiness; to uselessness at home, dissatisfaction with the monotony of ordinary life, horror of all useful work; in a word, to the worst forms of luxury and selfishness – to the most fatal effects arising from want of high principle and absence of tender feeling.

. . . It is this envy of the pleasures, and indifference to the sins, of these women of the demi-monde which is doing such infinite mischief to the modern girl.

Love in a cottage-that seductive dream which used to vex the heart and disturb the calculations of the prudent mother-is now a myth of past ages. The legal barter of herself for so much money, representing so much dash, so much luxury and pleasure-that is her idea of marriage; the only idea worth entertaining. For all seriousness of thought respecting the duties or the consequences of marriage, she has not a trace. If children come, they find but a stepmother's cold welcome from her; and if her husband thinks that he has married anything that is to belong to him – a tacens et placens uxor pledged to make him happy – the sooner he wakes from his hallu-cination and understands that he has simply married some one who will condescend to spend his money on herself, and who will shelter her indiscretions behind the shield of his name, the less severe will be his dis-appointment. She has married his house, his carriage, his balance at the banker's, his title; and he himself is just the inevitable condition clogging the wheel of her fortune; at best an adjunct, to be tolerated with more or less patience as may chance. For it is only the old-fashioned sort, not Girls of the Period pur sang, who marry for love, or put the husband before the banker. But the Girl of the Period does not marry easily. Men are afraid of her; and with reason. They may amuse themselves with her for an evening, but they do not readily take her for life.

E. Lynn Linton, *The girl of the period and other social essays,* vol. 1, London: Richard Bentley & Son (1883), pp. 1–7.

2.25   Domestic violence

At MARLBOROUGH-STREET, GEORGE FINLEY a carpenter, 1 Marlborough- mews was charged with ill-using his wife, Mary Finley. Mr Moor of the Associate Institute for Enforcing the Laws for the Protection of Women, watched the case. The complainant, who was poorly clad, said on the 13th inst. her husband struck her on the head, having been prevented from throwing the kettle at her which he took off the fire for that purpose. He was seldom sober, and was constantly ill-using her. She had been obliged to bring him to that court before. He worked for several good firms, and could earn 4 l. a week. On the day when she was assaulted she had asked him for a little money to get food for herself and children. He reluctantly threw down 6d and when she sent for twopennyworth of bullock's liver he seized the pan and flung it down. Poole, the assistant gaoler, said the woman was respectably conducted and from what he knew of the parties it was a very bad case. Mrs Camp of Blenheim-street, said owing to the ill-treatment of the complainant by her husband she had frequently taken pity on her and given her food. She believed the complainant would have died from cold but for the assistance she gave her. She had seen the prisoner throw things at his wife, which had they struck her must have killed her. The prisoner asked if the witness did not encourage his wife to come to her place. Mrs Camp said she did. She came with her infant to warm herself. Police-constable Fowkes lodged in the same house. He saw the prisoner take a kettle of water from the fire to throw at his wife, but he prevented him, and afterwards he saw the prisoner strike his wife. The prisoner was given to drinking, but he never saw the wife the worse for drink. Mr Knox sentenced the prisoner to three months' hard labour, and at the expiration of the time to find bail in 20l. for a further period of three months.

Receipt was acknowledge of 1l. from Mrs A. W. Campden-hill for the poor-box.

The Times, 27 January 1871.

2.26   Less than justice for women

The Women's Suffrage Journal, 1 July 1871 commented on the above extract:

'Less than Justice for Women'

Now the point to which we desire to call special attention in these cases is – not the assault, – wife beating is so common that it has come to be regarded as a natural condition of things, calling for no special remark nor interference – but the state of the law which permits the wife of a man who can earn £4 a week to be dependent on the charity of a neighbour for the food and fire needful to keep body and soul together. Observe, she asked her husband for money to but food – he reluctantly threw down sixpence – and when she had obtained her two pennyworth of cat's meat, he destroyed it . . .

The magistrate could lock up her husband for beating her, but he could do nothing to him for starving her so long as he did not starve to death. He could neither punish him for neglecting to supply her with food and fire, nor make an order on him to provide for her future necessities. By reason of this cruel defect in the law, vast numbers of women and children are suffering the pangs of hunger, because it is left to the absolute will and pleasure of a married man to determine whether his earnings shall go to the support of his family or to the public house.

2.27   Wife-torture in England

Wife-beating exists in the upper and middle classes rather more, I fear, than is generally recognized; but it rarely extends to anything beyond an occasional blow or two not of a dangerous kind. In his apparently most ungovernable rage, the gentleman or tradesman somehow manages to bear in mind the disgrace he will incur if his outbreak be betrayed by his wife's black eye or broken arm, and he regulates his cuffs or kicks accordingly. The dangerous wife-beater belongs almost exclusively to the artisan and labouring classes. Colliers, 'puddlers', and weavers have long earned for themselves in this matter a bad reputation, and among a long list of cases before me, I reckon shoemakers, stonemasons, butchers, smiths, tailors, a printer, a clerk, a bird-catcher, and a large number of labourers. In the worst districts of London (as I have been informed by one of the most experienced magistrates) four-fifths of the wife-beating cases are among the lowest class of Irish labourers – a fact worthy of more than passing notice, had we time to bestow upon it, seeing that in their own country Irishmen of all classes are proverbially kind and even chivalrous towards women.

There are also various degrees of wife-beating in the different localities. In London, it seldom goes beyond a severe 'thrashing' with the fist – a sufficiently dreadful punishment, it is true, when inflicted by a strong man on a woman; but mild in comparison of the kickings and tram-plings and 'purrings' with hobnailed shoes and clogs of what we can scarcely, in this connection, call the 'dark and true and tender North'. As Mr Serjeant Pulling remarks,[10] 'Nowhere is the ill-usage of woman so sys-tematic as in Liverpool, and so little hindered by the strong arm of the law, making the lot of a married woman, whose locality is the "kicking district" of Liverpool, simply a duration of suffering and subjection to injury and savage treatment, far worse than that to which the wives of mere savages are used'. It is in the centres of dense mercantile and man-ufacturing populations that this offence reaches its climax.

... The general depreciation of women as a sex is bad enough, but in the matter we are considering, the special depreciation of wives is more directly responsible for the outrages they endure. The notion that a man's wife is his PROPERTY, in the sense in which a horse is his property (descended to us rather through the Roman law than through the customs of our Teuton ancestors), is the fatal root of incalculable evil and misery. Every brutal-minded man, and many a man who in other relations of life is not brutal, entertains more or less vaguely the notion that his wife is his thing, and is ready to ask with indignation (as we read again and again in the police reports), of any one who interferes with his treatment of her, 'May I not do what I will with my own?' It is even sometimes pleaded on behalf of poor men, that they possess nothing else but their wives, and that, consequently, it seems doubly hard to meddle with the exercise of their power in that narrow sphere!

... not only is an offence against a wife condoned as of inferior guilt, but any offence of the wife against her husband is regarded as a sort of Petty Treason ... Should she be guilty of 'nagging' or scolding, or of being a slattern, or of getting intoxicated, she finds usually a short shrift and no favour – and even humane persons talk of her offence as constituting, if not a justification for her murder, yet an explanation of it. She is, in short, liable to capital punishment without judge or jury for transgressions which in the case of a man would never be punished at all, or be expiated by a fine of five shillings. ...

Frances Power Cobbe, *Contemporary Review*, 32, April 1878, pp. 55–87.

2.28 A destitute family

As the details of a few individual cases may convey more vivid impres-sions that any general statement, I will make no apology for inserting the following. The first is from a letter from one of the visitors of the 'Society for Benevolent Visitation of the Destitute Sick', in which he writes, 'I investigated the case of Mrs. —, Calton: I found her in a wretched abode, no glass in the window, no furniture of any kind except an old chair, not a handful of straw to lie upon, and blanket or rug was out of the question. The family must have spent a miserable winter. Her husband had been a drunkard and enlisted; has sailed for the Indies, and left her and four children, the eldest a girl of nine years of age, the youngest an infant of about a year old, who is ill of inflammation of the lungs brought on by cold, and not likely to live long. They are so destitute of clothing that they can scarcely cross the threshold. Though mid-day, they had got no breakfast, and one of the neighbours told me they were whole days without food, but that she never knew children bear hunger so patiently. The mother is a weaver, but with a sick child can earn little. These are the facts of the case'.

Inquiry in to the Sanitary Condition of the Labouring Population: Scotland (1842), HL, xxviii, p. 176.

2.29 'I was awfully poor'

My first girl was born before I attained my twentieth year, and I had a stepmother who had no children of her own, so I was not able to get any knowledge from her; and even if she had known anything I don't suppose she would have dreamt of telling me about these things which were supposed to exist, but must not be talked about. About a month before the baby was born I remember asking my aunt where the baby would come from. She was astounded, and did not make me much wiser. I don't know whether my ignorance had anything to do with the struggle I had to bring the baby into the world, but the doctor said that my youth had, for I was not properly developed. Instruments had to be used, and I heard the doctor say he could not tell whether my life could be saved or not, for he said there is not room here for a bird to pass. All the time I thought that this was the way all babies were born . . .

My third child, a girl, was born in a two-roomed 'nearly underground' dwelling. We had two beds in the living-room, and the little scullery was very damp. Had it not been for my neighbours, I should have had no attendance after the confinement, and no fire often, for it was during one of the coal strikes. My fourth child, a boy, was born under better housing conditions, but not much better as regards money; and during the carrying of all my children, except the first, I have had insufficient food and too much work . . .

In spite of all, I don't really believe that the children (with the exception of the oldest boy) have suffered much, only they might have been so much stronger, bigger, and better if I had been able to have better food and more rest.

Cleanliness has made rapid strides since my confinements; for never once can I remember having anything but face, neck, and hands washed until I could do things myself, and it was thought certain death to change the underclothes under a week.

For a whole week we were obliged to lie on clothes stiff and stained, and the stench under the clothes was abominable, and added to this we were commanded to keep the babies under the clothes.

I often wonder how the poor little mites managed to live, and perhaps they never would have done but for our adoration, because this constant admiration of our treasures did give them whiffs of fresh air very often.

My husband's lowest wage was 10s., the highest about £1 only, which was reached by overtime. His mother and my own parents generally provide me with clothing, most of which was cast-offs.

Maternity letters from working-women, London: Bell & Sons (1915), 11, pp. 30–1.

2.30 The problems of dirt

Amidst these scenes of wretchedness, the lot of the female sex is much the hardest. The man, if, as is usually the case, in employment, is taken away from the annoyances around his dwelling during the day, and is generally disposed to sleep soundly after his labours during the night; but the woman is obliged to remain constantly in the close court or neglected narrow alley where she lives, surrounded by all the evils . . . ; dirty children, domestic brawls, and drunken disputes meet her on every side and every hour. Under such circumstances, the appropriate employments of a tidy housewife in brushing, washing, or cleansing, seem vain and useless efforts, and she soon abandons them.

R. A. Slaney MP on the state of Birmingham, state of large towns, 2nd report; P.P. (1845), vol. XVIII, Appendix, p. 18.

2.31   Making ends meet

... Mrs. Smith, an excellent housewife, with a steady husband and three children at home. Her house is scrupulously clean and tidy. Mr. Smith is in regular work and earns 20s. per week. He keeps 2s. a week for himself, and hands over 18s. to his wife. ... Mr. Smith spends 1d. per day on beer, 3d. a week on tobacco, puts 3d. into the children's savings-box, and clothes himself out of the remainder. One new dress, Mrs. Smith tells us, will last for years. For everyday wear she buys some old dress at a jumble sale for a few shillings. Old garments, cast off by some wealthier family, are sometimes bought from the ragman for a few coppers; or perhaps they are not paid for in cash, but some older rags and a few bones are given in exchange for them. Garments so purchased are carefully taken to pieces, washed, and made up into clothes for the children ... She regularly pays 6d. a week for sick clubs, 4d. for life insurance, and 3d. per week into the clothing club held in connection with her church ... she kept detailed accounts for her total income and expenditure during two months.

Her 18s is usually spent as follows: –

	s.	d.
Food (five persons)	11	0
Rent	3	2
Coal and light	2	0
Soap, etc.	0	5
Sick club	0	6
Life insurance	0	4
Clothing club	0	3
	17	8
In addition to this sum ... Mr. Smith keeps 2s per week for his personal expenditure	2	0
If this sum is included the average weekly total is brought up to	19	8

... with such a normal expenditure there was no appreciable sum available for 'extras.' 'Then how do you do, Mrs. Smith,' ... 'when you have to meet any extraordinary expenditure, such as a new dress, or a pair of boots?' 'Well, as a rule,' was the answer, 'we 'ave to get it out of the food money and go short; but I never let Smith suffer – 'e 'as to go to work, and must be kept up, yer know! And then Smith 'as ollers been very good to me. When I want a new pair of shoes, or anythink, 'e 'elps me out of 'is pocket money, and we haven't to pinch the food so much.'

Here, then, is a family where the husband is in regular work and is absolutely steady, where the rent is less than the average for the class, and the wife is an exceptionally clever and economical housekeeper, and yet every extra must be bought out of the food money. This at its normal level is 4s. 5d. per week below the sum which would be required to provide such a family with the diet supplied to able-bodied paupers in York Work-house. This illustration . . . serves to show what can and cannot be made out of a pound a week, with clever management. Under average management the standard of living . . . will be distinctly below that which is here described . . .

Life of the Women in Class 'D'.

No one can fail to be struck by the monotony which characterises the life of most married women of the working class . . . with advance in the social scale, family life becomes more private, and the women, left in the house all day while their husbands are at work, are largely thrown upon their own resources. These, as a rule, are sadly limited, and in the deadening monotony of their lives these women too often become mere hopeless drudges. Especially does illness in the family, not infrequent with three or four growing children, tell heavily upon the mother, who has then to be nurse, cook, and housemaid all in one. The husband . . . seldom rises even to the idea of mental companionship with his wife. He rarely ill-treats her; but restricted education and a narrow circle of activities hinder comrade-ship and lack of mental touch tends to pass into unconscious neglect or active selfishness.

B. Seebohm Rowntree, *Poverty a study of town life*, Macmillan and Co., 2nd edn (1910), pp. 55–7, 77–8.

2.32   Middle-class standards

It is also easier for the middle-class housekeeper to dilate on the dirt and want of management she observes in mean streets than to consider exactly how she would herself conduct domestic life in these localities. It is easier to attack the problem of infant mortality by founding Babies' Institutes, and by endeavouring to screw up to a still higher level the self-sacrifice and devotion of the normal working-class woman, than to incur the wrath of vested interests by insisting on healthy conditions for mothers and infants alike . . .

The general rise in the standard of comfort on which social reformers congratulate themselves has made life harder for the mothers. 'When I was ten years old,' said one, 'I was helping my parents by gathering stones for the farmers; now, I send four girls to school every day with starched pinafores and blacked boots. Except on Sundays, my father never had anything but bread and cold bacon, or cheese, for his dinner; now I have to cook a hot dinner every day for the children and a hot supper every evening for my man.' ...

Of course, the home-makers of the mean streets are not to be judged by middle-class standards. Theoretically, most people acknowledge the evolutionary nature of manners and morals; practically, they fail to see that a code which works well enough in the household of a prosperous professional man would often prove disastrous in the household of a dock labourer. Take, for instance, the question of order and cleanliness. Not to have beds made till 8 o'clock in the evening would reasonably be considered to show bad management in the case of a rich woman; to have them made earlier would sometimes show lack of organising power in the case of a poor one. 'How do you manage about the housework if you are out all day?' a member of No. 39 was recently asked. 'I rise at 4.45, sweep the place a bit, and get my husband his breakfast. He must be off before six. Then I wake and wash the children, give them each a slice of bread and butter and the remains of the tea, and leave out the oats and sugar for Harry to prepare for the rest later on. (Harry is ten years old.) Then I open up the beds and take the baby to Mrs. T. My own work begins at 7 a.m. At 8.30 the firm sends us round a mug of tea and I eat the bread and butter I have brought with me. I used to come home in the dinner hour, but my feet are now so bad that I get a halfpenny cup of coffee in a shop and eat the rest of what I have brought. At 4.30 I have another cup of tea and get home a little before 7 p.m. I do the hearth up, get my husband his supper, and make the beds. Then I get out the mending and am usually in bed by 11. On Saturday I leave work at noon so as to take the washing to the baths.' ...

But nothing is so astonishing as the prevalence of the belief that the wives are bad managers and housekeepers. A moment's reflection will show that, if this were true, the families could not live at all. Any analysis of the incomes makes manifest that, when the wives have paid rent, coal, gas, soap, insurance, and have set aside a small sum for tiny incidental expenses and for renewal of boots and clothes, they seldom have left more than from 10s to 14s to provide food for two adults and three or four children. The husband, of course, costs more than his proportional share; luckily, the men insist on being well fed, or incapacity through illness would be even more common among the wage-earners that it is at present ...

Mrs. D., in answer to a question as to how she was feeding her husband and five children last winter on the occasional shillings she earned by charing, replied: 'Well, you see, nobody can manage better than I do. I get a halfpennyworth of carrots, halfpennyworth of onions, three pounds of potatoes for a penny. When they are nearly cooked I cut in two cold faggots. This makes a rich broth, and, with a pennyworth of bread, gives me and the children as much as we can eat for 3½d. Sometimes I can do better still. I get threepennyworth of pork rinds and bones from the butcher, a halfpennyworth of rice, a pennyworth of potatoes (3 lbs.), and a pennyworth of pot-herbs. This gives us all, father included, a good dinner, and leaves enough for next day if I boil another pennyworth of potatoes, so I reckon I get fourteen hot dinners for 6½d.'

Anna Martin, *The married working woman: A study*, London, National Union of Women's Suffrage Societies (1911), pp. 2, 6–9, 11, 13.

2.33 The views of the woman in the home

For many generations, and with special emphasis in the last fifty years, we have been told that woman's place is the home. If women are to accept this position, they must also claim a right to have that home built according to their own desires. The war gave rise to a new phrase when the Prime Minister made his declaration that with the coming peace houses must be built fit for heroes to live in. She wants her house to be fit for a hero to live in, but she wants also to free herself from some of that continuous toil which is the result of the bad housing conditions of the past, and has prevented her from taking her full share of work as a citizen, wife and mother.

Though it has been so largely the concern of women to keep the house, the working woman has had very little to say in the past as to the kind of house that she should keep. When a well-to-do family build their own house, the architect consults, not only the husband, but also the wife. But the working woman, to whom it is so infinitely important to secure a comfortable and convenient home, has never been consulted at all. In the main, working-class housing has been in the hands of the builders, and of jerry builders at that, who have considered cheapness as far more important than health and comfort. Even when housing has been a matter of municipal concern instead of private enterprise, no effort has been made to learn the opinion of working women before deciding upon the plans . . .

... there would be the healthiest and most convenient arrangements for cooking, bathing, and cleaning; there would be enough space and sufficient rooms to give healthy sleeping and living accommodation for all; the house would get the full benefit of sunshine and yet give protection from excessive cold and wet. But the home must not be just a place to live in; it must provide a centre for social life and for the reasonable use of leisure; and still more, it must be a good setting to the lives of those who inhabit it, and nourish the best qualities of their characters – in five words, it must be a pleasure to live in it ...

... there is the question of housework. The present demand for shortening the hours of labour is not only found in the workshop, the factory, and the mine; the woman in the home desires to see her work curtailed in order that she may preserve her health, widen her mental resources, and attain a higher standard of life herself. She therefore seeks to have a house in which she can reach a high level of cleanliness and comfort without working continuously at the drudgery which has been her common lot ... For many women the chief task of life has been to gain a series of victories in the constant struggle against dirt. From day to day the working woman has fought a constant battle with the poorest weapons against this foe ...

A. D. Sanderson & M. Phillips, *The working-woman's house*, London: The Swarthmore Press (1919), pp. 9, 11, 21.

2.34 Surplus women

Dr. R. Murray-Leslie delivered a lecture yesterday at the Institute of Hygiene on the subject of the disproportion of the sexes. He said that there could be no real social rest without feminine contentment and, in our own country, where women formed the bulk of the population, the effect of their sex preponderance seemed to be almost wholly injurious and to have little compensating advantage.

The female excess was greater in Great Britain than elsewhere, and the war had aggravated this disturbing factor, because the men who had fallen all belonged to the age-group which represented either potential or actual husbands and fathers. There were now over 1,000,000 excess females of reproductive age.

The social effects of sex disproportion were demonstrated in the crumbling of the old ethical standards. The freedom of the modern independent girl from the supervision of her parents; the tendency to rebel against discipline and conventional trammels; the cry of pleasure for pleasure's sake – all these tended to the encouragement of a lowered standard of morality.

It was in regard to marriage and family life that female preponderance was playing the most important part. Never had there been so many unhappy marriages. Many married women were demanding divorce by mutual consent, as it was contended that the present rigid law condemned many to the society of an utterly uncongenial companion; while married men often sought happier relations among the numerous unattached women. Speaking from his own medical experience, he had no hesitation in saying that much of the existing unhappiness was traceable to clandestine relations between young women and married men.

An extraordinary diversity of type had emerged as a direct outcome of sex disproportion. The domestic type still formed the bulk in the industrial classes, but was becoming rarer in the so-called middle and upper classes. The social butterfly type had probably never been so prevalent as at present. It comprised the frivolous, scantily-clad, jazzing flapper, irresponsible and undisciplined, to whom a dance, a new hat, or a man with a car, were of more importance than the fate of nations. The type contained a large proportion of physically attractive girls with strong reproductive instincts, and they were ever vying and competing with each other for the scarce and elusive male. In many cases they strove by means of dress, or the lack of it, to appeal to man's lower nature instead of exercising the power to elevate his ideals. Young men had dance invitations four and five deep, and our boys and young men were being spoilt before our eyes.

The intellectual type, represented by the professional workers, married in very small proportion, but to them was due the driving force that secured amelioration of the conditions of employment of their sex, and it was they who influence legislation designed to safeguard maternity and to promote child-welfare. Racially it was the intelligent type that was most important and best fitted to undertake the present complex responsibilities of marriage. There was a great difference between intellectuality and intelligence. The purely intellectual woman was, usually, not sexually attractive, but the intelligent woman was well read and in touch with new movements, while she equally appreciated the charms of dress refinement, and other social amenities.

The Times, 5 December 1920.

2.35   Problems of surplus women

To the Editor of The Times
Sir, The social reform . . . might succeed if the world were quite different
from what it is.

If, for instance, there were many more men than women in existence it would be possible for every woman to become a wife and
mother, and thus to fulfil what the Comtists consider to be her only true
vocation.

Unfortunately, however, there are many more women than men; it is,
therefore impossible unless we take to polygamy, for every woman to be
a wife. There are a great number of single women and widows, and the
practical question is how best to provide for them. Mr Harrison says that
they ought not to work, and that 'their true function is to educate not
merely children but men'; but he does not enter into details, and tell us
how this is to be done. How would he dispose of the thousands and thousands of women now engaged in textile factories? Would he give them
each 10s a week, and send them about as missionaries 'to educate men'?
Who would pay the 10s a week, and would the men stand being educated
to such an extent?

It would be interesting to know what the Comtists really do wish to
do. I hope they do not mean to shut all the unmarried women up in con-
vents. If they do, in the name of 'humanity' I protest against the plan . . .
    I am, sir, yours faithfully
    A Woman

The Times, 12 September 1891.

2.36   The size of families

. . . The large, haphazard families of former days have a fine record, but,
like most things haphazard, they fit with difficulty into an organized social
fabric. A suitable interval between one birth and the next is often advantageous to a woman's health, helps to maintain her youth and vigour, and
gives her the opportunity of continuing an intelligent interest in outside
things, to the advantage not only of herself, but also of her husband and
children. There is often a distinct disadvantage in her youth being too continuously occupied in child-bearing . . .

. . . The too small family is disadvantageous to itself, to its parents, and to the nation. There is an idea prevalent that the bearing of children is detrimental to the maintenance of a woman's youth. The contrary is the truth. Imagine a young woman of 30 with, say, two children, finally extinguishing at that early age the maternal side of her nature. Far from saving her youth, she is prejudicing it, and in addition she is inviting shrinkage of mind and sympathy. The woman who maintains best her youth of body and mind is the one with the larger family wisely distributed through the years.

Nor does the happiness of the family fare better. Children need each other — youth needs youth. Isolated children are often pathetic figures — over sensitive, unchildlike, and more difficult to maintain in health and cure of disease. Their parents, for their part, are over-anxious and apprehensive . . .

Of the many lessons which the war has taught us, surely there are few more patent than the mistake of the small family. What cup of bitterness could be deeper than the loss of the only son when there might have been others! This war has kindled afresh the flame of patriotism; it is going to re-enthrone the things which matter. This Empire needs to be peopled by Britishers, and no greater service can be rendered to it than the production of healthy families as large as the means of parents renders possible.

Your obedient servant,
PHYSICIAN.

The Times, 3 October 1916.

2.37   Maternity and Child Welfare Act 1918

Lord Downham recalled that he had the honour of piloting the Maternity and Child Welfare Act through Parliament. The nation, he said, was suffering from too many empty cradles. Motherhood must be made healthier and more attractive. Fees at the home would be reduced or waived in necessitous cases, but it was in no sense a pauper institution. By combating malnutrition and ignorance the homes and its Maternity Committee would save many lives.

The Times, 7 November 1919.

2.38   Position of unmarried mothers

Mr. HAYES FISHER, President of the Local Government Board, replying to a deputation from the Associated Societies for the Care and Maintenance of Infants on the problem at how to deal with unmarried mothers and their infants, said he was glad to find the anticipation of a large increase in illegitimacy falsified. His view was that maternity and child welfare schemes should be available equally for married and unmarried mothers, and for legitimate and illegitimate children, and that in matters of health there should be no distinction. Unmarried mothers, however, must not be put in a favoured position as compared with widows and deserted wives. The Local Government Board already had authority to pay grants for maternity homes established, and aided by local authorities, and they hoped soon to be able to extend them to homes for children whose mothers could not look after them properly and also to crèches. He recognized the importance of keeping the mother and child together. He did not rule out the question of paying grants otherwise than through local authorities to such institutions, and he was prepared to recognize a good society, subject to efficient Government inspection. Cooperation between local authorities and voluntary agencies was essential, and such homes as were set up must not become a safety valve for immorality.

The Times, 23 February 1918.

2.39   Harsh treatment of unmarried mothers

... One woman was sent to a mental institution in 1916 when, as an unmarried girl, she became pregnant. Although some women were released in the late 1950s when the law was repealed, she was by then institutionalised and is still there, now [1991] aged 92.

The stigma of illegitimacy was so strong that people appeared willing to accept the idea that unmarried mothers were mentally defective. One woman, born in London in 1918, remembers her mother whispering to her every night that she must not have sex before marriage or she would go mad. 'She didn't question why women were in mental institutions. She just thought, oh well, they deserved it; they'd had sex and they'd gone mad.'

71

Pamela Johnson, born in Grimsby in 1930, became pregnant when she was 16. She told her mother, who informed the authorities. 'I was arrested, took to court, and sentenced to 28 days in Steep Hill remand centre, Lincoln, for psychiatric and emotional reports. At Steep Hill I was put into a room with a bible to read. You did cleaning jobs, but mostly you were sat in the room on your own.' . . .

From the late 19th century to the last war, the only refuges available for destitute unmarried mothers were homes run by the Salvation Army, the Church Army or the workhouse. Gina ended up in a Church Army home in Brighton. 'It was a terrible place. You scrubbed and cleaned and you had no rest time and there was no recreation except church. You had to go to church three times a day and you were marched through the streets in the condition you were in, which was degrading.'

Ann Allen, a colonel in the Salvation Army who worked in one of their maternity homes in the 1920s, says: 'The girls came in great distress because they had been made to feel that it was such a disgrace to have an illegitimate child that they . . . really were the worst kind of people that ever were. The atmosphere in the maternity ward was very tense. The girls were in pain and they thought that these labour pains were part of the punishment for the' sin which they had committed.' . . .

Joy Melville, *New Statesman and Society*, 21 March 1991.

2.40   The nation's young lives

Sir,- Mr. Galsworthy, in his article in to-day's Times on 'The Nation's Young Lives,' strongly advocates the adoption of widows' or mothers' pensions, and the proper protection and care of unmarried girl mothers and their illegitimate children. His words are opportune. No amount of Welfare Centres can do anything radical to help the children of widows or those born out of wedlock, until the State has awakened to its grave responsibility for their welfare.

I have, within the last two days, been present at a meeting of a committee of women Poor Law Guardians in one of our great provincial cities. They were engaged, no doubt unconsciously, in a game which, for want of a better name, I must call girl-baiting. I saw a young expectant mother cruelly handled, and tortured with bitter words and threats; an ordeal which she will have had to endure at the hands of four different sets of officials by the time her baby is three weeks old. These guardians told her, in my presence, that they hoped she would suffer severely for her wrong-doing, that they considered that her own mother, who had treated her kindly, had been too lenient, and that her sin was so great that she ought to be ashamed to be a cost to self-respecting ratepayers. They added that the man who was responsible for her condition was very good to have acknowledged his paternity, but expressed the belief, nay, rather the hope, that he would take an early opportunity of getting out of his obligation. Meanwhile, a pale, trembling girl, within a month of her confinement, stood, like a hunted animal, in the presence of such judges.

We pray constantly in our churches for 'all women labouring of child, sick persons, and young children, the fatherless, the widows, and all that are desolate and oppressed,' and yet we continue this oppression of the desolate.

Yours faithfully,
DOROTHEA IRVING
10, Sudbury Hill, Harrow, February, 22,

The Times, 23 February 1918.

2.41   Women and the Bill

To the editor of *The Times*
I quite see that Mr. Lloyd George, knowing of the greater mortality amongst the children of employed married women and unmarried women, and desirous of doing something to prevent infant mortality, has made the benefits to mothers in paid employment and to the unmarried mothers greater than to the married mothers whose arduous home work is unpaid. My sympathy with the unmarried mother is great, for I know from experience how often she is an exploited and inexperienced girl; but I do strongly protest against a 'national' Bill which encourages married mothers to remain in paid employment and offers greater benefits to them and to unmarried mothers than it does to the wife of the working man who does his best to provide a home for his wife.

The Times, 14 July 1911.

2.42 Approximate proportion of marriages terminated by divorce 1911–1968, England and Wales and Scotland

Year	Petitions filed	Petitions per 100 marriages contracted annually 5–15 years earlier	Estimated percentage of marriage terminated by divorce
ENGLAND AND WALES			
1911	859	0.3	0.2
1921	2790	1.0	0.8
1937	5750	1.9	1.6
1950	29,096	7.9	7.1
1953	29,845	7.8	7.0
1954	28,347	7.4	6.7
1961	31,905	8.7	
1968	55,007	15.9	
SCOTLAND			
1911	236	0.7	0.7
1921	520	1.6	1.5
1937	643	1.9	1.9
1950	2216	5.2	5.1
1953	2420	5.4	5.2
1954	2271	5.0	4.9
1961	1830	4.3	
1968	4803	11.6	

Note: 1911 to 1954 figures are taken from *Royal Commission on Marriage and Divorce.* 1961 and 1968 figures are calculated from data obtained from the Registrar-General. No estimate is made of percentages of marriages terminated by divorce.
Sources: Royal Commission on Marriage and Divorce, Cmd 9678, 1956.
Registrar-General's *Annual Report for Scotland,* Part II, 1968.
Registrar-General's *Statistical Review for England and Wales,* 1968, Tables of Population.

From: A. H. Halsey, *Trends in British society since 1900,* Macmillan (1972), p. 49.

2.43   Unmarried mothers

Sir,- The object of the National Council for the Unmarried Mother and Her Child is to help with one of the most difficult of all social problems - that of the unmarried mother and her unwanted child.

... we have to face the fact that some thousands of illegitimate children are born yearly in this country, and that the burden of their maintenance falls almost always upon the mothers. In the eyes of the law the unmarried mother is the sole legal parent of her child; in actual fact she is usually its sole means of support. The inevitable result of her economic position, her physical and mental agonies, is the appalling death rate among children born out of wedlock, and the still more appalling damage rate among those who survive.

... The mothers who come to us are not abandoned or depraved women; they are the victims of folly and ignorance. Given a little help, a little timely guidance, they are anxious to face their position, and to do what they can for the children who are so gravely handicapped by the sin of their parents. We do not condone that sin, but we try to save the helpless babies from suffering, and their mothers from the river or the streets. We find them shelter, and we try to find work for the mother; we provide advice of all kinds, legal and medical among others.

The Times, 24 October 1922.

2.44   Professions for women

You who come of a younger and happier generation may not have heard of her – you may not know what I mean by the Angel in the House. I will describe her as shortly as I can. She was immensely sympathetic. She was immensely charming. She was utterly unselfish. She excelled in the diffi-cult arts of family life. She sacrificed herself daily. If there was chicken, she took the leg; if there was a draught, she sat in it – in short she was so constituted that she never had a mind or a wish of her own, but preferred to sympathize always with the minds and wishes of others. Above all – I need not say it – she was pure. Her purity was supposed to be her chief beauty – her blushes, her great grace. In those days – the last of Queen Victoria – every house had its Angel. And when I came to write I encountered her with the very first words. The shadow of her wings fell on my page; I heard the rustling of her skirts in the room. Directly, that is to say, I took my pen in my hand to review that novel by a famous man, she slipped behind me and whispered: 'My dear, you are a young women. You are writing about a book that has been written by a man. Be sympathetic; be tender; flatter; deceive; use all the arts and wiles of our sex. Never let anyone guess that you have a mind of your own. Above all, be pure'.

Michele Barrett, *Virginia Woolf on women & writing*, London: The Women's Press (1979), pp. 58–9.

2.45   Man's declining status

There was a time, our elders assure us, when man was the respected head of the house. Silence reigned in his presence and none dared to disturb him without permission. His word was law. His order was obeyed without question and without delay. No important decision was made till he gave assent. Meals were served when he was ready; no sooner, no later. But social progress, as the humorists call it, has changed all that. Man's status has shrunk as rapidly as his domestic labours have grown. He has become cook and kitchenmaid, gardener and nurse, laundryman and interior decorator. If by some happy chance, he is able to snatch a moment's rest, it is an exhausted Jack-of-all-trades who sinks into the seat once so proudly filled by his sires.

It is, of course, no coincidence that the tasks thrust upon him have become infinitely more difficult and exacting than they were a generation ago. Consider shopping for example. Before the war a list was given to the grocer and within an hour or so the articles were delivered, fresh and neatly packed. Those were the bad old days. Now the list is handed to the husband and he is cast adrift on the stormy sea of humanity that ebbs and flows through the shop doors. There the waves of what were once female forms will pound him against the rocks of baskets and elbows, thrust him this way and that, displace him from his rightful position while someone asks in a voice ringing with scorn, 'Are you in this queue, Sir?' If his patience lasts and if, as so rarely happens, he is in the right queue, he must undergo a gruelling examination on varieties and brands of which he knows little, and on points and periods, of which he knows less. Conjuring with change, ration books, parcels, hat, pipe, pouch, and other essentials, he may then take his place in the line at the bus stop to face the disapproval of his wife.

Yet shopping is only one of the many trials man now has to face. The tyranny of soap and water is no less burdensome. Few will deny that occasionally a man should help with the washing; but the handicap under which he works is not fully appreciated by the opposite sex. Whenever a man puts his hands in water, he is dogged by the demons of the washtub. They make the water so hot that it scalds, or so cold that it chills; they fling suds on his flannels or on the newly distempered kitchen wall. Nor is that all. It is notorious that in a man's hand a broom is immediately bewitched into a weapon of destruction; a peeler is sharp on his fingers and blunt on the potato; a needle jabs his flesh as surely as it refuses to enter the eye of the button. Even the children, if they are left in his care, immediately develop some troublesome complaint, if indeed, they are not completely lost; and disillusion, or worse, awaits the man who hopes his misfortunes will bring him relief. Women are relentless taskmasters. Like Blake, they believe that a fool must persist in his folly to become wise.

The Times, 28 April 1950.

2.46   Divorce Reform Bill carried

There were loud cheers from its supporters when the Divorce Reform Bill completed its passage through the Commons at 2.15 p.m. The Bill's third reading was carried by 109 votes to 55, a majority of 54.

MR. ALEC JONES (Rhondda, West, Lab.), sponsor of the Bill, moving the third reading, said that if they sought to discourage divorce they could not do it by law, but by practising and encouraging others to follow a far higher moral approach to human relationships.

He quoted from a letter which typified the feelings of many of the people who, he hoped, the Bill would serve well.

The letter said: 'There are many harsh cases such as mine and we can do so little to help you. I am 68 years of age and in 1936 I left my legal spouse, due to the conduct she meted out to me. That was 33 long, long years ago.

'She refused to divorce me and after many years of sadness I met a gracious lady in 1945 and in 1949 we came to live here as man and wife. We have no children; neither had I any by my legal spouse.

'We just go on hoping, hoping and hoping, that one day before one of us is called home we may be legally married and so complete our loyal love and affection. Will you help our dream come true? Please do try.'

That was what the Divorce Reform Bill would do–serve people like this and serve them well.

MR. PETER MAHON (Preston, South, Lab.) said the Bill was an open-ended attack on marriage and therefore on the family. As divorce became easier, marriage would become weaker. For the first time in English law, a defaulter would benefit from a wrong doing. A man could walk out on his wife with someone else's wife.

... This is legislation for marital pandemonium, or if you prefer it, the law of the jungle. With this Bill we are giving this country eternal promiscuity. As this Bill makes its mark there will be indubitably a philanderer's paradise.

MRS. LENA JEGER (Holborn and St. Pancras, South. Lab.) said this was a small turning point in the social history of the country. Women of the future would rejoice at what the Commons had done today.

She said 'women of the future' advisedly, because surely the Bill attempted to raise the status of both parties in a marriage. It was part of women's attitude generally to higher status, equal pay, and greater opportunity in professional and working life.

MR. EMERY (Honiton, C.) said it seemed to him a realistic and logical advance that for the first time in this country it should be accepted that the breakdown of marriage should be established as the reason for divorce. The concept that in any divorce there was just one guilty person was just not so.

The Times, 14 June 1969.

2.47 Pressure on women to marry

The supervisor was a spinster. She was a cow! In her fifties. We thought she was ghastly, fancy being a miss. We were horrible, but that was the pattern. In those days you really despised anyone who wasn't married by at least twenty-five. These poor souls. It was pitiful really. There was one – she was always writing to Lonelyhearts clubs. Rather like Jean Rhys, that type of person. She was always heavily painted – rouge, lipstick, ginger hair. Just to try and get a man. I don't think she ever got anybody. It was terribly sad. But, of course, we used to laugh at her. When I joined women's liberation, and I thought back to all those things, I felt terribly ashamed. But a lot of it still goes on, right?

I was twenty-six when I met Dad. I was really on the back of the shelf, covered in dust, beginning to give up hope. My elder sister had said, 'Look, Luce it's time you got married, and if you don't hurry up, you've had it'. People used to say to my mum, 'Isn't it terrible Lucy's not married'. I think my poor old Mum felt a bit funny about it. She'd say, 'Well, she doesn't like men'. It was just something to say. But, of course, it was the worst thing she could've said.

Spare Rib, 31 January 1975.

2.48   Family allowances

Miss Rathbone said that the Family Allowances Act was only the first. There would be other Acts to follow. Unless Britain was to become a second-class nation people must be enabled to have families. They did not want to bribe parents into having children, but to remove the economic barrier to parenthood. Better provision must be made against the pains and perils of maternity.

The Times, 14 November 1945.

2.49   Equality at home

Sir, I hope that a good number of your male readers will have seen the important Women's Page, feature on the role of women in Swedish society (March 5th). It is pleasing to find an article recognizing that emancipation is about something even more fundamental than equal pay, equal opportunity and equality before the law. Even if the day dawns when women are able to enjoy these rights, full emancipation will not be achieved until men abandon the secret belief that they are, in some indefinable but very definite way, superior to their female counterparts.

The root of the problem lies in the home, where the husband allows his wife to get the early morning tea and dress the children and make the breakfast and do the washing up – when he is quite capable of doing them all himself. Many a man with a working wife never goes near the kitchen, or, if he does, it is only to don an amusing apron and prepare a natty little dish that he fancies. Once in a while he may clear out the garage or mow the lawn or even give his wife breakfast in bed, but on the whole he is not much interested in the domestic round. Each morning he leaves his partner to make the beds, while he goes off to tackle the nation's business!

I am honestly amazed that housewives continue to put up with it. They have spoilt us men for far too long.

Yours faithfully
Gyles Brandreth
New College, Oxford, March 5

The Times, 8 March 1969.

Notes

1 See Chapter 1, 'Women and the law'.
2 Margaret Cole, *Marriage past and present*, London: Dent (1939), p. 135.
3 Dr James Fordyce, *The character and conduct of the female sex*, London (1776), p. 40.
4 W. H. Thornton, 'Devonshire matrimonial market', *Devon notes and queries*, 4 (1970), pp. 54–5, quoted in J. R. Gillis, *For better, for worse, British marriages 1600 to the present*, Oxford: Oxford University Press (1985), p. 216.
5 A. Wohl (ed.), *The Victorian Family*, London: Croom Helm (1978), p. 10.
6 William Thompson, *Appeal of one half the human race, Women, against the pretensions of the other half Men, to retain them in political, and thence in civil and domestic slavery*, London (1825) p. 79.
7 See Chapter 1, 'Women and the law'.
8 Margery Spring Rice, *Working-class wives*, Harmondsworth: Penguin (1939), p. 14.
9 A two-wheeled open carriage.
10 *Transactions Social Science Association* (1876), p. 345.

3

Education

Timeline

1833 Government granted £20,000 aid to churches for the construction of schools for poor children.

1839 Government grants increased to £30,000 for the construction and maintenance of schools: switched to voluntary bodies; conditional on satisfactory inspection.

1840 Grammar Schools Act: expanded Grammar School curriculum from classical studies to include science and literature.

1869 Hitchin College founded.

1870 Forster Elementary Education Act: partially state funded board schools to be set up to provide elementary education in areas where existing provision was inadequate. Board schools managed by elected school boards.

1873 Girton College, Cambridge founded.

1874 London School of Medicine for Women.

1876 Women allowed to register as physicians.

1878 Women admitted to degrees at London University.

1880 Elementary Education Act: education free and compulsory up to the age of ten.

1891 Free Education Act: state payment of school fees up to ten shillings per week.

1892 BMA admits women doctors.

1893 Elementary Education (School Attendance) Act: school leaving age raised to eleven and later to thirteen.

1897 Voluntary Schools Act: grants to public elementary schools not funded by school boards.

1900 Higher elementary schools recognised – providing education from the age of ten to fifteen.

1902   Balfour's Education Act created local education authorities
       (LEAs): took over responsibility for board schools from the
       school boards. Grammar schools also funded by the LEA.
1911   Miss E. Davis-Colley first female fellow of the Royal College
       of Surgeons.
1918   Fisher Education Act: secondary education compulsory up to
       fourteen; state responsible for secondary education schools.
1929   Local Government Act: Poor Law schools became state funded
       elementary schools.
1936   Education Act proposed raising the school leaving age to
       fifteen: postponed because of the War.
1944   Butler Education Act established the Tripartite System; Primary
       and Secondary education split at eleven; marriage bar for
       teachers abolished.
1947   School leaving age raised to fifteen.
1951   O and A levels introduced.
1972   School leaving age sixteen.

Common to ideas on female education, went a belief that women
were inferior to men in terms of intellectual abilities and this made
them unable to deal with academic subjects. (**3.1**) After all, Eve
had been an afterthought, made from Adam's rib. As with all aspects
of a woman's life, a class dimension was present, with middle-class
girls receiving an education which would enable them to attract a
husband, while working-class girls were to be taught skills necessary
for employment. As Elizabeth Sewell put it 1865, 'the aim of education is to fit children for the position of life which they are hereafter
to occupy'.[1]

Middle-class girls were subjected to a battery of advice and conduct
manuals. Thus Gregory's *A father's legacy to his daughter* (1808)
advised modesty, delicacy, chastity and reserve while warning against
wit and indelicate conversation. A girl should be careful how she used
humour and also hide any learning because it would put men off. (**3.2**)
Care had to be taken over dress and appearance with great delicacy
again required 'The finest bosom in nature is not so fine as what imagination forms'. Adam Smith (**3.3**) praised the fact that women were
not educated publicly 'in every part of her life a woman feels some
conveniency or advantage from every part of her education'. As far as
Dr Gregory was concerned, a 'woman's province' was domestic
economy. Where girls did learn a skill such as needlework, this was

only to enable her to judge the quality of others' work and to fill the many empty hours which she would have.

Hester Chapone advised girls to 'appear to be interested in what is said'. Where education was concerned the emphasis was on accomplishments. She suggested reading, 'well-chosen and properly educated', writing legibly, basic arithmetic, music and dancing (but only if the girl had ability). She also advised against the classics since, 'the labour and time that they require, are generally incompatible with our natures and proper employments' and cautioned against 'the danger of pedantry'. (3.4) Chastity was of supreme importance. (3.10)

Not all commentators favoured accomplishments. *The Times* agreed with the *Universal Register* that they were acting against the interests of the country since they encouraged tradesmen's daughters to refuse to work in their fathers' shops. (3.5) Both Maria Edgeworth and Hannah More were contemptuous of the idea that accomplishments would be the means of attracting a husband. (3.6, 3.7) More even went as far as to say that the trickle down of accomplishments to the middle and tradesman classes was altering the 'character of the age', leaving them 'unfit for their active duties', and leading to the 'abundant multiplication of superficial wives, and of incompetent and illiterate governesses'. Instead they should be trained to be 'daughters, wives, mothers, and mistresses of families'. More pointed out that women were unable to generalise and see the bigger picture. She was typical of one type of educated woman in that she saw no contradiction in her being able to write learned books herself and denying such opportunities to others. (3.8)

Mary Wollstonecraft was anxious to demonstrate the lack of choices open to a woman who had only been educated in accomplishments and had failed to find a husband: ladies' companion or governessing at best, prostitution at worst. What was needed was an education which would enable girls to enter business and therefore free themselves from the need to be supported by a man. (3.9)

Some critics were very far-sighted. Mary Robinson, the pseudonym of Anne Frances Randall, proposed, in 1799, a university for women where they would be classically educated and argued for a system of 'fines' on the wealthy to ensure that those in need could also attend and dealt with a common fear that education would unsex a woman. (3.11) Paradoxically, the education of working-class girls followed that of boys from the 1830s. The Whig Government made small grants in 1833 and 1839 towards the building of schools controlled by the

Church of England and instituted a system of inspection. Working-class radicals and Owenites also advocated education for women to ensure that mothers were in a position to educate their children and claim their rights. (**3.12, 3.13, 3.14**) The need for women to be educated for the good of society was an argument that was to continue throughout the century. (**3.16**)

The poverty of middle-class education was brought to public attention by the Schools Inquiry Commission (1864) headed by Lord Taunton. Originally designed to deal with boys' education, the work of Emily Davies and Dorothea Beale ensured that girls' education was also considered. This demonstrated quite clearly that education for working-class girls often surpassed that of the middle classes. (**3.15**) The question was how to improve the situation. The 1869 Endowed Schools Commission allowed the use of endowments from old grammar schools to set up girls' schools. The model for this was seen to be the North London Collegiate School established in 1850.

The next stage was to tackle Higher Education. (**3.16**) Emily Davies and her supporters met tremendous hostility from those convinced that women's smaller brains would be unable to cope, though as Emily said, 'why should simple equations brighten their intellect and quadratic equations drive them into a lunatic asylum?' When Davies set up Hitchin College in 1869, the precursor of Girton College, Cambridge (1873), she enlisted the support of medical men to disprove contemporary ideas that higher education would turn women into desexed man-hating viragos at best or cause their smaller brains to explode. The struggle for women's university education (**3.17**) has been well documented and there is no doubt that many despaired at its introduction. It was feared that education would threaten the sanctity not only of marriage and the family but also the entire future of the human race. (**3.18, 3.19**) The question was: should girls' education be improved to be the same and equal to men's, or the same, but different? Reformers like Emily Davies were keen to ensure that there should be no difference because this should be seen as condoning inferiority and would not allow women to develop their full potential. However they were faced with a double standard, this time of how to achieve equality in academic subjects while remaining ladylike. Not all feminists, however, agreed with Davies. The North of England Council for promoting the higher education of women was set up by Josephine Butler and Anne Jeminia Clough and this joined those who wished an alternative form of higher education; thus, Newnham

College provided special lectures and classes for girls. Nevertheless education gradually expanded, with London University awarding degrees on the same terms as men in 1878. A particularly difficult area for women to penetrate was that of medicine. (**3.17**) Elizabeth Garrett, for example, took her degree in Paris. Medicine was deemed incompatible with womanly qualities which should be devoted to nursing. (**3.20**) Gradually, however, women gained access to it, though there were still attempts to ban them as late as 1928. (**3.21**)

In 1870 Forster's Elementary Education Act set up a system of compulsory education for girls and boys aged between five and thirteen. These schools were to be administered by School Boards (**3.22**) which would be elected by all ratepayers, including women, who could also sit on them. The Boards were empowered to make by-laws such as compulsory attendance for those aged between five and thirteen with some exemptions for certain ten to thirteen year olds. Women were seen to have the particular qualities needed to work on School Boards though Balfour's Act of 1902 removed responsibilities to local government, thus reducing women's roles. The education of girls, however, still centred on domestic science: having received a grant in 1874, it became a compulsory subject in 1878, quickly followed by cookery (specific subject) in 1882 and laundry in 1889.

To cope with the need for elementary school teachers, training colleges were set up. By 1880 there were forty one such colleges of which thirty five were denominational. On 24 January 1885, Edge Hill, a true non-denominational college, was set up in Liverpool. It had no doubts of the qualities needed in a teacher. (**3.23**) These colleges were another avenue for girls to achieve higher education since some such as Edge Hill and Homerton also provided the chance of taking a degree.

The Cross Commission (1888) further emphasised the place of domestic subjects thereby reflecting fears that were girls to receive too much education, they would forget their true role – that of wife and mother: in contrast, in Scotland, parents considered that school should provide 'book learning' and the home, domestic skills.

By the beginning of the twentieth century, women's education was still heavily influenced by gender and class expectations. Despite the 1918 Education Act, which raised the school leaving age to fourteen, the half time system, whereby children worked for half the week, continued in the agricultural and textile areas into the 1920s. Furthermore a mere 15 per cent of girls aged between eleven and seventeen actually went to secondary school in the 1930s; the majority simply attended the elementary school till they reached fourteen. As for higher education, the figures were even lower with only 0.5 per cent attending in the 1920s.

The Butler Education Act (1944) established the 'eleven plus examination' where passing led to grammar school and failing to the secondary modern. However, more girls than boys passed, and so the system was adjusted in favour of boys, with more places being allocated to them. The argument here was akin to that of Campbell in 1891! (**3.24**) This led to many girls being denied a more academic education and feeling that they were failures.[2] Furthermore, domestic science was rarely taught in grammar schools. John Newsom had no doubts that there should be a separate curriculum for girls. (**3.25**) He also despaired of the unmarried female teacher as a good role model, arguing instead that they should be attractive and, since the 1944 Act had removed the marriage bar, there should be an equal number of married women teachers. Even within teaching, however, women were not equal to men, something which Miss Hale, principal of Edge Hill, had pointed out in 1895. (**3.26**) Equal pay may have been introduced in 1956, but most women teachers did not attain the position of head; even in primary schools, this was usually the preserve of men.

3.1 Women less intellectual than men

The science of legislation, or jurisprudence, of political economy; the conduct of government in all its executive function; the abstruse researches of erudition; the inexhaustible depths of philosophy; the acquirements subordinate to navigation; the knowledge indispensable in the wide field of commercial enterprise; the arts of defence, and of attack by land and by sea . . . these, and other studies, pursuits and occupations, assigned chiefly or entirely to men, demand the efforts of a mind endued with the powers of close and comprehensive reasoning, and of intense and continued application, in a degree to which they are not requisite for the discharge of the customary offices of female duty. It would therefore seem natural to expect, and experience, I think, confirms the justice of the expectations, that the Giver of all good, after bestowing those powers on men with a liberality proportionate to the subsisting necessity, would impart them to the female mind with a more sparing hand . . .

Thomas Gisborne, *An enquiry into the duties of the female sex* (1797), 1816 edn, London: T. Cadell & W. Davies, pp. 20–3.

3.2   Conduct and behaviour

One of the chief beauties in a female character, is that modest reserve, that retiring delicacy, which avoids the public eye, and is disconcerted even at the gaze of admiration, – I do not wish you to be insensible to applause; if you were, you must become, if not worse, at least less amiable women. But you may be dazzled by that admiration, which yet rejoices your hearts.

When a girl ceases to blush, she has lost the most powerful charm of beauty. That extreme sensibility which it indicates, may be a weakness and incumbrance in our sex, as I have too often felt; but in yours is peculiarly engaging . . .

This modesty, which I think so essential in your sex, will naturally dispose you to be rather silent in company, especially in a large one. – People of sense and discernment will never mistake such silence for dullness. (*sic*) One may take a share in conversation without uttering a syllable. The expression in the countenance shews it; and this never escapes an observing eye . . .

Converse with men even of the first rank with that dignified modesty which may prevent the approach of the most distant familiarity, and consequently prevent them from feeling themselves your superiors.

Wit is the most dangerous talent you can possess: it must be guarded with great discretion and good-nature, otherwise it will create you many enemies. Wit is perfectly consistent with softness and delicacy; yet they are seldom found united. Wit is so flattering to vanity, that they who possess it, become intoxicated, and lose all self-command.

Humour is a different quality, it will make your company much solicited: but be cautious how you indulge it. – It is often a great enemy to delicacy, and a still greater one to dignity of character. It may sometimes gain you applause, but will never procure you respect.

Be even cautious in displaying your good sense. It will be thought you assume a superiority over the rest of the company. – But if you happen to have any learning, keep it a profound secret, especially from the men, who generally look with a jealous and malignant eye on a woman of great parts and a cultivated understanding.

A man of real genius and candour is far superior to this meanness: But such a one will seldom fall in your way; and if by accident he should, do not be anxious to shew the full extent of your knowledge. If he has any opportunities of seeing you, he will soon discover it himself: and if you have any advantages of person or manner, and keep your own secret, he will probably give you credit for a great deal more than you possess. – The great art of pleasing in conversation, consists in making the company pleased with themselves. You will more readily hear them talk yourselves into their good graces . . .

Consider every species of indelicacy in conversation, as shameful in itself, and as highly disgusting to us. All double-entendre is of this sort . . . Virgin purity is of that delicate nature, that it cannot hear certain things without contamination. – It is always in your power to avoid these . . .

The intention of your being taught needlework, knitting, and such like, is not on account of the intrinsic value of all you can do with your hands, which is trifling; but to enable you to judge more perfectly that kind of work, and to direct the execution of it in others. Another principal end is to enable you to fill up, in a tolerably agreeable way, some of the many solitary hours you must necessarily pass at home . . .

The domestic economy of a family is entirely a woman's province, and furnishes a variety of subjects for the exertion both of good sense and good taste. If you ever come to have the charge of a family, it ought to engage much of your time and attention, nor can you be excused from this by any extent of fortune, though, with a narrow one, the ruin that follows the neglect of it may be more immediate.

I am at the greatest loss what to advise you in regard to books. There is no impropriety in your reading history, or cultivating any art or science to which genius or accident may lead you . . .

Dress is an important article in female life. The love of dress is natural to you, and therefore it is proper and reasonable. Good sense will regulate your expence in it, and good taste will direct you to dress in such a way as to conceal any blemishes, and set off your beauties, if you have any, to the greatest advantage. But much delicacy and judgement are required in the application of this rule. A fine woman shews her charms to most advantage, when she seems most to conceal them: The finest bosom in nature is not so fine as what imagination forms . . .

Accustom yourselves to an habitual neatness, so that in the most careless undress, in your most unguarded hours, you may have no reason to be ashamed of your appearance. – You will not easily believe how much we consider your dress as expressive of your characters. Vanity, levity, slovenliness, folly, appear, through it. An elegant simplicity is an equal proof of taste and delicacy.

Dr Gregory, *A father's legacy to his daughter* London: Brettell & Co. (1774, 1808 edn), pp. 141–3; 148–9.

3.3 Benefits of lack of schools

There are no public institutions for the education of women, and there is accordingly nothing useless, absurd or fantastical, in the common course of their education. They are taught what their parents or guardians judge it necessary or useful for them to learn, and they are taught nothing else. Every part of their education tends evidently to some useful purpose; either to improve the natural attractions of their person, or to form their mind to reserve, to modesty, to chastity, and to economy; to render them both likely to become the mistresses of a family, and to behave properly when they have become such. In every part of her life, a woman feels some conveniency or advantage from every part of her education. It seldom happens that a man, in any part of his life, derives any conveniency or advantage from some of the most laborious and troublesome parts of his education.

Adam Smith, *The wealth of nations* vol. ii (1776), London: World Classics edn, (1910), p. 416.

3.4 On politeness and accomplishments

Many are of the opinion, that a very young woman can hardly be too silent and reserved in company; and, certainly, nothing is so disgusting in youth, as pertness, and self-conceit. But, modesty should be distinguished from an awkward bashfulness, and silence should only be enjoined, when it would be forward and impertinent to talk. There are many proper opportunities for a girl, young even as you are, to speak in company, with advantage to herself; and, if she does it without conceit or affectation, she will always be more pleasing than those, who sit like statues, without sense or motion. When you are silent, your looks should shew your attention and presence to the company: a respectful and earnest attention is the most delicate kind of praise, and never fails to gratify and please. You must appear to be interested in what is said, and endeavour to improve yourself by it . . . Then, when called upon, you must not draw back as unwilling to answer, nor confine yourself merely to yes or no, as is the custom of many young persons who become intolerable burthens to the mistress of the house . . . In a young lady's behaviour towards gentlemen, great delicacy is certainly required . . .

Men of loose morals or impertinent behaviour must always be avoided: or, if at any time you are obliged to be in their company, you must keep them at a distance by cold civility. But, with regard to those gentlemen whom your parents think it proper for you to converse with, and who give no offence by their own manners, to them I wish you to behave with the same frankness and simplicity as if they were of your own sex. If you have natural modesty, you will never transgress its bounds . . .

With regard to accomplishments, the chief of these is a competent share of reading, well chosen and properly regulated . . . Dancing, and the knowledge of the French tongue, are now so universal, that they cannot be dispensed with in the education of a gentlewoman; and indeed they both are useful as well as ornamental; the first, by forming and strengthening the body, and improving the carriage; the second, by opening a large field of entertainment and improvement for the mind. I believe there are more agreeable books of female literature in French than in any other language; and, as they are not less commonly talked of than English books, you must often feel mortified in company, if you are too ignorant to read them. Italian would be easily learnt after French . . .

To write a free and legible hand, and to understand common arithmetic, are indispensable requisites.

As to music and drawing, I would only wish you to follow as genius leads . . . it is but seldom that a private person has leisure or application enough to gain any high degree of excellence in them . . . but with regard to yourself, it is of great consequence to have the power of filling up agreeably those intervals of time which too often hang heavily on the hands of a woman, if her lot be cast in a retired situation . . .

As to the learned languages, though I respect the abilities and application of those ladies who have attained them, and who make a modest and proper use of them, yet I would by no means advise you, or any other woman who is not strongly impelled by a particular genius, to engage in such studies. The labour and time which they require, are generally incompatible with our natures and proper employments: the real knowledge which they supply, is not essential . . . The danger of pedantry and presumption in a woman, – of her exciting envy in one sex and jealousy in the other, – of her exchanging the graces of imagination for the severity and preciseness of a scholar, would be, I own, sufficient to frighten me from the ambition of seeing my girl remarkable for learning. Such objections are, perhaps, still stronger with regard to the abstruse sciences.

H. Chapone, *Letters on the improvement of the mind addressed to a lady*, London: Brettell & Co. (1808), pp. 89–90; 92–5.

3.5 On the education of girls from twelve years upwards

Is it enough the tradesman's daughter can hurry through a novel from the Circulating Library? Is it sufficient she can scribble a letter full of bad spelling, about this here and that there? Is she completely educated, having learnt French but cannot speak it, or having learnt to dance, without being taught good manners? For what do our schools qualify girls? Not for business, for industry they are never taught. – What is the end of their education? Why, Miss, at fourteen, is delivered into the hands of her parents a smart young lady, understands every etiquette of dress, and is complete for the Park or Playhouse.

Much has been said in favour of their appearance behind the counter; but will they go behind it? – No, thanky Pa, says the daughter of my old friend Dipping – why should I go behind a counter? The Miss Lambs, the Miss Sturgeons, nor the Miss Pattypans, ever appear in the shop; and you have as good a trade as they, are worth as much money, and have given us as genteel an education. I am sure the boarding-school we were at has turned out as many smart young ladies as any about town. I ask you to go into the shop, to qualify yourself for an honest tradesman's wife, says the old man. Indeed, Pa, you must excuse me, I never can marry a tradesman . . .

Look into the tradesmen's houses, and you will see the girls are unmarried – ask why? – the answer is, they are trained in pride and extravagance, and the young men had rather travel in pursuit of happiness, than venture on a London fine Lady. The fact is, the girls are introduced into life too early; they are educated with a boldness that destroys their modesty; and it is common to meet girls in every street, girls not fifteen, without a cap, hair frizzed, and a hat cocked on one side, with a look as much as to say, Ruin me if you dare.

'Train up a child in the way she should go, and when she is old, she will not depart from it.' This is an old but a wise lesson, and must be put in practice by parents before you see a reformation of manners in this country.

From the *Universal Register*, quoted in *The Times*, 20 August 1787.

3.6   Women's qualities

In almost all that comes under the description of polite letters, in all that captivates by imagery, or warms by just and affecting sentiment, women are excellent. They possess in a high degree that delicacy and quickness of perception, and that nice discernment between the beautiful and defective which comes under the denomination of taste. Both in composition and action they excel in details; but they do not so much generalise their ideas as men, nor do their minds seize a great subject with so large a grasp. They are acute observers, and accurate judges of life and manners, as far as their own sphere of observation extends; but they describe a smaller circle. A woman sees the world, as it were, from a little elevation in her own garden, where she makes an exact survey of home scenes, but takes not in that wider range of distant prospects which he who stands on a loftier eminence commands. Women have a certain tact which often enables them to feel what is just more instantaneously than they can define it. They have an intuitive penetration into character, bestowed on them by providence, like the sensitive and tender organs of some timid animals, as a kind of natural guard to warn of the approach of danger, beings who are often called to act defensively.

Hannah More, *Strictures on the modern system of female education* (1799), London (1800), pp. 225–6.

3.7   Female accomplishments

Accomplishments, it seems, are valuable, as being the objects of universal admiration. Some accomplishments have another species of value, as they are tickets of admission to fashionable company. Accomplishments have another, and a higher species of value, as they are supposed to increase a young lady's chance of a prize in the matrimonial lottery. Accomplishments have also a value as resources against ennui, as they afford continual amusement and innocent occupation. This is ostensibly their chief praise; it deserves to be considered with respect.

. . . to judge of what will please and attach men of superior sense and characters, we must observe their actual conduct in life, and listen to their speculative opinions. Superficial accomplishments do not appear to be the objects of their preference. In enumerating the perfections of his wife, or in retracing the progress of his love, does a man of sense dwell upon his mistress's skill in drawing, or dancing, or music? No. These he tells you, are extremely agreeable talents, but they could have never attached him; they are subordinate parts in her character; he is angry that you can rank them amongst her perfections; he knows that a thousand women possess these accomplishments, who have never touched his heart . . .

With respect to sentimental stories, and books of mere entertainment, we must remark, that they should be sparingly used, especially in the education of girls. This species of reading cultivates what is called the heart prematurely, lowers the tone of the mind, and induces indifference for those common pleasures and occupations which, however trivial in themselves, constitute by far the greatest portion of our daily happiness. Stories are the novels of childhood.

M. & R. L. Edgeworth, *Essays on practical education*, 3rd edn, London: J. Johnson (1811), vol. ii., pp. 174, 178–9; vol. i., pp. 426–7.

3.8   On the education of women

This word [accomplishments] on its original meaning signifies completeness, perfection. But I may safely appeal to the observation of mankind, whether they do not meet with swarms of youthful females, issuing from our boarding schools, as well as emerging from the more private scenes of domestic education, who are introduced into the world, under the broad and universal title of accomplished young ladies, of all of whom it cannot very truly and correctly be pronounced, that they illustrate the definition, by a completeness which leaves nothing to be added, and a perfection which leaves nothing to be desired.

This phrenzy of accomplishments, unhappily, is no longer restricted within the usual limits of rank and fortune; the middle orders have caught the contagion, and it rages downward with increasing and destructive violence, from the elegantly dressed but slenderly portioned curate's daughter, to the equally fashionable daughter of the little tradesman, and of the more opulent but not more judicious farmer. And is it not obvious, that as far as this epidemical mania has spread, this very valuable part of society is declining in usefulness, as it rises in its ill-founded pretensions to elegance, till this rapid revolution of the manners of the middle class has so far altered the character of the age, as to be in danger of rendering obsolete the heretofore common saying, 'that most worth and virtue are to be found in the middle station.' . . . Their new course of education, and the indolent habits of life, and the elegance of dress connected with it, peculiarly unfit them for the active duties of their own very important condition; while with frivolous eagerness, and second-hand opportunities, they run to snatch a few of those showy acquirements which decorate the great. This is done apparently with one or other of these views; either to make their fortune by marriage, or if that fail, to qualify them to become teachers of others: hence the abundant multiplication of superficial wives, and of incompetent and illiterate governesses.

Comparison of the modes of female education in the last age with the present.

The profession of ladies to which the bent of their instruction should be turned, is that of daughters, wives, mothers, and mistresses of families. They should therefore be trained with a view to these several conditions, and be furnished with a stock of ideas, and principles, and qualifications, and habits, ready to be applied and appropriated, as occasion may demand, to each of these respective situations. For though the arts which merely embellish life may claim admiration; yet, when a man of sense comes to marry, it is not merely a creature who can paint, and play, and sing, and draw, and dress, and dance; it is a being who can comfort and counsel him; one who can reason, and reflect, and feel, and judge, and discourse, and discriminate; one who can assist him in his affairs, lighten his cares, soothe his sorrows, purify his joys, strengthen his principles, and educate his children.

Almost any ornamental acquirement is a good thing, when it is not the best thing a woman has; and talents are admirable when not made to stand proxy for virtues.

The benefits of restraint

Girls should be led to distrust their own judgement; they should learn not to murmur at expostulation; they should be accustomed to expect and to endure opposition. It is a lesson with which the world will not fail to furnish them; and they will not practise it the worse for having learnt it the sooner. It is of the last importance to their happiness, even in this life, that they should early acquire a submissive temper and a forbearing spirit.

They must even endure to be thought wrong sometimes, when they cannot but feel they are right. And while they should be anxiously aspiring to do well, they must not expect always to obtain the praise of having done so.

Hannah More, *Strictures on the modern system of female education* (1799), 12th edn, London: Cadell & Davies (1818), vol. i., pp. 71–4, pp. 109–11; 180.

3.9 'Unfortunate situation of females, fashionably educated, and left without a fortune'

But many who have been well, or at least fashionably educated, are left without a fortune, and if they are not entirely devoid of delicacy, they must frequently remain single.

Few are the modes of earning a subsistence, and those very humiliating. Perhaps to be an humble companion to some rich old cousin, or what is still worse, to live with strangers, who are so intolerably tyrannical, that none of their own relations can bear to live with them, though they should even expect a fortune in reversion. It is impossible to enumerate the many hours of anguish such a person must spend.

Above the servants, yet considered by them as a spy, and ever reminded of their inferiority when in conversation with the superiors. If she cannot condescend to mean flattery, she has not a chance of being a favourite; and should any of the visitors take notice of her, and she for a moment forget her subordinate state, she is sure to be reminded of it . . .

A teacher at a school is only a kind of upper servant, who has more work than the menial ones.

A governess to young ladies is equally disagreeable. It is ten to one if they meet with a reasonable mother; and if she is not so, she will be continually finding fault to prove she is not ignorant, and be displeased if her pupils do not improve, but angry if the proper methods are taken to make them do so. The children treat them with disrespect, and often with insolence. In the mean time life glides away, and the spirits with it; 'and when youth and genial years are flown', they have nothing to subsist on; or, perhaps, on some extraordinary occasion, some small allowance may be made for them, which is thought a great charity.

The few trades which are left, are now gradually falling into the hands of the men, and certainly they are not very respectable.

It is hard for a person who has a relish for polished society, to herd with the vulgar, or to condescend to mix with her former equals when she is considered in a different light ...

If what I have written should be read by parents, who are not going on in thoughtless extravagance, and anxious only that their daughters may be genteelly educated, let them consider to what sorrows they expose them; for I have not over-coloured the picture ...

Business of various kinds, they might likewise pursue, if they were educated in a more orderly manner, which might save many from common and legal prostitution. Women would not then marry for a support, as men accept of places under Government, and neglect the implied duties; nor would an attempt to earn their own subsistence, a most laudable one! sink them almost to the level of those poor abandoned creatures who live by prostitution. For are not milliners and mantua-makers reckoned the next class? The few employments open to women, so far from being liberal, are menial ...

It is a melancholy truth; yet such is the blessed effect of civilization! the most respectable women are the most oppressed; and, unless they have understandings far superior to the common run of understanding, taking in both sexes, they must, from being treated like contemptible beings, become contemptible. How many women thus waste life away the prey of discontent, who might have practised as physicians, regulated a farm, managed a shop, and stood erect, supported by their own industry, instead of hanging their heads surcharged with the dew of sensibility, that consumes the beauty to which it at first gave lustre; nay, I doubt whether pity and love are so near akin as poets feign, for I have seldom seen much compassion excited by the helplessness of females, unless they were fair; then, perhaps, pity was the soft handmaid of love, or the harbinger of lust ...

Mary Wollstonecraft, *Thoughts on the education of daughters: with reflections on female conduct, in the more important duties of life*, London: J. Johnson (1787), pp. 69–77; *A Vindication of the Rights of Women*, London: J. Johnson 1792, pp. 162, 163.

3.10   Chastity

But the most difficult part of female education, is to give girls such an idea of chastity, as shall arm their reason and their sentiments on the side of this useful virtue. For I believe there are more women of understanding led into acts of imprudence by the ignorance, the prejudices, and the false craft of those by whom they are educated, than from any other cause founded either in nature or in chance. You may train up a docile idiot to any mode of thinking or acting, as may best suit the intended purpose; but a reasoning being will scan over your propositions, and if they find them grounded in falsehood, they will reject them with disdain. When you tell a girl of spirit and reflection that chastity is a sexual virtue, and the want of it a sexual vice, she will be apt to examine into the principles of religion, morals, and the reason of things, in order to satisfy herself on the truth of your proposition. And when, after the strictest enquiries, she finds nothing that will warrant the confining the proposition to a particular sense, she will entertain doubts either of your wisdom or your sincerity; and regarding you either as a deceiver or a fool, she will transfer her confidence to the companion of the easy vacant hour, whose compliance with her opinions can flatter her vanity. Thus left to Nature, with an unfortunate bias on her mind, she will fall a victim to the first plausible being who has formed a design on her person . . . the great difference now beheld in the external consequences which follow the deviations from chastity in the two sexes, did in all probability arise from women having been considered as the mere property of the men; and, on this account had no right to dispose of their own persons: that policy adopted this difference, when the plea of property had been given up; . . . The snares, therefore, that are continually laid for women, by persons who run no risk in compassing their seduction, exposes them to continual danger; whilst the implacability of their own sex, who fear to give up any advantages which a superior prudence, or even its appearances, give them, renders one false step an irretrievable misfortune. That, for these reasons, coquettry in women is as dangerous as it is dishonorable . . .

C. Macaulay, *Letters on education*, London, Part One, *Letter XXIV*, 'Chastity' (1790), pp. 218–21.

3.11   Need for education

Let these mental despots recollect, that education cannot unsex a woman; that tenderness of soul, and a love of social intercourse, will still be hers; even though she become a rational friend, and an intellectual companion. She will not, by education, be less tenacious of an husband's honour; though she may be rendered more capable of defending her own.

A man would be greatly shocked, as well as offended, were he told that his son was an idiot; and yet he would care but little, if every action proved that his wife were one. Tell a modern husband that his son has a strong understanding, and he will feel gratified. Say that his wife has a masculine mind, and he will feel the information as rather humbling than pleasing to his self-love. There are but three classes of women desirable associates in the eyes of men: handsome women; licentious women; and good sort of women. – The first for his vanity; the second for his amusement; and the last for the arrangement of his domestic drudgery. A thinking woman does not entertain him; a learned woman does not flatter his self-love, by confessing inferiority; and a woman of real genius, eclipses him by her brilliancy . . .

Had fortune enabled me, I would build an university for women; where they should be politely, and at the same time classically educated; the depth of their studies, should be proportioned to their mental powers; and those who were incompetent to the labours of knowledge, should be dismissed after a fair trial of their capabilities, and allotted to the more humble paths of life; such as domestic and useful occupations. The wealthy part of the community who neglected to educate their female offspring, at this seminary of learning, should pay a fine, which should be appropriated to the maintenance of the unportioned scholars. In half a century there would be a sufficient number of learned women to fill all the departments of the university, and those who excelled in an eminent degree should receive honorary medals, which they should wear as an order of literary merit.

Mary Robinson, pseud. Anne Frances Randall, *A letter to the women of England on the injustice of mental subordination* (1799), pp. 55–7, 92–3. Hypertext version: www.rc.umd.edu/editions/robinson/mrletterfrst.htm/

3.12   On female education

While the working classes are looking in a thousand ways for the means by which to extricate themselves from poverty, and all the miseries and vices attendant thereon, one of the most fruitful sources of these evils is seldom thought of: – the education of our female population: – for what is termed education, is so little suited to their wants – so ill calculated to prepare them for the important stations they fill in society – that it is unworthy of the name. And so long as man ungenerously and unjustly pays so little attention to this subject, so long will he be poor, miserable, and vicious . . .

The women of today, are to be the wives, the helpmates, the companions of the men of today; – and more, to be the mothers, the nurses, and the first instructors of those who will be the men of tomorrow. If their habits and dispositions will influence those of their partners; – if on them will depend, in a great degree, the interests of their families; – if in their keeping is the happiness of the present race; – if on the care that has been bestowed on their minds and bodies depend the mental and corporeal qualifications of the succeeding human race; – how tremendously important is the education of woman?

The education of the females of the lower classes, in many cases does not even extend even so far as a knowledge of their letters; – in the aggregate, to sew and to read (and that but very indifferently) is the sum of their acquirements. Yet these females are to be the bosom friends of the most useful portion of our population. – The mothers and nurses of the next race of artizans and labourers. What companions are they, even for men having the slight pretensions to knowledge their partners possess? – How little that is valuable can they teach their offspring?

And in what consists the superiority of the education afforded to the females of the middle classes? They are these: – in addition to reading and writing, they are taught to play a few trifling pieces on the pianoforte, to dance, and perhaps to gabble a few sentences of bad French; or to translate them into worse English. And in exchange for these accomplishments (which are seldom used after leaving school) they are taught to despise every useful employment; and often treat with indifference approaching to contempt, their industrious parents who toil day and night to give them this superior education.

The Pioneer, 28 September 1833.

3.13 To the females of the working class

... Men, in general, tremble at the idea of a reading wife, being taught to believe it an evil by designing tyrants. Woman's rights, like man's; have been withheld from motives purely political, by deep concerted plans of early oppressors. The sage priests of olden time well knew, if woman's penetrative and inquisitive mind was allowed its liberty, their well-laid schemes of bigotry and superstition would soon have come to light.

The Pioneer, 8 February 1834.

3.14   Female education

It has generally been the crafty ambition of kings, aristocrats, and priests, to keep the female mind in a state of childhood, and thereby prevent mothers from becoming the great primary instructors of their children in philosophical and political knowledge . . .

Come my female friends, and let us reason together: I wish you still to be religious and virtuous, but I also wish you to understand philosophical and political sciences, and to be able to teach them to your children. I wish to see a nation of philosophical, intelligent, and political mothers – a nation of such mothers will teach knowledge to their children, and rear up a race of intelligent men and women. And where is such knowledge to be acquired? but in philosophical and political institutions, of which you ought to be members.

. . . there must be a great political change before a proper system of 'national education' be established . . . in the meantime, to accelerate that change, you ought to instruct yourselves, not only in the common and ornamental branches of female education, but also in the profound elements of experimental philosophy and political science. . . . In this way you may rear up a race of men who not only understand their rights, but sternly assert and wisely exercise them. The world will then advance in liberty, equality, and happiness.

The Chartist Circular, 23 November 1839, pp. 35–6.

3.15   On secondary instruction as relating to girls

In the great controversy which, having been begun by the debates on the Report of the Public Schools' Commission, is now extending itself over almost the whole department of secondary instruction, there is an omission which seems to call for remark. Throughout the discussion . . . the question has hitherto been treated exclusively in reference to boys, it having been tacitly assumed that male education only is a matter of concern to the general community. This feature is the more remarkable, inasmuch as it is peculiar to the present agitation. In the effort made some years ago for the improvement of primary education, ignorant boys and ignorant girls were recognised as having similar claims. National and British Schools for the girls are inspected, mistresses are trained, female pupil-teachers are apprenticed, and speaking generally, the education of the daughters of the labouring classes is as carefully watched over as that of their sons. Why is the case altered when we advance a few steps higher in the social scale? With regard to the Public Schools, the reason is obvious enough. As there are no Etons for girls in existence, they could not be made the subject of investigation. Probably the sisters of Public School boys are for the most part taught by governesses at home. Their education is therefore clearly beyond the scope of a Commission of Inquiry . . . But this consideration does not apply to the daughters of the middle-class, and it is difficult to understand why their early training should be regarded as a matter of less importance than that of their brothers . . .

Public writers are occupied with the busy world around them, in which men only are to be seen, and it is perhaps not much to be wondered at, if they think only of training the boys, who are hereafter to do the more conspicuous part of the world's work . . . Women . . . are largely responsible for the general carelessness they are generally ready enough to profess themselves perfectly satisfied with things as they are, and to echo doubts as to whether 'so much education is necessary for girls.' Some, who are conscious of their own deficiencies, are afraid that the manifestation of a desire to help others may be mistaken for an assumption of great enlightenment in themselves. Others, who by unusual energy and perseverance have succeeded in gaining knowledge, and the power that it brings with it, are, by their very superiority, cut off from the multitude. They look down from their heights, with little sympathy, on the mass of women tamely giving way before difficulties which they have known how to overcome. Others again shrink from prominence in any cause whatever; their dread of publicity is so overpowering that they would rather see a whole generation drowning before their eyes in ignorance and sloth, than run the slightest risk of being spoken of as taken part in the rescue . . . that it is one of the duties imposed upon women of this generation to speak out, careless of the cost, on those questions of which they can most fitly judge . . .

The impression is conveyed to the public mind that the education of girls is an affair of very little consequence – that it is, in fact, one of the things which may safely and properly be left to take care of themselves. It is no wonder that so agreeable an untruth should meet with ready acceptance . . .

There is a method by which we may test the quality of the schools:– we can look at the quality of the thing produced. Anybody, or at least any woman, may know what girls are after leaving school, and we may fairly judge of the process by its results, making allowance, of course, for extenuating circumstances in the shape of vitiating home influences.

I ask then, what are girls worth when their education is finished? What are they good for? Are they in vigorous health of mind or body? What is there that they care about? How are their lives filled up? What have they to talk about? What do they read? I am speaking, let it be remembered, not of children, but of grown-up women. Does anybody care for their opinions on any but the most trivial matters? Have they thought beyond the circle of petty cares?

. . . On all sides there is evidence that as regards intelligence and good sense, English women of the middle class are held in small esteem. 'A woman's reason' means, in popular phrase, no reason at all. A man who lets it be known that he consults his wife, endangers his own reputation for sense. A habit of exaggeration, closely verging upon untruthfulness, is a recognised feminine characteristic . . . it will be admitted that the popular estimate of a woman's mental worth is somewhat low.

Emily Davies, in *Thoughts on some questions relating to women, 1860–1908* Cambridge: Bowes and Bowes (1910), pp. 63–8. (Read at the Annual Meeting of the National Association for the promotion of Social Science, 1864.)

3.16 Female education in the middle classes

What advances can 1858 shew either in education itself, or in the ends it proposes? Have these accomplishments been replaced by more solid training, in which individual capabilities and tendencies and not fashion, lead the way? Has the full and free development of woman, as a human being, superseded the blind and narrow prejudice which sought to make her first, man's plaything, and then his slave? In short, is modern female education, in any substantial respect, different to what it was fifty years ago? Looking to externals only, the answer is unsatisfactory. Fashionable governesses and fashionable boarding schools still hold their ground. Colleges, it is true, have of late sprung up, where, at the discretion, or rather, indiscretion of the parents, girls can be exposed to a forcing process hitherto unequalled, and which can be compared to nothing but the gardener's exertions to produce early blossoms at the expense of the plant . . . Does a knowledge of all the languages under the sun, serve either to train the intellect, or to form the character? – does a woman better fulfil her duties as daughter, sister, wife and mother, because she can chatter bad French and worse German, or rattle the keys of a piano in a slap dash style which, at best, only serves to drown in noise and clamour the deficiency of real musical knowledge, the utter want of taste, feeling and expression? And if we look beneath the surface, what shall we find? Imagination naturally so vivid in woman, kindled and excited at the expense of her reasoning faculties; as an eloquent French writer has it, 'study without object, knowledge without practice, modern education enlarges the circle of woman's wants, but adds nothing to their satisfaction.'

Sensitive and impressionable by nature, the education of the nursery, the school room, and the drawing room, tends to foster and develop qualities which in after years too often sap and destroy the springs of existence. Quick in her sympathies, ardent in her affections, but too prone to a life of emotion and feeling, female education, instead of counteracting these dangerous tendencies, fatally excites and stimulates them ... Nor is it only in the business of education that women would influence the destiny of men. If women knew more, men must learn more – for ignorance would then be shameful – and it would become the fashion to be instructed. The instruction of women improves the stock of national talents, and employs more minds for the instruction and amusement of the world; it increases the pleasures of society by multiplying the topics upon which the two sexes take a common interest; and makes marriage an intercourse of understanding as well as of affection, by giving dignity and importance to the female character. The education of women secures public morals; it provides for every season of life, as well as for the brightest and the best; and leaves a woman when she is stricken by the hand of time, not as she now is, destitute of everything and neglected by all, but with the full power and the splendid attractions of knowledge – diffusing the elegant pleasures of polite literature, and receiving the homage of learned and accomplished men.

The whole social condition of women during these fifty years has undergone a thorough revolution. Then, to some extent at least, home duties and household occupations furnished employment for heads and hands, which now, listless and unoccupied, leave their owners a prey to that curse of modern middle-class existence, that death in life, ennui. Now, more than ever, is there need of solid education for our girls, that our women may be fitted and trained to open other paths for themselves than the stereotyped and worn out one of matrimony ... Till women of the middle classes are educated as responsible human beings, trained to take their part in active life, they will never truly be man's mate and companion.

English Woman's Journal, vol. i. (1858), pp. 217–18, 221–3.

3.17   Female education

The one thing men do not like is the man-woman, and they will never believe the College, or University, woman is not of that type. Sensible men will always like sensible and cultivated women; but they will always prefer that their good sense and cultivation should have come through channels which they recognise as suitable for the womanly character. The learned woman does not make the best educator of children. We require the well-trained and well-balanced woman. The duties of women do not to any great extent lie in the intellectual direction. Their sprightly intuition is often, in practical matters, worth far more than the reasoning faculty which a laborious education has developed in man . . .

But, if it is conceded that a special training is necessary for school teachers and governesses, the advantages may well be held to outweigh the disadvantages. May we give a word of kindly advice? We would say let it be a true College for women. Let its promoters give up the ambitious notion of an institution on the same footing as a man's College . . . Let all the arrangements be made with reference to the special work of the College, the training of teachers . . . Thus simplicity of living, the strictest economy, so as to suit governesses; training in housekeeping, regular needlework, and, if possible, actual school teaching, should be parts of a system to which all should with very slight exceptions conform . . . If the College is to succeed, there will be no such thing as free permission to read as much and as late as enthusiastic students may desire. The health of women cannot stand, much evening reading. Nature is imperative in these matters. Reading aloud should be cultivated and might be made exceedingly useful if some were to read out to others, who, in various self-arranged sets, practised making their own dress, or worked for others as in the mission-working parties now happily becoming common in many places. Nothing could be more useful to governesses, who seldom at present possess this often necessary and always feminine accomplishment; while the relief from the constant strain upon minds ill prepared for hard and regular study, as most of them will be, may make the whole difference in the bill of health.

With all respect for the ladies who are about to make this interesting experiment, no one of the slightest experience can contemplate without very great alarm the effect of indiscriminately applying the system of men to women. As we have already said in regard of boys and girls, the former have gone through a mingled discipline of physical and mental labour which enables them, when they have reached manhood, to grapple with the tasks of the real student, to apply any amount of patient study, and to suffer but little from the strain of the stiffest examinations. Even among them it is well-known how many, from want of proper care, break down before they arrive at the goal. It is an ascertained physiological fact that the actual capacity of the average male brain is considerably greater than that of the female . . .

Keep the male and female types essentially distinct. For those young ladies who cannot obtain 'a higher education' through their parents, brothers, friends, and books at home, or by means of Lectures in cities, let a refuge be provided with the training governesses; but for heaven's sake, do not let us establish the 'University-woman' as the modern type. We want to entice our 'golden youth' into matrimony, not by wiles and plots and match-making warfare, but by the exhibition of a true, modest, retiring, useful, womanly character.

M. Burrows, *Quarterly Review*, vol. 126 (1869).

3.18   Sex in mind and education

It will have to be considered whether women can scorn delights, and live laborious days of intellectual exercise and production without injury to their functions as the conceivers, mothers and nurses of children. For it would be an ill thing, if it should so happen, that we got the advantages of a quantity of female intellectual work at the price of a puny, enfeebled, and sickly race.

Henry Maudsley, *Fortnightly Review*, 21 April 1874.

3.19   False notions of propriety

It is contended by some that a certain degree of helplessness in women is not only becoming but useful, as a stimulus to exertion in men. This is scarcely a fair argument, unless it could be proved that it is also good for women to sit with folded hands admiring the activity of men.

A fear has indeed been expressed that, if women had anything else to do, they would be unwilling to marry, and a diminution in the number of marriages (justly regarded as a serious evil), would ensue. But those who entertain such an apprehension must surely look upon matrimony as a very unhappy estate. If women can only be driven into it by ennui, or as a means of earning a livelihood, how is it that men are willing to marry? Are the advantages all on their side? The experience of happy wives and mothers forbids such a supposition. It is likely, on the contrary, that, by making women more capable, the number of marriages would be increased, as many men would be glad to marry, who are now deterred from doing so by prudential considerations.

In conclusion, I may be permitted to say a few words to those liberal-minded persons who are favourable to the movement now in progress, but who content themselves with standing aside and wishing it God-speed, under the impression that that is all thy can do. You can – nay, you must – either help this movement forward, or, in a greater or less degree, retard it. If you are a medical man, you can throw the weight of your influence into the scale in favour of extending to women the educational advantages you have yourself enjoyed; if you are a merchant or a banker, you may be able to make such arrangements in your office as would render it practicable to employ female clerks and cashiers; if you are a master-tradesman, you can make known your willingness to receive female apprentices; if you take part in the government of hospitals, prisons, &c., you can encourage the increased employment of women as officers in these and kindred institutions. Whoever and whatever you are, you can testify against the notion that indolence is feminine and refined; and that if a lady may, in certain cases, be permitted to work, her labour must at any rate be unpaid. You can assist in breaking down those false notions of propriety by which women are hampered in so many directions. And so you may help them to exchange a condition of labour without profit, and leisure without ease, for a life of wholesome activity, and the repose that comes with fruitful toil.

Emily Davies, *The higher education of women*, London: Strahan (1866).

3.20 Medicine

. . . The practice of medicine by women would for the present have been regarded by us merely as a curious American 'institution,' were it not for the fact that Dr. Elizabeth Blackwell has lately again honoured this metropolis with her presence. Her mission has been in part to give a course of public lectures on physiological and hygienic matters, and in part to propagate her doctrines on the expediency of qualifying women for treating their own sex and children – that is to say, for supplanting such men as Sir Charles Locock, Professor Simpson, and Dr. West, in the performance of those duties which have been, as it seems, erroneously entrusted to them . . .

But is not the idea of a female practitioner, . . . lamentably ridiculous? Imagine . . . a Fergusson in woman's outward guise, amputating a thigh, or removing a diseased jaw or elbow-joint, aided by assistants of like sex and mind, and surrounded by a host of fair damsels, who regard the proceedings of the operator with that appreciation of the cool head and the ready hand which medical students so well know how to feel . . . Call to mind all things that are done in the ordinary course of hospital duties, or even of general practice in town or country; and imagine, good reader, if you can, a British lady performing them.

It may perhaps be said, that there is no intention of proceeding so far; that women are to be educated only with the view of treating the ailments peculiar to their own sex and to children; but that, in special cases, the aid of the male practitioner is to be called in. This is no argument . . . Women who would practise medicine and surgery must do so wholly; there is no shirking the obligation. If they attempt to do less, they will fail in the duty they undertake; and the male sex will have an unfair advantage over the female, in being able to command a higher exercise of professional skill and knowledge.

An argument which is, we believe, prominently put forward in favour of females being professionally attended by persons of their own sex, is the indecency of male attendance . . . Is it compatible with the attributes of woman, that she should arm herself with a medical education and medical diplomas, and put herself forward to practise medicine? Certainly not. There has been a great deal of nonsense talked in late years about the rights of woman, strong-minded women, and so forth. Granted, that much of this is the result of a reaction; that the female mind has not been properly appreciated; still we are as far as possible from partaking in the extreme views of those who cheer on in their course the Doctors Blackwell and other lady-doctors. Woman has her full share of duty to perform as well as man, and she has been endowed with the qualifications both of mind and of body necessary for the fulfilment of her duty; but there are classes of duties which are peculiar to each sex, and the attempt to perform which, otherwise than by those to whom they have been assigned, is a failure . . .

In the sick-room, the exercise of the moral attributes is divided between the two sexes. From the male are especially expected judgment, decision, and promptness in action: in the female there shine forth most brightly sympathy, tenderness, and devotion to duty; and in the exercise of these she possesses the highest claims to our respect.

Does any one hint that there is no greater incompatibility with feminine attributes in the proceedings of Dr. Elizabeth Blackwell than in those of Florence Nightingale in her attendance on the hospitals of Scutari and the Crimea? There is, we fear, a wide difference between the two cases. The mission of Florence Nightingale was one of mercy and benevolence: she went, that she might afford to the sick and wounded the treatment which woman alone could give them. The mission of the lady-doctors of medicine is – what is it? We lament to record our conviction that it is one of arrogance and self-glorification ... When woman undertakes, as a habit, the duty of man, then she goes beyond her province, and loses all title to our respect.

We must not be understood as wishing to shew the slightest disrespect to Dr Elizabeth Blackwell, or to any dominæ doctores, as ladies. It is the principles and practices they have engrafted on the womanly status that we attack. Doubtless they possess excellent intellectual and moral qualities; let them exercise these in performing the proper duties of woman as they are recognised by civilised nations ... We have alluded above to the public teaching of physiology and hygiene by Dr Elizabeth Blackwell. With this, beyond the very questionable taste, to our minds, of lectures by ladies, we have no fault to find. There can be no question that women ought to know more than they do at present of the processes of life, and of the means of preserving health. But this is altogether another matter from undertaking the treatment of disease. The knowledge we have here briefly advocated can detract nothing from the worth and excellence of woman; the habitual usurpation of functions which are not hers must put her beyond the pale of respect. But there is no fear that the British matron and the British damsel will be tempted, by any cry of woman's dignity or of false delicacy, to do aught that shall diminish the esteem and affection with which they have ever been regarded.

'Room for the Ladies!' *British Medical Journal*, 9 April 1859, pp. 292–4.

3.21 Proposed ban on women medical students, 1928

London Hospitals and Proposed Ban
It is hoped that an acceptable compromise will be reached on the subject of the proposed exclusion of women students from the medical schools of most of the London hospitals ... the intention of King's College, Charing

Cross, and Westminster Hospitals is believed to tend towards the exclusion of women medical students, and if these hospitals take that step there will only remain the Royal Free Hospital and University College Hospital (with a maximum of 12) still open to women.

It is only since the days when, owing to the absorption of men by the War, male students fell off in numbers that women have been admitted to any of the London hospital medical schools other than that of the Royal Free Hospital, where the students are exclusively women. Some of the hospitals, including Guy's, St Bartholomew's, and St Thomas's, have never admitted women students. For 40 years the Royal Free Hospital alone accepted women . . .

The one [reason] offered by most members of the medical profession is that the hospitals regard this as one means of relieving the overcrowding in the profession . . . This is perhaps one way of stating the objection of some of the men students to women on the ground that their presence in a school of limited numbers reduces the total of men from whom sports teams may be drawn . . .

From the point of view of London University the situation is delicate, since all the medical schools receive grants from its funds and one of its statutes provides that no disability shall be imposed on the ground of sex. This clearly could not be interpreted as meaning that there may be no school for men or women exclusively, or the position of the Royal Free Hospital would be no more tenable that that of Guy's or St Bartholomew's. It must apparently be taken to mean that there shall be no disability arising from lack of facilities for either sex. Supporters of the women students will maintain that such a disability would be created if the hospitals carried out their present threat. It is hoped, however, that neither side will act hastily and that a way of solving the difficulty will be found.

The Times, 2 March 1928.

3.22 Women on school boards

If we compare the enormous number of large towns in England where School Boards exist, with the very small number of women who are serving on them, the need for some better organised action will be very evident; especially when we consider how many ladies are fitted both by nature and by training to undertake the really feminine duties of the Boards, the attention to details in housing, warming and teaching so many thousands of children with due regard to economy and at the same time to thoroughness. There are special services in connection with the education of children; the sanitary accommodations of the schools, the guidance of the teachers, the friendly consultations with the parents, which no one thinks outside the province of women. Opinion may be very divided about the share that women ought to take in political matters; but in the politico-domestic sphere of the School Board nearly every one agrees that women do good by participating and accordingly it has generally happened that when a lady has announced her willingness to serve the public upon the School Board, the electors have been very ready to give her the opportunity. Apart from her specially intellectual qualifications a woman is useful upon a School Board by reason of her womanliness, for her kind heart, ready tact, sympathetic insight into the troubles and requirements of the small and weak, and of her patience in working out the small details which added together make the sum of public as of domestic life. The presence of a lady is sufficient sometimes to humanise a whole Board of Directors, . . . in the every day matters which occupy the attention of the Board, and which have reference to the three subjects which women understand best; the management of children, the direction of servants or employees, and intercourse with the poor . . .

The importance of women on the school boards is still more manifest in the case of the girls' schools. Until lately our legislators and educators have hardly seemed aware of the fact that there are as many girls in the world as boys, for their education was invariably overlooked or postponed as secondary in importance to that of the boys. Even now there is a continual tendency to give them an inferior education, to diminish the supply of books and school appliances in the girls' schools, or shorten the hours of instruction. Sometimes another course is adopted, and a system of cooking and needlework is introduced, so elaborate that though these sciences are useful and necessary, they trench upon the hours of study. Ladies are needed to superintend and regulate all these details, that their due importance should be recognized without absorbing too much time . . .

It is not only the children who benefit by the constant vigilance and kindness of the lady members of the school board. Rather more than half the teachers are women – the greater portion of them young women. They are often inexperienced, frequently strangers from another town, in new and difficult positions, with imperfectly understood duties, and with many trials to their tact and temper. A large portion of the work of each member of the Board lies in directing the teachers. Numberless troubles and doubts and jealousies arise in which a young woman teacher requires aid or advice. The Members of the Board are ready to give it, but will she confide in any but ladies, or would it be desirable if she did?

The English Woman's Review, LXXVI, 15 August 1879, pp. 353–6.

3.23   Qualities required in a teacher

Alertness, pleasantness of manner, responsiveness, some amount of individuality, a real desire for the work – these are the characteristics which with a suitable home environment make themselves fairly evident. No lethargic, stolid, unobservant, unattractive – whether in speech or manner – or unsympathetic person, however physically strong, mentally well-equipped, and even morally sound should be accepted for the teaching profession ... there should be no hesitancy on the part of the authorities in rejecting any who show lack of teaching aptitude.

Edge Hill College magazine 17 (1908), p. 15.

3.24   Woman an undeveloped man

The average woman, whose mental development has hitherto been left very much to chance, is in these respects more on a par with the child than is the average man; but as the education of the two sexes more and more approximates, less difference between them will be observable. I have not found the capacity for abstract thought less in educated women than in educated men.

   ... the woman more than the man maintains throughout life the mental characteristics of the child, and this leads me to touch briefly upon the question, so frequently discussed nowadays, whether the man is mentally superior to the woman. The general drift of my remarks hitherto has obviously been in favour of the view that the man is the more intellectual of the two ... How are we to account for the fact that women acquit themselves as brilliantly as, or more brilliantly than, men in examinations open to both sexes? In reply I would point out that the mere capacity for storing away facts – and examinations are very largely a test of this capacity

– does not necessarily ... go along with the highest order of mind. It is further probable that women think more quickly than men, and this also helps them in examinations, though here again the capacity for rapid thought is not a necessary mark of a high order of intellect ... originality of thought is of little help in most examinations, which rather require the assimilation of facts and of other men's opinions. Finally – and I venture to lay particular stress upon this mental evolution is much more rapid in woman than in man, and the difference is observable at a very early age. Thus, to take a particular instance, a little girl two and a half years old is intellectually ahead of her brother, who is fifteen months older, and the observation is made constantly that girls are more precocious than boys. It is therefore unfair to pit a girl of sixteen or seventeen against a boy of the same age, who probably does not arrive at her stage of mental evolution until he is twenty-one or twenty-two years old.

I believe that, taking one individual with another, there is greater intellectual equality between the sexes than is generally supposed; that is to say, that the thoroughly stupid members of either sex are proportionately about equal in number, and also the rank and file, and even the talented members ... ; it is only when we pass into the region of genius that we see the intellectual disparity of the two sexes unmistakably revealed. Genius of the highest order is practically limited to the male sex. Nor can this be explained on the ground that women have not been allowed the same opportunity as men. Opportunity undoubtedly accounts for much, but not for all, for, as has been well said, 'Genius does what it must, talent what it can;' and we cannot doubt that, had a woman Shakespeare or Beethoven potentially existed, the world would have heard of her in spite of unfavouring external circumstances.

H. Campbell, *Differences in the nervous organisation of man and woman physiological and pathological*, London: H. K. Lewis (1891), p. 171.

3.25   Women's role is that of a housemaker

Women possess certain particular needs based on their psychology, physiology, and their social and economic position ... The fundamental common experience is the fact that the vast majority of them will become makers of homes, and that to do this successfully requires the proper development of many talents.

J. Newsom, *The education of girls*, London: Faber and Faber (1948), p. 110.

3.26 Attitudes to teachers' pay

It is terrible heresy, no doubt, and would lead to a great upheaval in the present order of things, but why also should not a *woman* teacher be paid at the same rate as a *man*? She does the same kind of work, puts in more rather than less, hours per day, and may be as highly certificated. Even when she is working under precisely the same conditions, say as Assistant in a boys' department, her salary falls very much below that of her fellow-assistant, just because he is a man, and for no other reason.

Edge Hill College magazine 4 (1895), p. 6.

Notes

1 E. Sewell, *Principles of education* (1865), vol. ii, p. 219.
2 C. Skelton, 'Women and education' in D. Richardson and V. Richardson, eds, *Introducing women's studies*, London: Macmillan, 2nd edn (1997).

4

Work

Timeline

1802   Health and Morals of Apprentices Act: children in textile mills limited to twelve hours per day; no night work.

1819   Cotton Mills and Factories Act: no child under nine to work in cotton mills; over nine, maximum twelve-hour day.

1825   Cotton Mills and Factories Act: children under sixteen years limited to twelve hours per day; 5am–8pm with half an hour off for breakfast and one hour for lunch.

1831   Truck Act prohibited in certain trades payment of wages in goods, tokens or otherwise.

1832   Sadler's Report of the Select Committee on the Bill for the Regulation of Factories: proposed ten-hour day for under eighteens.

1833   Mills and Factories Act (Althorp's Act): no work for under nines; nine to thirteen, no more than forty nine hours in one week or nine hours in one day; thirteen to eighteen, no more than sixty nine hours in a week or twelve in one day.

1842   Mines and Collieries Act: no employment underground of women and children under ten in mines and collieries; inspectors appointed.

1844   Labour in Factories Act: machinery to be guarded; the age at which children might be employed reduced from nine to eight years; maximum hours of work for children and women prescribed.

1847   Ten Hours Act: ten hours per day and fifty eight hours in any one week; maximum hours of work for women and children.

1850   Factories Act: total hours which could be worked by young people and women restricted to sixty per week.

1864 Factory Acts (Extension) Act: extended coverage of industries.

1867 Factory Acts (Extension) Act: all factories employing more than fifty people under the terms of all existing Factory Acts; no employment of children, young people and women on Sundays.

1867 Workshop Regulation Act: no employment of children under the age of eight years in any handicraft.

1867 Agricultural Gangs Act: no employment of children under the age of eight in public agricultural gangs; no gangs of mixed sex; all gangmasters to be licensed by local magistrates.

1868 First report of the Royal Commission on the Employment of Children, Young Persons and Women in Agriculture.

1871 Criminal Law Amendment Act: no intimidation, violence, obstruction and picketing against an employer or other employees.

1871 Bank Holidays Act: Easter Monday, Whit Monday, the first Monday in August and 26th of December (if a weekday) official holidays.

1872 Metalliferous Mines Regulation Act: no boys under the age of 12, women or girls in mines.

1873 Agricultural Children's Act: children eight to ten years could be employed in agriculture only if the parent signed a certificate stating that the child had completed 250 school attendances, and if the child was over ten, fifty attendances in the preceding twelve months. No enforcement.

1874 Factory Act: minimum working age nine; working day for women and young people limited to ten hours in the textile industry, between six am and six pm; working week reduced to fifty six and a half hours.

1875 Conspiracy and Protection of Property Act: peaceful picketing lawful.

1878 Factories and Workshops Act: banned children from work involving white lead.

1878 Phillipa Flowerday appointed as nurse to J. & J. Colman (Norwich) to work among the factory people, and to visit them at home when they were ill.

1880 Employers' Liability Act: extended the law regarding injuries to employees.

1886 Shop Hours Regulation Act: the hours of work of children and young persons in shops not to exceed seventy four per week, including meal times.

1891 Factory and Workshop Act: minimum age for employment in factories eleven years; no factory owner to knowingly employ a woman within four weeks of giving birth.

1892 Shop Hours Act: responsibility for inspection placed on local councils.

1893 Women factory inspectors introduced.

1895 Factory and Workshop Act.

1897 Workmen's Compensation Act: persons injured at work should be compensated.

1898 Thomas M. Legge appointed as the first medical inspector of factories.

1917 Women's Land Army established.

1917 Women's Royal Air Force (WRAF).

1918 The Women's Royal Naval Service (WRNS).

1919 Restoration of Pre-War Practices Act.

1930 First woman Chief Inspector of police force (Lilian Wyles).

1938 Women's Voluntary Service for Civil Defence (later the Women's Royal Voluntary Service).

1938 The Auxiliary Territorial Service (ATS), the women's army, is formed.

1939 Women's Land Army re-launched under the leadership of Lady Gertrude Denman.

1941 The National Service Act: introduced conscription for women. All unmarried women between the ages of twenty and thirty called up for war work. Later extended to include women aged up to forty three and to married women, though pregnant women and those with young children could be exempted.

1941 Trades Union Congress pledged itself to principle of equal pay.

1941 The Auxiliary Territorial Service (ATS): given equal military status with men.

1942 Post Office took on 5,000 women engineers.

1946 Royal Commission on Equal Pay recommends teachers, local government officers and civil servants should all receive equal pay.

1946 Marriage bar abolished in the Post Office, Civil Service and BBC.

1946 Dame Alix Kilroy: most senior woman civil servant (under-secretary to the Board of Trade).

1949 ATS (the Auxiliary Territorial Service): transformed into a permanent force – Women's Royal Army Corps (WRAC).

1955   Dame Evelyn Sharp: first woman permanent secretary in the Civil Service, as Head of the Housing Ministry.

1955   Government agreed to equal pay for civil servants, though this not fully implemented until 1973.

Work has been at the forefront, from the very beginning, of writings on women's history. When defined as labour which received monetary reward, it obviously discounted much of a woman's work. There is no doubt however that at least up until the middle of the nineteenth century the majority of women did take part in paid work. Women worked in domestic service and agriculture. Employment conditions in domestic service were very hard, with long hours, poor pay, little personal freedom and the possibility of sexual exploitation. Women's work in agriculture was physically heavy and time consuming. (**4.1**) Dairy work involved long hours: milking two or three times a day, making butter in balls weighing fourteen to nineteen kg and cheese which could weigh more than the women herself (sixty four kg plus). Women took part in all aspects of arable agriculture: sowing, weeding, hoeing and harvesting. (**4.7**) Despite the importance of women's labour, however, it was devalued. Such apprenticeships that existed were designed to prepare girls for their life of domesticity – the work which was seen as appropriate for women. Furthermore wages lagged far behind men's. (**4.3**) K. D. N. Snell's work shows a decrease in employment opportunities for women in arable areas but an increase in pastoral areas. Snell, however, believes that women's participation rates were determined by economic factors (such as the replacement of the sickle by the scythe) whereas feminist historians put more weight on attitudinal influences.

In the late eighteenth century Mary Wollstonecraft pointed out that 'very few trades were open to women' and those that were, such as lacework, often had deleterious effects on women's health.[1] (**4.4**) Domestic ideology had much to do with what was considered suitable work for women, thus mining with its image of half-naked women working in the presence of men was seen to have detrimental effects on a woman's morality and her ability to be a good wife and mother. (**4.5**) The 1842 Mines Act was the first piece of gender legislation, i.e. legislation affecting only one sex. It failed to take into account, however, the lack of alternative employment for women in mining areas. This meant that it had the opposite effect to that intended.

Instead of protecting women, it led many women to ignore its provisions and therefore work without protection.

In a similar way, the 1844 Factory Act, by reducing the number of hours that a woman could work, effectively cut her wages, since she was no longer able to clean her machine at the end of her shift. Such legislation classed women as children and many later reformers did not want 'protective legislation' (**4.6**) for women since it constructed women as dependants not equals. Rather than excluding women from the public workplace, it merely restricted their earning capacity. And as late as 1911, when attempts were made to extend legislation to pit brow women, protestors against the measure pointed out that,

> Over 5,000 women are engaged in the work which has been proved to be suitable for them, to be neither detrimental to their health or morals nor dangerous to their limbs. The women like the work and bitterly resent this attack on their livelihood. As a class they compare favourable with any other class of working women, and it will be a great injustice to the women of the country if Parliament debars them from engaging in this work.[2]

There is no doubt, however, that women's work did contribute to the national economy, as radical politicians pointed out (**4.7**), though women were also disproportionately to be found among the poor. (**4.8**) By the middle of the nineteenth century, men dominated five sectors of the economy – mining, building, transport, clerical and general labouring – while women were only prominent in two – domestic service and 'unoccupied', though the latter also encompassed children. In terms of numbers rather than percentages, women were most often to be found in manufacture (textiles), agriculture, domestic service and 'dealing' (shop work). In all areas, however, men had the more important jobs, thus in agriculture men ploughed, mowed, harvested and took care of animals while women planted, weeded and gleaned. This was even more marked in the professions where women were confined to the lower ranks of teaching and medical occupations. Official sources like the census, however, do not tell a full story of women's working experiences. Much of women's work was part-time, seasonal and did not fit easily into census categories.

Nevertheless the gender division of labour was more pronounced by c. 1850, with working-class women increasingly employed in areas associated with the home and motherhood. Only in factory work was this not the case. Furthermore even if the numbers employed in a sector did not decline, their skills levels did. This gender division cannot be explained by women's lack of strength or being more adept with their hands. As noted above, women working in agriculture did undertake heavy labour, while tailoring, jewellery and watch-making despite their need for delicate accurate work were overwhelmingly male-dominated occupations. Education (or the lack of it) is important. A girl's education was designed to enable her to acquire domestic skills and therefore gain a husband. This was true of both the middle and the working classes.[3] Women's work in agriculture was now seen to unsex her. (**4.9**)

As the century progressed, social reformers increasingly concentrated on the moral aspects of employment. The Society for Promoting the Employment of Women (1859), with its patron Lord Shaftesbury, was designed to find suitable employment for women, particularly of those above the labouring classes, since the options open to them were limited due to their lack of an adequate education. (**4.10**) Reformers stressed that large numbers of women needed to earn their own livings and had no visible means of support. (**4.11**, **4.12**) The 'traditional' option of governessing was also seen to be exploitative. (**4.13**) Furthermore the need for women to undertake paid employment was driving down wages. (**4.14**) Low wages for women were often justified on the grounds that women worked only for 'pin money'. If they did have dependants, then they would have fewer than a man. (**4.17**, **4.18**) Feminists fought to override this impression and isolated men like Lord Haldane agreed that women civil servants should be paid the same as men. (**4.19**)

The rise of clerical work at the end of the century seemed heaven sent. It enabled women to work without women losing their essential feminine qualities: it was clean, did not involve prolonged contact with inferiors and did not debar a woman from marriage. Secretarial work had originally been a male occupation and once it was taken over by women its standing was devalued. Women should receive enough for decency but no more, otherwise they might be tempted to abandon their true vocation of wife and mother. Skill was being defined in a gendered way and men felt threatened. Thus women were encouraged to join unions so that they would not undercut men. (**4.14**) 'Surplus' women's choices were limited to emigrating to the colonies, being a ladies' companion or trying to find a career in such areas as medicine and teaching.

Despite the increase in opportunities for women, it was still assumed that paid work was simply an interlude before marriage. For working-class women, however, work was essential to ensure the family income. Notions of respectability nevertheless meant that they often had to keep such work 'hidden' by working at home and taking in lodgers and/or laundry. They were also to be found in the sweated industries (**4.15**) and it was gradually being realised that there was no way a married working-class woman could afford a period of maternity leave. (**4.16**) World War I increased the scope of women's work. Women worked in munitions (women's employment at the Woolwich Arsenal had been 125 women in 1914, but by 1917 was 28,000), transport, the armed services and the police, but this was to be short-lived and they did not receive equal pay. (**4.20**) In the National Shell Factories, women received up to £2.22½ p. per week, while men could earn up to £4.32½ p. Employers always tried to avoid direct substitution of skilled male workers, both to cut costs and appease the unions. Women therefore were still seen as a threat to the skilled male worker. It was generally agreed that men, given the sacrifices that they had made, should receive their jobs back. After all, they were the natural breadwinners. And women did not disagree though many would have liked to continue working in their new jobs. Demonstrations took place such as that at the Woolwich Arsenal in November 1918 of women protesting about being laid off. Once the Armistice was signed, however, women were swiftly removed from the labour force. From January 1919, 1,500 women a week were dismissed from the Woolwich Arsenal. Women, however, did not want to return to the traditional work of domestic service even if it mean losing the 'out of work donation' of £1, though they were only eligible for this if they had paid National Insurance contributions pre-war.

The Times discourse at this time is interesting. Having happily praised women's war efforts, it quickly turned to criticising and downgrading women's work. Thus on 20 November 1918 it made reference to 'the expensively-gowned, highly-paid munitions worker of whom so much has been heard'. (**4.21**) By 29 January 1919, it complained that women were scorning employment in domestic service because they had 'tasted the joys of high wages, constant companionship and limited hours of work' (**4.22**) and on 16 April 1919 stated boldly that, 'The trouble seems to be that a considerable proportion of the unemployed girls are not sufficiently competent to command the confidence of employers.' (**4.23**) As R. Strachey commented, 'The tone of the Press swung, all in a moment, from extravagant praise to the opposite extreme, and the very same people who had been heroines and the saviours of their country a few months before were parasites, blacklegs and limpets'.[4]

By 1921, following the onset of the slump in the autumn of 1920 which particularly hit employment opportunities in the North and Wales for both sexes, no more women were employed than had been in the pre-war economy. And, the marriage bar further restricted women's employment. The inter-war years demonstrated that the economy was still structured by male ideals (**4.25, 4.26**) though in certain areas such as the Midlands women were to be found in the light engineering industries where women were supposed to be better able to withstand the boredom of the repetitive work! Women were to be admitted to the Civil Service on the same terms as men, but not to receive the same salary. *The Times* was wary that this would become the 'precursor of other and perhaps, greater changes' (**4.27**) The majority of feminists (Monica Whately being a notable exception) restricted their campaign for equal pay throughout the 1930s to teaching and the Civil Service (**4.28**) since they felt this was where they had their best case. Sometimes they received support from enlightened men such as Sir William Beveridge. (**4.29**)

World War II again saw women taking over men's jobs with great success. (**4.30, 4.32, 4.33**) though they were not always welcomed by men. Women were to be called up both to the armed service and work on the home front, though those responsible for childcare could be exempted along with those in 'vital war work'. (**4.31**) By 1941, most women were working a twelve-hour day, five and a half days a week in industry. Hours were reduced in theory, in 1942, to fifty five hours but any single woman working less than fifty five hours had to do compulsory fire watching. By 1945, women were being urged to return to their pre-war jobs and the unions were in favour of laying off women first. Women's participation in both World Wars, therefore, was thought of as a temporary phenomenon: women's proper place was still the home.

A shortage of manpower in the 1950s and 1960s led to Commonwealth immigration and the introduction of the 'twilight shift' which enabled a woman both to work and fulfil her domestic responsibilities. (**4.34**) Since 1951 the number of married women working in the public economy has risen from 26 per cent in 1951 to 71 per cent in 1991 though much of this reflects the growing trends towards part-time work. Britain now has one of the highest percentages of working women in the EU but one of the worst records as regards childcare. What has changed over the last two hundred years? Men still outweigh markedly women in managerial and supervisory positions. Women still do much work in relation to domesticity and caring and these continue to be undervalued in terms of financial recompense.

4.1 Women's work in agriculture

It is painful to one . . . to behold the beautiful servant maids of this county toiling in the severe labours of the field. They drive the harrow, or the ploughs, when they are drawn by three or four horses; nay, it is not uncommon to see, sweating at the dung-cart, a girl, whose elegant features, and delicate, nicely-proportioned limbs, seemingly but ill accord with such rough employment.

A. Pringle, *General view of the county of Westmoreland: With observations on the means of its improvement*, Edinburgh: Chapman (1794), p. 265.

4.2 A labourer's wife's earnings

In Gloucestershire, the average earnings of a labourer's wife were given as 6 d a week by spinning for 39 weeks, and a total of £2 11 s 6 d for the other 13 weeks employed in agriculture. Her time was spent in the following manner:

	£	s	d
Bean or pease setting, for 3 weeks at 7 d a day		10	6
Fruit picking, 2 weeks at 4 d		4	0
Hay-making, 2 weeks at 4 d		4	0
Gleaning, or leasing 5 bushels at 5 s 6 d per bushel	1	11	6
	2	11	6

David Davies, *The case of labourers in husbandry, stated and considered*, London: Robinson (1795), p. 162.

4.3 Men's wages compared to women's

The wages of men-servants in husbandry who are hired from half-year, are from 9 to 12 guineas a year; whilst women, who here do a large portion of the work of the farm, with difficulty get half as much. It is not easy to account for so striking an inequality; and still less easy to justify it.

F. M. Eden, *The state of the poor: Or, an history of the labouring classes in England*, London: J. Davies (1797), vol. 2, p. 47.

4.4 Working conditions

Girl. It [lace running] is a very bad trade for the eyes. Where I sit I can't see the hands and figures on the clock-face a bit.

Second Girl. Me! I can see the clock very well, but I can't tell what time it is. I can't see which is hands and which is figures . . . None of us [five girls] can see much except the youngest; she has not been at it so long. We earn at this work 3s 6d a week the most of us; some only 3s . . . It's a trade that makes you subject to headache.

First Girl. I like it better than the factory, though we can't get so much. We have our liberty at home, and get our meals comfortable, such as they are.

PP (1833), vol. XX, p. C2, 18.

4.5 Women in mines

137. West Riding of Yorkshire: Southern Part – The following may serve as examples of the evidence given on this subject by the several classes of witness in this district:

Matthew Lindley, collier, Day and Twibell's Barnsley: 'I wish the Government would expel all girls and females from mines. I can give proof that they are very immoral, and I am certain that the girls are worse than the men in point of morals, and use far more indecent language. It unbecomes them in every way; there is not one in ten of them that know how to cut a shirt out or make one, and they learn neither to knit or sew. I have known myself of a case where a married man and girl who hurried him had sexual intercourse often in the bank where he worked'. (J. C. Symons, Esq., Evidence No. 109: App. Pt. I, p. 251-1. 13) Mr George Armitage, aged thirty-six years, Hoyland: 'I hardly know how to reprobate the practice sufficiently of girls working in pits; nothing can be worse. I have no doubt that debauchery is carried on, for which there is every opportunity; for the girls go constantly, when hurrying to the men, who work often alone in the bank faces apart from every one. I think it scarcely possible for girls to remain modest who are in pits, regularly mixing with such company, and hearing such language as they do. I dare venture to say that many of the wives who come from pits know nothing of sewing or any household duty, such as women ought to know – they lose all disposition to learn such things; they are rendered unfit for learning them also by being overworked, and not being trained to the habit of it. I have worked in pits for above ten years, where girls were constantly employed, and I can safely say it is an abominable system. I think that girls ought to be prevented from going into pits, whatever may be the consequence; the effect of preventing them could not be worse than that of letting them be in'.

Appendix to the first report of the Commissioners on the employment of children in mines (1842), p. 31.

4.6 Women factory workers

Observe the appalling progress of female labour; and remember that the necessity for particular protection to females against overwork is attested by the most eminent surgeons and physicians . . .

'Mr E a manufacturer (says the writer), informed me that he employs females exclusively at his power-looms; it is so universally; gives a decided preference to married females, especially those who have families at home dependent on them for support; they are attentive, docile, more so than unmarried females, and are compelled to use their utmost exertions to procure the necessaries of life'.

Thus, Sir, the virtues, the peculiar virtues, of the female character to be perverted to her injury – thus all that is most dutiful and tender in her nature is to be made the means of her bondage and suffering! . . .

'The small amount of wages', says inspector Saunders, 'paid to women, acts as a strong inducement to the mill-occupiers to employ them instead of men, and in power-loom shops this has been the case to a great extent'
...
So much, Sir, for their physical, and, if I may so speak, their financial condition; the picture of their moral state will not be more consolatory ... the females not only perform the labour, but occupy the places of men; they are forming various clubs and associations, and gradually acquiring all those privileges which are held to be the proper portion of the male sex. These female clubs are thus described – Fifty or sixty females, married and single, form themselves into clubs, ostensibly for protection; but, in fact, they meet together, to drink, sing, and smoke; they use, it is stated, the lowest, most brutal, and most disgusting language imaginable ... Whence is it that this singular and unnatural change is taking place? Because that on women are imposed the duty and burthen of supporting their husbands and families; a perversion as it were of nature, which has the inevitable effect of introducing into families disorder, insubordination, and conflict. What is the ground on which the woman says she will pay no attention to her domestic duties, nor give the obedience which is owing to her husband? Because on her devolves the labour which ought to fall to his share, and she throws out the taunt, 'If I have the labour, I will also have the amusement'.

Hansard, 15 March 1844 cc. 1099–100.

4.7   Women's work in agriculture

... It is a most incontrovertible fact, that woman contribute to the wealth and resources of the kingdom. The population in Great Britain in 1831, consisted of 16,255,605, which may be classified under the head of agriculture, mining, and manufacturing; from these three sources the wealth of a country is raised ... In the first place, the dairy is managed almost exclusively by woman and girls; the small live stock, such as poultry, &c., wholly so ... In the fields, again, we find women performing every kind of labour except draining, hedging, ditching, fencing, ploughing, and mowing. We find them driving, sowing, setting, harrowing, drilling, manuring, weeding, hoeing, picking stones, gathering potatoes, turnips, pulling carrots, mangel wurzel, shearing, binding, gathering, hay-making, &c. &c ... In the barn, with the exception of thrashing and handicraft work, women perform every other occupation. There is no country in Europe where the women are such slaves upon the soil as they are in Scotland . . . Debased is the man who would say women have no right to interfere in politics, when it is evident, that they have as much right as 'sordid man.' None but a tyrant, or some cringing, crawling, hireling scribe, succumbing to the footstool of power, would dare to say so.

R. J. Richardson, *The rights of woman* (1840) reprinted in Dorothy Thompson, *The early chartists*, London: Macmillan (1971), pp. 118–19.

4.8   Women among the poor

. . . of the sessional poor, in all, on 1st August last, 1220, there were of the following:

Description	Males	Females	Total
Clippers	"	22	22
Hawkers	3	75	78
House work, or lodgings	"	132	132
Knitters of stockings	"	20	20
Labourers	44	"	44
Porters	20	3	23
Sewers	"	139	139
Tambourers	"	32	32
Unfit for work or of no occupation	4	118	122
Weavers	62	1	63
Washers	"	46	46
Winders of yarn	6	335	341
Of other occupations, in all	113	45	158
Total	252	968	1,220

The very great proportion of females may at first sight appear striking, but will not astonish any one acquainted with the poor in our large cities and towns, or with those of other countries: 'Les femmes (says M. Leuret, in his 'Notice sur les Indigens de la Ville de Paris') 'tombent dans la misère en plus grande proportion que les hommes'.

Sanitary conditions of the labouring population: Scotland (1842), p. 180.

4.9   Work in agriculture unsexes women

I refer to the employment of females of whatever age or condition upon the labours of the farm . . . It is universally admitted that such employment, not so much from causes inherent in it as from circumstances by which it is surrounded, is to a great extent demoralizing. Not only does it almost unsex a woman, in dress, gait, manners, character, making her rough, coarse, clumsy, masculine; but it generates a further very pregnant social mischief, by unfitting or indisposing her for a woman's proper duties at home. Some of the work on which women are frequently employed, such as serving the threshing machine, weeding high wet corn, drawing turnips or mangolds, is work to which, on physical grounds, they never ought to be put at all. Exposure to wet or cold, from which no farm labourer can claim exemption, is likely, owing to the greater susceptibility of the female constitution, to be specially injurious to them. The farmers, almost to a man, complain of the difficulty of getting dairymaids and other domestic servants; and almost to a man again, express the opinion that the proper place for a young single girl is in a household, and not upon the land. It is admitted that the intermixture of the sexes is one great cause of demoralization; yet such is the nature of farm work that it would be very difficult even by the best contrived arrangement – it would almost be impossible by legislation – to secure effective separation. It is said that a party of women almost necessitate the presence of a male superintendent to keep them steadily and methodically to their work; while even more corrupting than the intermixture of any number of men with women in their work is said to be the influence of two or three debased members of their own sex . . . The evil is to some extent being mitigated by natural and spontaneous influences. Everywhere I heard the same story, that women are found to be less and less disposed to go out to work upon the land. They will refuse unsuitable work; they will stay at home on wet days. Whether from the easier circumstances in which they live or from their having become intelligent enough to take a more accurate measure of loss and gain, there seems to be much less attraction for them in the farmer's 8 d or 9 d a day than there used to be.

1867 Commission on employing women and children in agriculture (1867–9),
4068, xvii.

4.10   Society for promoting the Employment
of Women

The terrible necessity which exists for providing women with other remunerative employments than the few yet open to them, is a fact too familiar to us all to need comment, . . . Mr Mackenzie dwelt upon the very imperfect manner in which women of all classes are instructed in arithmetic, and showed how necessary and useful a thorough knowledge of accounts would be, not only for those who are compelled to support themselves, but for those who lead a comparatively idle life, and merely have to superintend others. After referring to many occupations, where a knowledge of accounts was essential, and after some allusions to watchmaking, shoebinding, etc, Mr Mackenzie read the following paper by Miss Boucherett:

'. . . no less than forty-three thousand women in London get their livelihood by needlework of some sort or other. Of these, some can only earn four-pence a day, by working from five in the morning till eight at night.

The reason why such a large number of women rush into this overcrowded and ill-paid profession is made apparent by the remarks of numerous applicants for employment at the office of our society. Many of these persons belong to a class decidedly above the labouring poor. The story usually told is that they have lived at home with their parents since they left school, engaged in no particular occupation, until their father's death has reduced them to the necessity of providing for themselves. When asked of what employment they are capable? they generally answer that they can read and write and sew, but not earn enough by their needles to live upon. If asked whether there is anything else they can do? The usual reply is 'No, but I shall be glad to learn anything: I do not care what, only it must be something that can be learnt very quickly, as my means of living will be soon exhausted.' Of course, it is seldom possible to assist these poor creatures, as no remunerative employment can be learnt quickly . . .

The contrast between the wages earned by tolerably well and ill educated women, is very great. Fifteen shillings a week is the lowest rate of remuneration for saleswomen, and many earn twenty, thirty, or even forty pounds a year besides board and lodging. And this, although some of the tradesmen who employ them, complain that they experience inconvenience from the slowness with which the girls calculate when they first enter upon their situations.

It is probable that if girls were better educated, the number of women employed in shops might be multiplied almost indefinitely, as they would be more and more used if found well-qualified. The same kind of teaching would also enable them to become cashiers, accountants and clerks' . . .

. . . Sir W. Wood read the following paper by Miss Parkes: –

'It being conceded that in England a vast number of women are forced to earn their own livelihood, two distinct inquiries meet one at the outset of this question: – For what employments are women fitted by nature? And How is it possible to introduce them practically into new and renumerative spheres of labour?

Generally speaking, all the mechanical arts which demand perception and skill rather than strength, are intrinsically suited to the capacities of the average women of the middle and lower classes. . . . That women possess sufficient physical strength to pursue the mechanical arts, is proved by their extensive employment by thousands and tens of thousands in the factories of the north and elsewhere. The conditions of factory labour, in many ways, highly injurious to female health, are a sort of ultimate test, which being submitted to with results less fatal to the health of the population that causal inquirers would imagine, there is reason to hope that various other branches of industry, pursued at home, or in workshops adapted for a limited number, may be redeemed from reproach on the score of health. In any case, they form a better alternative than slop-work or starvation.

. . . it is . . . astonishing that in so very few instances are women employed as managers, in factories, where a large proportion of the inferior work is done by female hands . . .

The difficulty does not seem to lie so much in educating women for these artistic trades, as in effecting their subsequent introduction into renumerative labour. This is partly owing to the extreme timidity evinced by women themselves in seeking work, and in the social customs which render it unusual or inconvenient for them to work with men, to walk long distances at varying hours of the day or evening, and to conform in many ways to the ordinary regulations of workshops . . .

English Woman's Journal, 5, 1860.

4.11 Employment of women

In the first place, then, it appears that marriage, as a means of subsistence (to say nothing of the indecorum of looking forward to it in this light) is exceedingly precarious in two ways. The proportion of wives to widows and spinsters in 1861 was just about three to two, while of these wives themselves nearly one in four was occupied in other than domestic duties, either as her husband's coadjutor, as in farm-houses or shops, or, of necessity, as his substitute in cases of his desertion, or help-lessness, or vice. In the second place, the number of widows and spinsters supporting themselves, which in 1851 was two millions, has increased in 1861 to more than two millions and a half . . . Two and a half millions of Englishwomen without husbands, and working for their own subsistence! This is not an accident, it is a new order of things. Of the three and a half millions of women – wives, widows, and spinsters – engaged in other than domestic occupations, it is probable that scarcely a thousand make, without capital, and by their own exertions, one hundred pounds a year. The best paid are housekeepers in large establishments, a few finishing governesses, and professed cooks. 43,964 women are returned as outdoor agricultural labourers – a fact worthy of remembrance when it is said that women are too weak to serve in haberdashers' shops. Women, refused admission to such shops on the pretext that they are not strong enough to lift bales of goods, have been afterwards traced to the occupations of dock porters and coal-heavers. In practice the employments of women are not determined by their lightness, but by their low pay. One newspaper still scoffs at the desire of women to be self-supporting: but starvation is a sufficient answer to sneers. As a favourable symptom of the last few years, I may add that 1822 women are returned as employed by the Post-office. 213 women are returned as telegraph-clerks. It is instructive to note the way in which the salary of these women telegraph-clerks has fallen. When the telegraph companies were first formed, the pay of a female clerk was eight shillings a week, to be increased by a shilling yearly, until it reached fourteen shillings a week. So great, however, has been the com-petition of women for these situations, that the pay has been reduced to five shillings a week, a sum on which a woman can scarcely live unas-sisted. In France the women telegraph-clerks have met with a worse fate. The government took the management of the telegraphs, and dismissed the women, because they had no votes to bestow on the government candidates. The exclusion of women from the suffrage has been called a harmless injustice; but there is no injustice from which is not liable to become an injury.

At present the principal employments open to women are teaching, domestic service, and sewing. I come to consider the remuneration of the highest profession open to women.

In 1861 there were 80,017 female teachers in England, of whom the majority were governesses in private families. It is difficult to ascertain the average salary of governesses, because the Governesses'

Institutions in London and Manchester, which are the chief sources of information on the subject, refuse to register the applications of governesses who accept salaries less than £25 a year. The number of this lowest class may be guessed from the fact that for a situation as nursery governess, with a salary of £20 a year, advertised in a newspaper, there were five hundred applicants; as I have already stated, three hundred applied for a similar place with no salary at all.

Josephine E. Butler, *The education and employment of women*, London: Macmillan (1868), pp. 4–5.

4.12   Women's work

Every woman ought to read Miss Parkes's little volume on *Women's Work*
. . .

Now, we believe that no one can accomplish more good for womankind at present than by stating clearly and forcibly, truthfully and soberly, what is the precise position of the sex in the present stage of our civilization. Within living memory, the position of women in the world has sensibly altered . . .

It is but too easy to make mirth of petticoats. We have heard so much of woman's rights, and this whole subject of women has been so vulgarized by coarse treatment, has been so inflated by nonsense, that few now care to give it the serious attention which it deserves. In Miss Parkes's volume the reader will not find a word about women's rights – not a sentence which is disturbed by the spirit of Bloomerism. Her discourse is of woman's duties, woman's wants, woman's work. What is expected of women in the altered condition of modern society? How are women to get their living? And how can we assist them in their efforts?
. . .

Miss Parkes argues that the position of those ladies who have to earn their bread is not fairly recognized. It is the position of a minority of ladies; therefore it is treated as an exceptional position – therefore, also, as one which it is not necessary to recognize, to respect and to facilitate. We give pity to such a position, but pity, with all its kindliness, may be injurious. What is wanted is not that the women who have to earn their bread should have upon them the slur which is implied in pity, but that they should be recognized as engaged in a natural and honourable duty to which no social disadvantage should be attached.

. . . Miss Parkes . . . means not the work of the vast majority of women. The vast majority of women are engaged in the work of managing their homes. They are wives, and mothers and mistresses of households. The work which Miss Parkes thinks of is the work of those who either have no household cares, or have something more than a household to look after. If these are minority among the women of England, they are certainly a very large minority, when we consider the number of women among the lower classes who have to seek employment away from their homes, in great mills and factories, in cornfields and turnipfields, in domestic service, in shops, in dressmaking, in bookbinding, and in all the lighter trades. It is not, however, of women in the lower classes that Miss Parkes now writes. Their position as breadwinners is perfectly recognized, and if it were not recognized they would not much care . . . A girl of the lower class is not supposed to be out of her position when she leaves her father's home to become a chambermaid, to go into millinery, or to help in making steel pens. The whole difficulty concerns women of the middle class and especially women who are ladies or set up for ladies. In the middle class, and especially in the upper ranks of this middle class, the theory is that men provide for the women, and therefore that the women have nothing to do. Husbands, fathers, brothers, and sons take care for the most part of their female relatives – at least keep them from want if they cannot indulge them in affluence . . .

In truth, however, the exceptions are very numerous, – far more numerous than people suppose; we mean the cases of women, most of them ladies, who are forced upon the world, and who have to fight their way there. They are to be counted in this land, not merely by thousands, but by tens of thousands and hundreds of thousands. There are widows left penniless, and daughters left homeless; sisters whose brothers can afford them but the scantiest maintenance, and mothers who see the hunger of their babes that they cannot assuage. What is to be done for these? They can go out as governesses, and they can turn authoresses: what else can they do? There are heaps of things which they might do if only it were properly recognized that they might do them and that they ought to be prepared to do them. The theory is that no woman who is born in the position of a lady will ever require to do anything, and so she is never taught anything which she can afterwards turn to profit when she is thrown upon her own resources. Miss Parkes's argument is that this state of things should be recognized – that women in the position of ladies have to help themselves, and that we ought to facilitate their attempts to do so . . .

Ought it not to be arranged in her education that, as, however fair her prospects may be, there is always at least a chance of poverty overtaking her, and no help near at hand, she should be prepared by solid acquirements to encounter and overcome the miseries of such a lot? And when she is thus accoutred and can undertake duties different from those of a governess, or an authoress, or an artist – duties which women are not usually called upon to accept – need we pity her as a victim? need we brand her as strong minded? Why should we not accept her as an honest woman honourably doing her duty in her proper sphere? . . .

It is our duty to recognize the necessities of these women, and Miss Parkes will do not a little good if she can get the public generally to recognize the necessities of their position.

The Times, 31 August 1865.

4.13 Governessing

The phrase 'to become a governess' is sometimes used as if it were a satisfactory outlet for any unsupported woman above the rank of housemaid. When we see advertisements in the newspapers, offering 'a comfortable home,' with no salary, as a sufficient reward for accomplishments of the most varied character, we sometimes wonder at the audacity of employers; but when we learn that such an advertisement, offering the situation of nursery governess, **unpaid**, was answered by **three hundred women**, our surprise has in it something of despair.

Josephine E. Butler, *The education and employment of women*, London: Macmillan (1868), p. 3.

4.14 Women's industry

. . . Mrs. Peterson read a paper contending that it was desirable to organise the trades of women. It would benefit men indirectly by preventing the depreciation of their labour. It was also necessary to maintain the rate of women's wages, estimated to be around 12 s. a week in London. It would prevent women ignorantly offering their labour below the market price and would often save time that would otherwise be lost in search for employment. Women's unions did not encourage strikes, but exercised a moderating influence in the appropriation of a common fund. Unions were required to keep up good wages as well as to raise bad ones. The surplus of 900,000 women who could not marry would form a good many unions. Domestic service, at best, was in most cases a kind of slavery. At a meeting at Bristol she urged women earning 5 s. or 6 s. a week to seek domestic service; but the suggestion was scouted. There must be freedom of choice, and those who chose trades were none the less deserving of consideration and sympathy. Under the auspices of the Women's Protective and Provident League unions had been formed in London which had an aggregate membership of 1000, with a balance in hand of £363 after meeting their expenses out of subscriptions of 2 d. a week and entrance fees of 1 s. In Leicester the immediate effect of union in certain women's trades was the abolition of the sweating system by middle-men who netted exorbitant profits by simply acting as agents between employer and employed. In London the League promoted the social entertainment of the members, and that might be furthered by the formation of clubs, which ought to be as free and easy as men's clubs if they were to attract the right women, and ought to be equally exempt from charity and restraint. Miss Simcox, secretary of the Shirtmakers' Society and head of a co-operative shirt-making firm, contributed an argument in favour of the organization of self-supporting workshops, giving the workers the benefit of such economy as was promoted by the combination of capital with intelligence. All charitable attempts to provide work for the unemployed should be placed on a self-supporting basis, and carried out with due regard to the welfare of other branches of industry.

The Times, 17 March 1879.

4.15   The sweating system

The sweating system
. . . Goods were got by the middleman or sweater from the warehouse, and he got 2 s. for making up into trousers, coat, and vest. The sweatee received 6 d. a dozen for pressing trousers, about 40 pairs a day being possible to the most skilled worker. A vest was made outright for 5 d., and a woman could make four a day. Button-hole making was done at 3 d. a dozen, except in wholesale factories, where less was paid, but he was not at liberty to mention the price. A coat was made for $7\frac{1}{2}$ d. A woman could make four a day by working fifteen hours. Half a day in the week was lost in shopping, and half a day in cleaning up the house and washing the children, leaving four-and-a-half days a week, bringing

in about 8 s. 6 d. as wages. For making a child's knickerbockers suit, a woman got 4½ d. for making up the whole suit. The middleman or sweater got 7 d., making a profit of 2½ d.

... The sweater generally had his own workshops, but sometimes had neither machines nor workshops, and contributed nothing, merely extracting profit from labour. Fourteen hours' work seemed to be considered a day. He had the evidence of a Hungarian girl, 18 years old, earning 8s. a week at the best times, but more frequently only 3s. a week, working from a quarter to 7 in the morning till half past 8 at night. She lived with a woman whose husband slept upstairs, and she paid 1s. per week. In one workshop there were seven men and three women. There was only one sanitary convenience. He knew one case where there was only one sanitary convenience for 50 persons. The majority of men in the tailoring trade received from 4s. to 4s. 6d. a day, but they had to work from 15 to 17 hours. Women would get from 1s. 6d. to 3s. a day, but the latter rate was exceptional; and the tendency of late years had been to lower wages and increase the number of hours. In summer time the heat of the atmosphere in the workrooms, the exhalations from bodies not often washed and the smells from the wholly inadequate sanitary accommodation were most revolting. The houses in which the work was carried on were often most unhealthy, and the sanitary inspection was a farce ... It was quite impossible for the factory inspectors to cope with the evil under present regulations, because the staff of inspectors was too small, and as the sweaters were very numerous it was beyond the power of the factory inspectors to discover them. He had been round with a Home Office official, armed with a certificate, after 12 o'clock at night. In many cases they found women employed after that hour, which was against the Act. Once he watched from the other side of the street and saw the women run away before the official entered the room. Mr White further stated that in consequence of a letter he received he went to Chatham Marine Barracks, and there found that the master tailor gave out work to women, and paid them 1d. to 1½d. per article less than the regulation prices laid down by the Admiralty.

The Times, 21 April 1888.

4.16 Married women in factories

Miss Ada Heather Bigg, hon. secretary of the Women's Industrial Defence Committee, writes ...

'It is with much satisfaction that my committee has read Mr. Asquith's excellent reply to the deputation of medical men who urged him to put further restrictions upon the labour of married women. We know very well, being in constant touch with a large body of married working women, that Mr. Asquith speaks the saddest truth when he says that in many cases the mother is as much the bread-winner as the father. No one regrets this fact more than we do, but so long as there are multitudes of men who from incompetence, poor physique, or other causes are unable to keep a wife and children in decency, and who yet have wives and children to keep, so long will it be the grossest cruelty to prevent a wife and mother from securing by her own exertions the ordinary comforts of life. The cruelty becomes greater when it is remembered that the alleged connexion between excessive infant mortality and the industrial employment of women rests upon very insufficient evidence . . .

Five minutes' talk with any intelligent woman would have shown clearly that a law forbidding a married woman to work in a factory for three whole months after the birth of a child would not necessarily keep her in her home. The need remaining, women would simply be driven to substitute standing at the washtub in public washhouses, cleaning offices, or other hard work for the (perhaps) lighter work pursued by them in factories.

The Times, 22 November 1894.

4.17   Causes of low wages

Partly as a result of this ignorance, there has been a general tendency to take for granted either that the woman worker is not entirely self-supporting, or, at least, that there is no one for whom she has to provide except herself. The consequence of these assumptions has been twofold. First, while it is not asserted that the wages of any class or industry are determined by the number of workers' dependants, it is undoubtedly the fact that, whatever the real cause of the low wages of women, their supposed lack of dependants has constantly been used as an argument to explain and excuse an economic position which, for the vast mass of women workers, is intolerable. Secondly, although observers have been faced with the obvious fact that many women workers do support not merely themselves but other people, they have been in the habit of declaring that such women were in an exceptional position . . . It is essential for all workers and the nation as a whole, that these women shall be recognised as ordinary human beings who live by their labour. They must not be placed, even theoretically, at a disadvantage by reason of arguments which are not allowed to weigh in the determination of wages in general.

Ellen Smith, *Prefatory note to wage earning women and their dependants*, London: Fabian Society (1915).

4.18   Do women have dependants?

Women are seldom paid the same rate of wage as men, even when they do the same work. The generally accepted reason for this difference of payment is that a woman has only herself to keep, while the man has a wife and family. As a result, however, of the present shortage of male labour and the need of the nation to make more use of the work of women, this argument has been for the moment withdrawn, and we find a number of men, including practically all Trade Unionists, insisting that where a woman is undertaking work formerly done by men she should be paid the same rate of wage. Never before have men been so eager to impress upon employers the justice of the women's claim for equal pay for equal work, for they see the imminent danger that if women are allowed to enter trades hitherto reserved to men at a lower rate of pay, their own wages, together with the whole standard of living of the working class, may be permanently reduced. But the fact has to be faced that when the country returns to normal conditions, or, as is anticipated, there is an abnormally high rate of unemployment, women will be the worst sufferers; it is they who will be the first to be thrown out of employment, and the old argument that a woman has only herself to support will be effectively revived . . .

If, then, we apply our conclusions to the total number of the women workers of England and Wales, it would seem that 15 per cent are not entirely self-supporting. In our investigation we arrived at the conclusion that these were mostly young girls. And here it is interesting to note that in the Census of 1911, 15 per cent of the females engaged in occupations in England and Wales are shown to be either girls under 17 years of age (12.44 per cent) or women of 65 years and upwards (2.53 per cent).

According to our investigation, it would further seem that 33 per cent of the women workers of England and Wales support themselves and themselves alone, while slightly over 51 per cent maintain more than 1¾ persons besides themselves. In other words, 51 per cent of the women workers of England and Wales support a mass of persons the total of which, counting themselves, approaches three times their own number. If we distribute this responsibility over the whole of the self-supporting women, which forms 85 per cent (4,000,000) of the women workers of England and Wales, we find that they support among them, including themselves, a total which is more than equal to twice their own number.

Hitherto it has been taken for granted that the wives and families of the whole body of men in work were dependants. But, if our conclusions be accepted as approximately correct, it is evident that the total burden, up to now attributed to working-men, is shared to an appreciable extent by their wives and daughters. However, that may be, the economic position of the woman breadwinner, always admitted to be serious, is further complicated by the number of her dependants. If indeed the wage-earning women of England and Wales do support anything like 4,000,000 dependants the problem becomes still graver.

Ellen Smith, *Wage earning women and their dependants*, London: Fabian Society (1915), pp. 5, 35.

4.19   Equal pay?

. . . Replying to Miss Haldane, a member of the Commission, on the question of equal pay for women and men in the Civil service. Lord Haldane said that while he found it very difficult to make up his mind, he was inclined to think that, choosing between two evils, the lesser evil was to pay a woman on the same level as a man. Even when the bread winner, the man as the head of the family, was paid a good salary, the best salary that the Civil service offered to him, he was not really being highly paid; and he thought that a woman was entitled to be paid just as much, upon a comparison of the standards in other professions.

The Times, 29 May 1912.

4.20   Women's claim for equal pay

A strike of women tramway and omnibus workers in London on Saturday to enforce their demand for the same war bonus as that given to men was followed by a midnight meeting of the executive committee of the London and Provincial Union of Licensed Vehicle Workers, at which a general strike was declared. As a result Londoners were yesterday put to great inconvenience.

Mr Ben Smith, organizing secretary of the Vehicle Worker's Union, said that they all realized that the present was a serious time to take action, but the women were in a position to say, 'The employers told us that our rates should be the same as the men's. If they keep their word we will keep at work.' (Cheers.)

Mr. G. Beale, vice-president of the London district, National Union of Railwaymen, expressed the wish that the strike had been postponed for a fortnight. 'My reason is,' he added, 'that in a fortnight's time the railway women will be with you.' (Cheers.) . . .

Women and the war bonus
Some months ago the drivers and conductors, men and women, employed on the tramway and omnibus services, not in London alone, but throughout the country, applied for an extra war bonus.

On July 13 this committee made an award granting a bonus of 5s. a week to male drivers and conductors. They also decided that the case presented on behalf of the women did not justify their inclusion in the award, for the reason principally that the women do not work a full six day week like the men. It is suggested that the Committee of Production were further influenced by the fact that many of the women conductors are the wives of soldiers, receiving separation allowances, and, unlike the men, have most of them no families to support.

The women, however, resented being treated differently from the men and those in London made representations to their trade unions that they would not submit to it. The National Transport Workers' Federation then on August 3 wrote to the tramway and omnibus companies and asked them to take into consideration the case of the women. The reply, which was sent last week, was that the companies would give the matter immediate attention. It is said that it was this delay that drove the women to their precipitate action on Saturday in declining to go out with the omnibuses and the tramcars.

The Times, 19 August 1918.

4.21 Munition workers' demands

Whitehall was considerably astonished yesterday afternoon by the appearance of about 6,000 women munition workers, the greater number of whom came from Woolwich Arsenal, and the others from munitions factories all over London and its suburbs. The woman formed up in procession with many large and small banners, and each one of them wearing her munitions badge. They did not look in the least like the expensively-gowned, highly-paid munitions worker of whom so much has been heard, but rather represented the woman worker who is the permanent industrial product.

The idea of the demonstration was quite spontaneous, and originated at the Arsenal on the previous day, when it was found that many of the women were under notice, and they determined to go to the Ministry of Munitions and ask for immediate guarantees for the future . . .

The women carried a small banner, which had attracted much attention, with the inscription, 'Shall Peace bring us Starvation?' in red letters. The officials received them with courtesy and sympathy and provided them with tea, and afterwards they left for Kingsway Hall in motor-cars belonging to the Ministry.

Request for greater unemployed pay
The women's claim was for a living wage while working and for an adequate maintenance allowance on discharge. They urged that the promised £1 a week while unemployed was only worth 8s 4d. now, and claimed 30s. They also asked for increased pensions for soldiers and increased allowances to soldiers' widows, so that they might not compete with them.

The Times, 20 November 1918.

4.22   Women out of work

Case of Domestic Service
It is a familiar fact, and one inherent in the fluctuations of industrial employment, that at any given moment workers in various occupations may be unemployed in some districts while employers in other districts are calling for workers in those very occupations . . .

Servants and mistresses
The figures for women show very little demand for labour in occupations outside domestic service. There were 1,229 vacancies on January 10 for women book-keepers and clerical workers, and 9,948 applicants for such positions. The vacancies classified under 'domestic, hotel, servants, day-girls, charwomen' were far more numerous – namely 20,539. The

applicants for positions in that category – to be more precise, the women who gave 'domestic service' as their usual occupation – were 20,840. The number of women 'placed' in domestic service during the week ending January 10 was 2,168, but the extraordinary fact that at the end of that week there were roughly, 20,000 mistresses wanting servants and 20,000 ex-servants wanting mistressed – an accumulation on both sides of several weeks – creates a presumption that women and girls who left domestic service to take up war work are taking a more exacting view of what constitutes 'suitable employment' than they did before they tasted the joys of high wages, constant companionship and limited hours of work. It may perhaps be regarded as additional evidence for this conclusion that, of the total (53,708) of women's registration during the week only 9.4 per cent (5,078) came under the heading of domestic service occupations. Further support is supplied by the division of the domestic service group into day servants, charwomen, and private domestic indoor servants. The latest figures obtainable are for January 3, and these give the following interesting results:

	Registrations	Vacancies
Day Servants . . .	5,022	4,121
Charwomen . . .	6,229	2,210
Private domestic indoor servants . . .	2,008	7,956

We thus find that while there is a substantial excess of day servants and charwomen wanting work (11,251) over vacancies for such workers (6,331) this is more than balanced by the excess of vacancies over applicants in the case of domestic servants 'living in' . . . It is not necessary here to discuss the problem of rendering domestic service more attractive. It is sufficient . . . to point out, . . . that at least two-thirds of all the vacancies for women workers notified to employment exchanges and carried forward at the end of the week were for domestic servants, and that there were approximately enough women registered for domestic service (and drawing out-of-work donation) to fill all those places.

The Times, 29 January 1919.

___

4.23   Out-of-work women typists

Whitehall clerks not wanted in the city
Among the women who are at present receiving the out-of-work donation are 21,000 clerks and typists. In view of the fact that complaint is being

made in the City that typists cannot be obtained, this fact seems to require explanation. The trouble seems to be that a considerable proportion of the unemployed girls are not sufficiently competent to command the confidence of employers.

During the war there was no labour reserve, and inefficient clerical work had to be tolerated, not only in Government offices, but by commercial firms. Since the Armistice there has been a gradual weeding out of the less competent, and many young people who took a more serious interest in afternoon tea and gossip than in their work are now without employment. In the process of demobilizing some of the Government Departments the skilled and intelligent clerks have been transferred to other Ministries or have found posts with private employers, but the semi-efficient have found that their services are no longer required.

Statistics which are available concerning other unemployed women workers show that there is a very limited demand for charwomen. For every vacancy notified to the employment exchanges there are eight charwomen seeking work. Three times as many day girls are registered as there are vacant situations to be filled, and caretakers and doorkeepers are also in the position of not being wanted. In the case of domestic servants, willing to live in, the vacancies, on the other hand, are in excess of the applications for positions. Many tailoresses, dressmakers, and boot and shoe makers are drawing the out-of-work donation, although one would think that plenty of work was waiting for them, but here again the question of efficiency arises, and it is stated that large numbers of the women are not sufficiently skilled to fit them for vacancies which employers notify to the exchanges.

The Times, 16 April 1919.

4.24 Unemployed women war workers

Demand for factory amenities

More Ex-Soldiers in Work
Official figures now available show that during the week ended March 14, 998,619, men, women and young people were drawing the out-of-work donation.

There are special reasons why so many women discharged from war work remain unemployed. The majority of the women registering at the exchanges are anxious to be re-absorbed into industry, though there is continued resistance on the part of many former domestic servants to return to their pre-war occupation. An important factor is that large numbers of women workers are either the wives or widows of soldiers. The wives are expecting their husbands home again and are unwilling to go to posts which would take them far away or would involve special training. In some of these cases it is probably that no extension of the out-of-work donation will be granted. Soldiers' widows are in a different class, and employers wherever possible might give preference to them in filling vacancies.

In the case of single women the question why they do not take up such employment as is available may be asked with more force. The answer is that they have often little skill in the occupations in which they were engaged before they transferred to the munition factories. Dressmakers are required, and dressmakers are registered as unemployed. It is found, however, that many of those seeking situations were only learners before the war and that they have forgotten the greater part of what they had learned.

Further training required

These women must either go back to the work-rooms at a learner's-wage when they have passed the learner's age, or industrial training must be provided for them by local authorities, the State or employers. In some cases glove manufacturers, straw hat manufacturers, and similar firms have offered to give the necessary training to those willing to enter the industry. A drawback is the fact that for the period of training only a low wage is offered, and girls who have been well paid in munition factories are reluctant to make a new start on these terms.

Another matter which has to be faced is that women and girls who have worked in the well-equipped establishments built during the war have grown accustomed to the softening of industrial conditions by welfare schemes. They miss in the older type of factory the rest-rooms, canteens, and cloakrooms which have been at their disposal in the munitions works. There can be little doubt that, in future, employers who wish to make use of women's labour will have to realize that women must be properly treated, that adequate accommodation for meals must be provided, and that, generally, conditions must be improved.

Finally, there is the case of women workers who have become skilled in work which the trade unions regard as a close preserve of men. Here they are dependent on the decisions which the trade unions will make on the question of dilution. Many women who have become expert in acetylene welding, work in aircraft factories, and similar processes will be sorely disappointed if they are automatically shut out from employment in these industries.

The Times, 28 March 1919.

4.25 'Prejudiced men'

The resumed Conference of the National Union of Women Teachers at Manchester yesterday dealt with a series of issues involving the rights of women teachers as against the tendency to favour men. A resolution was moved protesting against the system of regarding the marriage of a woman teacher as a disability either for appointment or permanent retention by educational authorities, and demanding the immediate enforcement in all Government appointments of the Sex Disqualification (Removal) Act.

Miss Byell (Birmingham), who moved it, said that the system was as unsound economically as it was morally. It robbed the people of the best teachers and, by replacing them with the inexperienced and inefficient, resulted in a serious wastage of public funds. Marriage should not be classed with inefficiency and immorality as a cause for dismissal. To leave it so was to degrade the institution of marriage, and to so penalise it as to undo all the work of social reformers in correcting the shrinkage of the population.

Supporting the resolution, which was carried, Miss Kenyon (Oldham) gave instances in her own experience in which, time after time, youths, some of whom were only emerging from their teens, were placed in authority while the headmaster was away, over women teachers, many of whom had 20 years experience. Her great objection to the system – which, she said, prevailed in many parts of the country, was that it led even the children to imbibe ideas of the inherent superiority of man, and that it added force to the tragic tradition upon which women were robbed of their rights in the educational world.

Miss Walmsley contended that the system of preferring men was based solely on prejudice. If there was one thing worse than a prejudiced woman it was a prejudiced man. The only way to disturb and upset the prejudice was for women to protest even to the point of making themselves a nuisance.

Further resolutions claimed that married women's incomes should be assessed separately from those of their husbands and be subject to the same abatement; that the school leaving age should be raised to 15, and that the continuation school system should at once be enforced on a practical basis.

The Times, 6 January 1922.

4.26   Women's demonstration at Hull

A women workers' demonstration was held in Hull last night. Mr A.A. Purcell, MP, president of the Trades Union Congress, who presided, said there was greater need today for the organisation of women in trade unions than ever before. Their wages were extremely low and their hours long. In his opinion the conditions under which they were employed were a serious danger to society. Low wages among women were greater temptation to immorality than among men.

Miss Margaret Bondfield, Parliamentary secretary to the Ministry of Labour, moved a resolution expressing grave concern at the present industrial situation, especially as it affects women wage-earners, and calling upon all women workers to join their appropriate trade union for their own protection and for the furthering of measures required for the adequate treatment of unemployment and a raising of the standard of living of the workers generally.

Miss Bondfield said there was no reason why women should not do any process in industry for which she was fitted. The only thing they asked was that women should not sell their labour more cheaply than the recognised rate for the job. They had every right to say that the trade union organisation should take any steps it could to shut out that unfair kind of competition. They should not shut out women's labour simply because it was women's labour, but it was perfectly right to say that women coming into a trade must be asked to take their share of the responsibility for maintaining the standard of living in that trade. They should not be allowed to degrade the standard which others had spent their lives building up. It was in those trades in which women were mainly employed that they had the greatest difficulties to contend with in relation to the degradation of the standard of life.

The Times, 3 November 1924

4.27   Women civil servants

The vexed question of woman's ability to stand upon an equal footing with man in most branches of national activity bids fair to solve itself. The old barriers are falling one after another, and women can no longer complain that they are restricted in the choice of a profession, or denied great opportunities of advancement in any that they may select. Therefore, the part that they will play in the future, be it in public life, in the professions, or in the public service, will depend almost entirely upon themselves. The dislike of the average male to feminine competition in what he has been trained to regard as his own sphere, and the ingrained doubt of most men and a large number of women whether human nature is quite as compliant to human idealism as the convinced feminist claims, will remain to some extent a handicap on feminine advancement; but it is one which no legislation can remove. Otherwise, the way is open, and many even of those who heartily dislike and mistrust the tendency of the age now deem it best that women should be allowed to find their own place in the world without artificial hindrance. It is certainly the most reasonable attitude; and, though it implies the adoption of a general rule of sex equality, it need not be feared on that account, so long as that rule be not applied in obvious violation of the laws of common sense. Viewed from this standpoint, the Government proposals for the admission of women to the Civil Service, which Sir Robert Horne announced yesterday, startling though they might have seemed a generation ago, have much to commend them. After three years the mode of admission to the Civil Service is to be the same for both sexes, though the Civil Service Commissioners are to pay due regard to suitability in the allocation of successful candidates. Women are to be appointed and to hold their posts under the same regulations as men, in so far as classification, status, and authority are concerned. The remuneration of the sexes is not to be equal, for the simple reasons that the cost would be too great and that the rates paid in the public service are naturally governed by those that prevail in other walks of life. Thus women are given the fair start for which they have asked, and though there may still be some traces of discrimination, they can, we think, be justified in every case upon the ground that they are to the interests of women themselves.

The adage of an older generation of constitutionalists that Parliament is all-powerful, save that it cannot turn a woman into a man, has come to the test. Last December there were over 110,000 women in the Civil Service, or thirty-one per cent, of the whole. Under the more favourable conditions of the proposed regulations that percentage may increase.

Despite, however, the experience of war time, the employment of women in such large numbers is still, to some extent, in an experimental stage. People can even yet debate inconclusively upon the relative capabilities of the sexes in the public and other services. Certainly it is too soon to gauge their suitability for the higher grades. But, even though we dare not forecast the ultimate judgment of the country upon their employment, it seems possible that their entrance into the public service in such large numbers may affect the position of that service as a whole. The wild extravagance of recent administration has brought the organization and staffing of all the Government Departments under the closest public scrutiny. Economy is an all-compelling national necessity, and we fear the causes which have made it so will only too probably be accentuated in the future. If women do not justify the hopes reposed in them, their failure will provide yet another reason for bringing the whole establishment of the Civil Service into closer accord with the national requirements, and with the nation's power to pay. We wish these women well who may take advantage of the new opportunities; but we see in this new departure the precursor of other and perhaps, greater changes, destined inexorably to be effected when once this nation has squarely faced the facts of its position.

The Times, 6 August 1921.

4.28   Equal pay for equal work

Women civil servants' appeal
An appeal for equal pay for equal work in the Civil Service, without regard to sex, was made at a crowded meeting of women in Caxton Hall, Westminster, last night and at an overflow meeting at St. Ermins's nearby, organized by the London and National Society for Women's Service for the Joint Committee on Women in the Civil Service. Twenty-five organizations took part, representing opinion in many parts of the United Kingdom. The chairman, Professor Winifred Cullis, announced receipt of apologies for absence from 19 male Civil servants.

The meeting resolved to call upon the Government to establish one salary scale in each grade of the Civil Service which shall apply equally to all in it without regard to their sex . . .

Moving the resolution, Colonel D. Clifton Brown, MP, complimented women on their patriotic patience in allowing their claims to lie dormant in the whole period of acute financial stringency. It was not the sex struggle of a few man-hating spinsters seeking to wreak vengeance on men, but a genuine movement pursued in the belief that the principle of equal pay was in the best interests of the country as a whole.

Miss Ellen Wilkinson, MP, seconding, said the principle of equal pay had been accepted for higher grades under the London County Council and by a number of local authorities for all grades. Many women had dependants to support in common with men, and equal pay for women would not bring worse conditions for men in employment.

The state as employer

Lady Astor. MP, contended that the State as an employer was setting a bad example to employers in industry, where the payment of lower rates to women resulted in increasing unemployment among men. Part 13 of the Treaty of Versailles said it was of special and urgent importance that men and women should receive equal remuneration for work of equal value. Great Britain put her name to that clause, and the principle of equal pay was adopted in the House of Commons nearly 16 years ago. Since then in spite of repeated promises, nothing had been done.

Major J.W. Hills, MP, said that although parliament's resolution for equal pay in the Civil Service was confirmed the year after its adoption, action was postponed on the ground of the then financial stress, and reconsideration within three years was directed. Not merely had nothing been done; women were formerly paid equally with men in the National Physical Laboratory, but since 1933 women's pay was drastically reduced. There were many cases in the Civil Service where women in senior positions were superintending the work of men paid more than themselves.

The Times, 18 March 1936.

4.29   Work for educated women

The need for co-ordinating organisations concerned with the employment and training of educated women was emphasised last evening at a meeting held at 7, Green Street, W., the Dowager Lady Nunburnholme in the chair.

As a result of the deliberations the Women's Employment Federation was brought into being. The Federation proposes to arrange for a general pooling and collection of information in regard to training, loans, grants, and scholarships to assist training, openings for work for women . . .

Sir William Beveridge, Director of the London School of Economics, said that if a woman could do a job better than a man, by employing the woman the economic condition of the country was improved. He hoped the new organisation would be able to break down the last remaining barrier which made it difficult for women to get certain work simply because they were women.

Miss Grace Hadow, first president of the new federation, said that many women had to earn their living, but for lack of knowledge they were often forced into blind alley occupations. There was urgent need for such a central organisation, which could do much to help the younger generation. Equal pay for equal work

The Times, 24 January 1934.

4.30 Women's services during air raids

Comfort and clothing for homeless
Women everywhere in London have carried on right through the raids. Women wardens, women of the Auxiliary Fire Service, nurses, women ambulance drivers, women in charge of mobile canteens have all acted with cool competence without paying any attention to possible personal risk.

The Women's Voluntary Services were equal to every call made upon them. The biggest of their mobile canteens served 3,000 cups of tea on Monday night during the raids. The rest and clothing centres which they staff for the local authorities, where homeless people awaiting billeting are housed, fed, comforted, and clothed, are entirely manned by the W.V.S., and are known as 'The Third Line.' During the worst raids on the East End their drivers drove on with their stores of food and clothing to the schools and church halls where the homeless were temporarily housed. The drivers said that it was waste of time to stop and take shelter while hurrying to where they were needed.

The Times, 19 September 1940.

4.31 How women will be called up

The new National Service Bill, introduced in the House of Commons yesterday by Mr. Bevin, contains a declaration in the first clause that 'all persons of either sex for the time being in Great Britain are liable to national service, whether under the Crown or not, and whether in the armed forces of the Crown, in civil defence, in industry, or otherwise.'

The age limit of liability to compulsory service under the National Service (Armed Forces) Act 1939 is raised from 41 to 51; and, subject to the provision that women may be called up only for the women's auxiliary services, the National Service Acts 1939 to 1941 are made to apply in relation to women as they apply to men. This means that women, as well as men, are liable to compulsory service under the Acts up to the age of 51, although the Prime Minister has announced that at present only women from 20 to 30 will be called up.

A schedule to the Bill enumerates 10 categories of women exempt from liability to be called up. These comprise women already serving in the three auxiliary services; members of Queen Alexandra's Royal Naval Nursing Service, Queen Alexandra's Imperial Military Nursing Service, the Territorial Army Nursing Service, and Princess Mary's Royal Air Force Nursing Service; women medical practitioners serving in the Navy; and women employed with the R.A.M.C., the Army Dental Corps, and the Medical and Dental Branches of the Royal Air Force with relative rank as officers. As is explained in a White Paper (Cmd. 6324, price 1d.), which was issued with the Bill, women 'engaged in vital war work or service,' will also be reserved from calling up . . .

Other women may have their calling up deferred if it is in the national interest that they should not be moved from their present work.

'Vital war work or service' as at present defined by the Ministry of Labour includes work in aircraft and munitions factories, radio manufacture, transport services, civil defence services, nursing services, hospital domestics, the Women's Land Army; and the N.A.A.F.I. This list is to be extended, and teachers will be among those to be included . . .

A woman will generally be regarded as available for employment away from her home unless she is the wife of a man serving in the armed Forces or Merchant Navy, or a married woman with household responsibilities . . .

The Times, 5 December 1941.

4.32 Female farmers

The Minister of Agriculture is urging farmers in good time to make use of the labour offered by the Women's Land Army . . . No one will deny that the 9,000 members of the Women's Land Army now at work have shown themselves capable of undertaking a large variety of jobs on the farm, as their predecessors did in the last War. Apart from milking and care of livestock, in which women naturally excel, volunteers are employed as tractor drivers, shepherdesses, wagoners, and general farm hands. Through the severe weather of last winter they carried on manfully. Though in many cases they had to wade through deep snow to their work, they were up at five in the morning, sliding across the yard to milk the cows long before it was light.

The Times, 23 December 1940.

4.33   Women at work with R.A.F.

Replacing men in 25 trades
Members of the Women's Auxiliary Air Force are now engaged in 25 trades formerly followed only by men.

They are being trained as wireless telegraphy slip-readers and operators, instrument mechanics, fabric workers (aero), and fabric workers (balloon), sparking plug testers, equipment assistants, cooks; for administrative duties and various clerical duties; as teleprinter operators, radio operators and tracers, telephone operators, four kinds of aircraft hands, dental clerk orderlies, and sick quarter attendants. Some of the R.A.F. doctors are women, but they do not form part of the W.A.A.F.

Women who have been upholsterers, machinists, or tailoresses are found to be good at fabric work, while those who have had experience in factories or wireless shops usually make excellent instrument mechanics. Many former typists are employed as wireless telegraphy slip-reader operators, while among those whose task it is to trace in and colour maps are a number of women trained as commercial artists. The W.A.A.F. have their own officers. There is no direct entry for officers, all of whom are promoted from the ranks.

The Times, 12 March 1941.

4.34   Twilight shift recruits the mothers

Bathed in scent of lemon grass and lavender and an aroma of roses which never bloomed in Beeston gardens, Mrs. Patricia Fearn tips bags of soap into a thunderous machine.

As her husband tucks up the children at home and millions of other women sit knitting before the nation's television sets, Mrs. Fearn is one of 120 local women who cause one to think furiously about marriage a la mode. From five o'clock to nine, on five evenings a week, she works the twilight shift at the great factory of the Boots Pure Drug Company.

The firm is glad enough to have her. In no city in the country is the shortage of female labour more desperate. Every day the special buses go out to bring in full-time girls from as far off as Worksop and Rotherham. And Boots's only regret about the twilight shift is that its numbers are not a good deal higher . . .

The firm makes fairly stringent inquiries to ensure that someone will be minding the children while mother is away.

Nottinghamshire men appear to make obliging husbands to have about the house . . .

What persuades a woman to spend four hours of each evening in such surroundings away from husband and family?

Mrs. Gladys Wood took her job for the £4 a week and assured herself it would only be temporary. She has bought a big living-room carpet with the proceeds and she is thinking about a suite of furniture.

Mrs. Joan Curwood said: 'I got fed up with stopping at home to look after seven children. My husband only goes out at weekends. If I am at home we just sit in – so why do that when I can go out and earn money? If I were at home I should only be putting the children to bed, and washing them, and now my husband does that.

'You get to know more people like this. Working here in the last year I have got to know more local people than I did in the five years before that.'

. . . A young mother sheltering behind one of the yashmaks said she took the job 'to get out of the house'.

It is not, indeed, the £4 which is the only magnet. Is the success of the twilight shift not also a reminder that for a modern woman modern marriage can become pretty much of a bore?

The Times, 16 August 1965.

4.35 A woman's status

From Miss Audrey Bayley

Sir, When signing a legal document recently I saw that the marginal rubric said: 'If woman with no occupation insert status.' As the solicitor had designated me 'spinster' I informed him that I had an occupation – that of a publisher's editor. The reply came back: 'It is normal for a woman just to be described as spinster or married woman unless she happens to be a doctor or a solicitor.' How is it that these are the only professions which are considered noteworthy in the case of a woman?

The Times, 7 November 1972.

Notes

1 See Chapter 3, 'Education'.
2 National Archives, POWE 8/28/202217, no. 251.
3 See Chapter 3, 'Education'.
4 R. Strachey, *The cause: A short history of the women's movement in Britain*, London: Virago (1978), p. 371, quoted in S. K. Kent, *Sex and suffrage in Britain*, Princetown: Princetown University Press (1987), p. 223.

5

Politics

Timeline

1866 John Stuart Mill's attempt to enfranchise women defeated by one hundred and ninety four votes to seventy three.

1867 Second Reform Act.

1869 Jacob Bright: amendment to Municipal Franchise Act – all women ratepayers enfranchised for local elections.

1870 Elizabeth Garrett Anderson top of London School Board elections.

1872 *Regina* v. *Harrold*: restricted municipal franchise to unmarried women.

1875 Miss Martha Merrington elected as Poor Law Guardian for Kensington Board.

1883 Corrupt Practices Act.

1884 Third Reform Act.

1884 Women admitted to Primrose League.

1887 Women's Liberal Federation.

1892 Property qualification for Poor Law Guardians reduced to £5.

1894 Local Government Board order: committees of women to visit and inspect workhouse areas where women and children accommodated.

1894 Property Qualification abolished.

1900 London Borough Act reformed London's vestries and excluded women from Office.

1902 Town and County Councils became education authorities – women lost their electoral status.

1902 Northern England women textile workers present 37,000 petition to Parliament demanding votes for women.

1902 Midwives Act: established the Central Midwives Board which, for the first time, regulated midwives' training and practice.

1903   Women's Social and Political Union (WSPU) founded in Manchester by Emmeline, Christabel and Sylvia Pankhurst.

1904   Dora Montefiore, suffragette, refused to pay her taxes until women were enfranchised.

1905   10 October: Christabel Pankhurst and Annie Kenney, first suffragettes, arrested.

1906   'Suffragette' used for the first time, by the *Daily Mail*; intended as a derogatory name for women in the WSPU.
19 May: delegation of women from both the WSPU and the National Union of Women's Suffrage Societies (NUWSS) met Prime Minister, Sir Henry Campbell Bannerman.

1906   The National Federation of Women Workers: set up by Mary MacArthur.

1907   February, the NUWSS, led by Millicent Garrett Fawcett, organised its first national demonstration.

1907   *Votes for Women* launched by Emmeline and Frederick Pethwick Lawrence.
The Women's Freedom League (break-away movement from WSPU) formed by Teresa Billington-Grieg and Charlotte Despard.

1907   Qualification of Women Act: women can be elected on to borough and county councils and as mayor. Local government authorities open to women.

1908   17 January: suffragettes chained themselves to railings of 10 Downing Street.

1908   WSPU start stone-throwing campaign. Emmeline Pankhurst imprisoned for the first time.

1908   Elizabeth Garrett Anderson elected as first woman mayor of Aldeburgh in Suffolk.

1909   July: Marion Wallace Dunlop: first imprisoned suffragette to go on hunger strike. Force-feeding introduced.

1910   18 November: failure of the first Conciliation Bill. 'Black Friday': suffragettes and police clashed violently outside Parliament. Ellen Pitfield later died from injuries.

1911   Olive Schreiner, *Women and Labour*.

1912   East London Federation of Suffragettes established (Sylvia Pankhurst), predominantly for working class women in the East End.

1913   Emily Wilding Davison killed by the King's horse at the Epsom Derby.

1913 Prisoners' Temporary Discharge for Ill-Health Act ('The Cat and Mouse Act'): introduced for suffragettes who refused to eat.

1914 10 March: Mary Richardson slashed the 'Rokeby Venus' at the National Gallery.

1914 4 August: Britain declared war on Germany.

1914 Scottish Women's Hospitals movement set up by Dr Elsie Inglis (1864–1917).

1915 First Women's Institute, Llanfairpwll, North Wales.

1916 Women's Army Auxiliary Corps.

1917 Annie Besant: elected the fifth president of the Indian National Congress.

1918 Representation of the People Act.

1918 Parliamentary Qualification of Women Act: women can stand as MPs.

1918 Women voted in a General Election for the first time on 14 December.

1918 Constance Markiewicz elected as first woman MP for Sinn Fein; declined to take her seat.

1919 The National Union of Women's Suffrage Societies changed name to the National Union of Societies of Equal Citizenship. Millicent Garrett Fawcett retired, Eleanor Rathbone became leader.

1919 Sex Disqualification (Removal) Act.

1919 28 November: Nancy Astor elected MP for Plymouth South; the first woman to take her seat in the House of Commons.

1921 The Six Point Group founded by Lady Rhondda (1883–1958), to push for women's equality on six points: political, occupational, moral, social, economic and legal.

1922 *Good Housekeeping*, a new style of women's magazine, appeared. Contributors to the first issue included Nancy Astor and Helena Normanton.

1922 Infanticide Act. A mother cannot be hanged for the murder of her child if mentally unbalanced.

1927 Ethel Snowdon: first woman governor of the BBC.

1928 Equal Franchise Act: all women over twenty one enfranchised.

1929 'Flapper Election'.

1929 'A Week in Westminster' first broadcast on the BBC. Hilda Matheson to inform the newly enfranchised women about the workings of Parliament.

1929 The Townswomen's Guild.

1929 Women became 'persons' in their own right, by order of the Privy Council.

1929 Margaret Bondfield appointed Minister of Labour (first woman Cabinet Minister).

1930 National Birth Control Council, later the Family Planning Association (FPA). In line with the teaching profession and the Civil Service, the BBC introduced a marriage bar, and no longer employed married women, except under exceptional circumstances.

1938 Married Women's Association set up by Edith Summerskill to promote equality in marriage.

1939 Outbreak of World War II.

1943 Dame Anne Loughlin elected as the first woman president of the TUC.

1945 'Red' Ellen Wilkinson elected as first woman Minister of Education.

1945 Family Allowances introduced.

1948 National Health Service.

1958 Life Peerages Act: women to sit in the House of Lords for the first time.

1960 The National Housewives' Register set up by Mary Nichol.

1963 Betty Friedan, *The Feminine Mystique*: the first book to analyse the role of women in American society and raise issues of emancipation.

1963 Christine Keeler charged with perjury in the Profumo affair.

1964 Married Women's Property Act entitled a woman to keep half of any savings she had made from any allowance she was given by her husband.

1965 Barbara Castle appointed Minister of Transport – the first female Minister of State.

1966 In the USA, the National Organisation for Women (NOW) founded by Betty Friedan and other feminists to campaign for equal rights.

1968 850 women machinists at Fords of Dagenham struck for equal pay.

1969 Bernadette Devlin: youngest member of the British Parliament.

1969 Representation of the People Act: enfranchised eighteen year olds.

1970   The first national meeting of the women's liberation movement at Ruskin College.
1970   Equal Pay Act.
1970   Miss World Contest disrupted by women's liberation protesters.
1970   Germaine Greer, *The Female Eunuch*.
1970   Kate Millet, *Sexual Politics*.
1971   6 March: first women's liberation march in London (4,000 - plus women).
1972   *Spare Rib*, Britain's first feminist magazine, launched.
1972   Erin Pizzey established first women's refuge, in Chiswick.
1974   Women's Aid Federation (bring together refuges for battered women).
1975   Sex Discrimination Act: illegal to discriminate against women in education, recruitment and advertising.
1975   Employment Protection Act: statutory maternity provision; illegal to sack a woman because she is pregnant.
1975   Equal Pay Act takes effect.
1975   Child Benefit replaced Family Allowances.
1975   Margaret Thatcher elected leader of the Conservative Party.
1976   Equal Opportunities Commission: to oversee the Sex Discrimination and Equal Pay Acts.
1976   Domestic Violence Act: women could obtain a court order against their violent husband or partner.
1977   International Women's Day.
1977   Betty Williams and Mairead Corrigan won the Nobel Peace Prize for their peace campaign in Northern Ireland.
1977   First Rape Crisis Centre opened in London.
1979   4 May: Margaret Thatcher elected Britain's first woman Prime Minister.

Although excluded from formal politics for most of our period, women still played a role in many aspects of political activity and indeed, it is possible to define 'politics' so that it includes any public actions intended to change or shape political, social or economic conditions. Thus from food riot to trade unionism to local and national politics, women made a contribution. This received a varying reaction from men: some, such the Chartists, were willing to use women to further their cause, while others, particularly trade unionists, saw them as a real threat to their interests.

There is no doubt that women took a part and often a prominent one in food riots. (**5.1**) They were part of the 'moral economy' whereby each person had his or her role to play and consequent obligations. Allied to this was a concept of fairness. They did not object to the existing system as such, but rather to what they saw as exploitation.[1] Thus they would sell what they had seized at what they considered a fair price and then give the money received along with the sacks back to the original owners: 'at Malmesbury they [rioters] seized all the corn; sold it at 5s. a bushel, and gave the money to the right owners'.[2] It was the middle men to whom they objected. Women also took part in community action and riots against the introduction of new, large scale machinery (seen as unfair competition) and against the enclosure movements. Access to common land was particularly important to women since it provided an opportunity for the grazing of cattle and the collection of firewood and herbs (essential for medicine). During such encounters women could be violent, as at the enclosure riot in the Llŷn peninsula. (**5.2**)

Historians differ in their interpretation as to whether women's actions resulted from identification with the wider community, or the need to ensure their families' survival since they were the ones who would suffer price rises at first hand. The Hammonds and Thompson understood food riots to be female-dominated,[3] John Bohstedt, however, has suggested women were only present as adjuncts to men.[4] What can be said is that where women did act, they were often successful in preventing the movement of grain and fixing what they believed to be a 'fair' price. Nor can it be denied that purchasing food for their households ensured that women had more face-to-face dealings with the market than men. Their presence in food riots, as part of a community with ideas of what constituted 'fairness', is important and illustrative of the idea that women took action in defence of family interests.[5] Women were also involved in the Gordon Riots 1780: eighty women were prosecuted, twenty four convicted and seven hanged as a result of their activities. In contrast to Bohstedt's views that women were 'strikingly absent from the wave of riots that swept villages from Lincolnshire to Cumberland to protest against balloting for the Supplementary Militia Act of 1796',[6] women in Scotland acted against the Militia Act of 1797. (**5.3**) They also took part in election riots such as that in Trowbridge, Wiltshire, in July 1797. (**5.4**)

Unlike their sisters in France, however, who had formed their own clubs and debated political rights, British women did not take part in the new political radicalism of the 1790s. It was individual writers like Mary Wollstonecraft and Mary Robinson (**5.5**) who debated a woman's position and their need for political rights in print. There is no surviving evidence of women participating in the Corresponding societies of the decade which were established largely by artisans to campaign for manhood suffrage. Women's involvement dates from post-1815 when distress and discontent in the post-war economy led to renewed interest in radicalism. Now they organised their own associations (**5.7, 5.8, 5.9**), (taking care to massage male egos (**5.10**), and took part in main events such as Peterloo. Women were not, however, claiming rights for themselves but still campaigning for male rights, nevertheless the very fact of their activity meant they were challenging accepted notions of a woman's role. They did not therefore see themselves as victims. Radical women often concentrated on the role of the mother as educator. (**5.8, 5.11**)

Political education for women was also provided by the Owenite movement which through Owen's 'doctrine of circumstances' (people become what they are through the conditioning of their environment) provided the possibility for reviewing women's position within society. Women from the working classes and lower middle classes attended Owenite lecturers, spoke at meetings and contributed to its journal *New Moral World*. But despite its supposed emphasis on equality, women found that they were still expected to do domestic tasks and very few served as branch officials. Owenism, however, remained a minority moment.

Other areas where women were prominent included the struggle for the unstamped press and the agitation for the 1832 Reform Act. Due to government taxes on newspapers, the price of 'stamped' or legally produced papers was beyond most of the working classes. Radicals responded to this 'tax on knowledge' by producing cheap, unstamped newspapers, which espoused radical political ideas. Women distributed and sold the papers (criminal offences in themselves). At times, women even took over the actual running of individual papers while the male proprietors were in gaol, as Susannah Wright and Eliza Sharples (**5.12**) did for Richard Carlile (editor of the *Republican*) in 1832. Women, once more acting in defence of the family, set up organizations such as the Friends of the Oppressed (1832) to support the families of those men who were imprisoned.

In the struggle for the 1832 Reform Act, radical women both formed new female societies, such as the Female Radical Reform

Society of Manchester, and joined male organizations, such as the Birmingham Political Union. They took part in riots as at Bristol following the Lords' rejection of the Reform Bill on 7–8 October 1831. Female radicals also encouraged women to engage in 'exclusive dealing', that is, to buy only from shopkeepers who supported the cause which they justified on the grounds of a women's domestic responsibilities: 'The spending of money (especially in domestic concerns) is the province of women, in it we can act without the risk of being thought politicians'.[7] This was a tactic which was still being employed in the 1930s: 'As a protest against Germany's treatment of the Jews, . . . when women entered a shop they should note the origin of the product they wished to buy, and if it were marked "Made in Germany" they should decline to purchase it . . . If women declined to buy any German goods, the Germans would be forced to alter their methods. It was the only way to stop the injustice and tyranny that was occurring in Germany . . .[8]

The rise of feminist scholarship from the late 1960s has led to the restoring to visibility of those areas where women had previously been deemed to be absent. Chartism – the movement for a real reform of the political system with its demands for universal male suffrage, annual parliaments, the ballot, payment of MPs, no property qualifications for MPs and equal electoral districts – is a prime example of this. Chartism arose out of the disillusion following the Reform Act. Not only had the Whig government not furthered working-class interests – there had been no ten hour Factory Act and trade unions were outlawed – they had also seemed deliberately to go against them with the Poor Law Amendment Act 1834. Furthermore from 1837 the country was in the grip of recession. It was not surprising then that women should agitate both *against* the new Poor Law and *for* the Charter. They attended mass meetings, petitioned, took part in educational aspects and dealt only with shopkeepers who supported their cause. (**5.13**, **5.14**) Their aim was to defend family life against the onslaught of industrialisation. (**5.15**) Some women did, however, move on to claim the vote for themselves. (**5.17**, **5.18**)

Middle-class women from the stance of 'moral mission' took part in those political movements which reflected the concerns of their class: anti slavery, the anti-corn law movement (**5.19**) temperance and peace – a development of which *The Times* did not approve. (**5.20**) By 1850 both working-class and middle-class women were becoming increasingly politicised and while it could be argued that radical working-class women had developed a more advanced level of politi-cisation than middle-class women after 1850 it would be middle-class women who would continue to campaign for women's rights (as they did for example in the battle to repeal the Contagious Diseases Act).[9]

The *English Woman's Journal* founded in 1858 served as an organ for feminist campaigns on all aspects of inequalities. The Women's Co-operative Guild established in 1884 fought for better maternity care, housing and easier divorce.[10] Women, however, were no nearer gaining the suffrage. In 1866 John Stuart Mill's attempt to secure the fran-chise for women was defeated by one hundred and ninety four votes to seventy three, while an attempt to amend the Second Reform Bill by substituting 'person' for 'man' was similarly thwarted.

In August 1867 Lydia Becker set up the Manchester Women's Suf-frage Committee which was quickly followed by groups in Edinburgh and Bristol. These were the forerunners of the National Union of Women's Suffrage Societies [NUWSS] under the leadership of Millicent Fawcett. The basis of representation had always been communities not individuals, with the franchise seen as a privilege and not a right. Women therefore had to prove their fitness for admission to the body politic. In this, they were helped by their ability to play a role in local government. This was the result of Jacob Bright's amend-ment to the Municipal Franchise Act which gave all women ratepay-ers the right to vote for local councils. The case of *Regina* v. *Harrold* in 1872 restricted this solely to unmarried women ratepayers. Women immediately took up the challenge with regard to school boards[11] and from 1875 also became Poor Law Guardians. Up till 1892 when it was reduced to £5, the rating qualification for Poor Law Boards differed from board to board and in some areas it had been as high as £40. This effectively restricted service to the single and affluent. In 1894 it was abolished altogether. The work of women in these areas advanced their claims to participate in the body politic, though women's work on Poor Law Boards was often seen in terms of 'home management'. (5.21) After 1907 (5.22) all local government authori-ties were open to women but, as pre 1894, a property qualification was in force which again meant that it became the province of the single and affluent.

On the national scene, extension of the franchise in 1867 and 1884 meant the creation of a mass electorate and the 1883 Corrupt Practices Act restricted the amount of money which could be spent in campaigning. Political parties therefore needed large numbers of voluntary workers and women fitted the bill. They were admitted to the Tory Primrose League in 1884 and the Women's Liberal Federation established in 1887 as well as to various socialist organisations such as the Fabian Society, the Social Democratic Federation and the Independent Labour Party [ILP]. Socialist organisations stressed women's political inequalities and were important in that they provided an arena for working-class women to take part in politics. Such work encouraged women to demand the vote for themselves, although there was disagreement over who should be enfranchised: everyone or just single women? The question of the vote for women was to dominate the wider women's movement from 1900. (**5.25**) Emmeline and Christabel Pankhurst founded the Women's Social and Political Union [WSPU] in 1903 (**5.23**) to campaign for both socialism and the suffrage. In 1907 differences over tactics with the Pankhursts led to a breakaway movement – the Women's Freedom League [WFL] set up by Theresa Billington Grieg and Charlotte Despard.

In 1906, the Liberals won a landslide victory and it was during the election campaign that the WSPU began disrupting political meetings – a strategy which progressed to full-scale militancy after 1910. Suffragettes also went on hunger strike which led to force feeding which was often accompanied by brutality (**5.24**) while the 'Cat and Mouse Act' of 1913 allowed hunger strikers to be rearrested once they had regained their health. The suffrage movement was subject to many splits and militancy put off potential supporters. (**5.26**) The outbreak of war in August 1914 led to a cessation of suffrage activity as the WSPU supported the war effort and the NUWSS concentrated on relief work. In 1918 the Representation of the People Act enfranchised women over the age of thirty who already held the local government franchise. Historians have debated the extent to which women's work in the war effort contributed to enfranchisement and also reinterpretated the suffrage campaigns. Their analyses have shown the militancy was a complex strategy and that there was cross-over between the WSPU and NUWSS.

The inter-war period saw the dominance of the Conservative Party and the decline of the Liberals. With the granting of the franchise, there was no one single issue on which to focus. Many feminists turned to questions of maintaining peace and improving the welfare of working women.[12] Women were encouraged to join the Labour Party.

The NUWSS changed itself into the National Union of Societies for Equal Citizenship [NUSEC] with Eleanor Rathbone as its president. Rathbone argued that women would never achieve equality unless they obtained economic independence within the family. This again led to splits between those like the Six Points Group who believed that the similarities between the sexes should be emphasised and not a woman's traditional role as mother. World War II saw women undertaking war work with great success.[13]

The period from the 1920s to the 1950s did not see a lack of action by women's movement and indeed organisations (**5.27**) such as the Fawcett Society provided a link between these earlier movements and the Women's Liberation Movement (**5.28**) in the 1960s and 1970s. Furthermore, the late 1960s and early 1970s saw much legislation of women's issues partly as result of neither main party (Conservative and Labour) having a large majority which meant that they wanted to attract the woman voter.[14] Women also began to take control of their lives with their establishment of women's refuges (**5.29**, **5.30**) and rape crisis centres. In a celebrated case, Asian women joined those protesting about lack of union recognition, poor pay and conditions at the Grunwick photo processing lab in London, suffering intimidation and violence. (**5.31**) The Labour Government set up a Cabinet committee to investigate the issues and the strike itself was ended after 670 days. And while women still had not achieved full gender equality, they were certainly in a stronger position politically than they had been in the late 1780s.

5.1 Community action

Taunton, Somersetshire, June 25. Several hundred women and a great number of men, assembled in this town, in a tumultuous manner, and proceeded to a large weir, call'd the Town Mills, when the women went briskly to work demolishing it, and that so as to prevent any corn being ground at the mills. The men all the while stood lookers on, giving the women many huzzas and commendations for their dexterity in the work. Their reason for it was a dislike they had to the manager of the mills, whom they charge with sending flour to other parts, whereby they apprehend corn was advanced to a higher price than otherwise it would have been.

Politics

Gentlemen's Magazine (1753), p. 343, as quoted in Bridget Hill, *Eighteenth-century women: An anthology*, London: Routledge (1987), p. 254.

5.2 Enclosure riot

We had not been there an hour before about forty persons, men and women and children, assembled and after reasoning with the men for some time and telling them the consequences of opposing the Surveyor I think they had made up their minds not to molest them, until a fresh set of women from the neighbourhood of Llithfaen came up who immediately abused the men for their supineness and commenced a salute of sods upon the Commissioner and the Surveyor and the old women continued to do so until we came to the boundary of Nevin and Pistill when the action became general and the Commissioner, the Surveyor and myself were obliged to retreat.

D. Jones, *Before Rebecca: Rural protests in Wales, 1793–1835*, London: Allen Lane (1973), p. 47.

5.3 Scotch militia

Haddington, 31 August, 1797
The Deputy Lieutenants and Magistrates arrived at Tranent a little after 11 o'clock, escorted by a party of the Cinque Ports, and about 20 of the Volunteer Cavalry. On their arrival they were insulted and abused in the grossest language, by a multitude of people whom they found assembled. The women were particularly clamorous.

So formidable a body of military created much confusion and alarm in the street. The women, in particular, became exasperated, and began throwing stones at the windows of *Glen's* [the constable] house. The Cinque-Port Cavalry, some of whom were struck by the stones, grew impatient; and the women continuing to throw stones, the cavalry were ordered to charge through the people in the streets; which they accordingly did . . . The women again threw stones, and seemed regardless of the dragoons on their horses; they even seized the horses by the bridles and held them. The Commanding Officer now gave orders to the soldiers to load with ball-cartridges, and to fire. *Isabel Rogers*, a young woman, about twenty years of age, Servant to Mr. *William Nelson*, stocking-maker in Tranent, was the first who fell.

The Times, 5 September 1797.

5.4 Trowbridge election riot

On Tuesday night, about 10 o'clock, an infuriated rabble, consisting of many females (to their disgrace be it spoken), with men and boys, assembled in this town, and proceeded to acts of violence, in destroying the windows, window-frames, and shutters, of several of the inhabitants, whom they had previously marked out as the objects of their vengeance: at some houses not a pane of glass was left whole, and the desolation which the morning light presented was horrid . . .

The Times, 26 July 1819.

5.5 Political analysis

Let woman once assert her proper sphere, unshackled by prejudice, and unsophisticated by vanity; and pride (the noblest species of pride), will establish her claims to the participation of power, both mentally and corporeally . . .

Supposing that destiny, or interest, or chance, or what you will, has united a man, confessedly of a weak understanding, and corporeal debility, to a woman strong in all the powers of intellect, and capable of bearing the fatigues of busy life: is it not degrading to humanity that such a woman should be the passive, the obedient slave, of such an husband? Is it not repugnant to all the laws of nature, that her feelings, actions, and opinions, should be controuled (sic), perverted, and debased, by such an help-mate? Can she look for protection to a being, whom she was formed by the all wise CREATOR, to protect? Impossible . . .

In what is woman inferior to man? In some instances, but not always, in corporeal strength: in activity of mind, she is his equal. Then, by this rule, if she is to endure oppression in proportion as she is deficient in muscular power, *only*, through all the stages of animation the weaker should give precedence to the stronger . . .

The question is simply this: Is woman persecuted and oppressed because she is the *weaker* creature? Supposing that to be the order of Nature; let me ask these human despots, whether a woman, of strong mental and corporeal powers, is born to yield obedience, merely because *she is a woman*, to those shadows of mankind who exhibit the effeminacy of women, united with the mischievous foolery of monkies? . . .

If woman be the *weaker* creature, why is she employed in laborious avocations? why compelled to endure the fatigue of household drudgery; to scrub, to scower, to labour, both late and early, while the powdered lacquey only waits at the chair, or behind the carriage of his employer? Why are women, in many parts of the kingdom, permitted to follow the plough; to perform the laborious business of the dairy; to work in our manufactories; to wash, to brew, and to bake, while men are employed in measuring lace and ribands; folding gauzes; composing artificial bouquets; fancying feathers, and mixing cosmetics for the preservation of beauty? . . . Are women thus compelled to labour, because they are of the weaker sex?

Mary Robinson, pseud. Anne Frances Randall, *A letter to the women of England on the injustice of mental subordination* (1799), pp. 2–4, 12, 18–19. www.rc.umd.edu/editions/robinson/mrletterfrst.

5.6 A plea for woman

We shall now proceed to enumerate more precisely the disadvantages which, in this country, we conceive woman in general labours under. The principal of these seem to be: –

I.   Want of equal civil rights.

II. Enforcement of unjust laws.

III. Want of means for obtaining a good substantial education.

The second and third of these grievances are, in themselves, and essentially, evil and unjust. The first is, perhaps, principally of importance, because without it there are no sure means of obtaining and securing the others; but although the results of legislative powers are what render those powers chiefly desirable, still they are also desirable on their own account; free institutions being one of the most important and elevating influences which can be brought to bear on the human mind. We, therefore, place the deprivation of civil rights first; being the fertile source of many other evils, as well as most injurious in itself.

The ground on which equality is claimed for all men is of equal force for all women; for women share the common nature of humanity, and are possessed of all those noble faculties which constitute man a responsible being, and give him a claim to be his own ruler, so far as is consistent with order, and the possession of the like degree of sovereignty over himself by every other human being . . .

We do not mean to enter into the question of the claim of all men to equal rights, but simply . . . show that the first principles on which it does rest apply to all mankind, without distinction of sex . . .

Of course, we do not mean that all women should possess a privilege which has, as yet, only been conferred on particular classes of men; we only mean to insist that the right is the same in both sexes . . . The class of women corresponding to the privileged class among men have still a claim; and the *onus probandi* against them lies with those who advocate the continuance of the system of exclusion.

The exercise of those rights would be useful in two ways: it would tend to ennoble and elevate the mind; and it would secure the temporal interest of those who exercise it . . .

The consciousness of responsibility which the possession of a vote would bestow the dignity of being trusted, the resolution to justify the faith placed in her trust and judgment, would all call forth, in woman, noble powers which, hitherto, have been too much suffered to lie dormant: powers which, when they have occasionally peeped forth in an individual, have but too often been greeted with laughter and ridicule, sometimes even with more serious obloquy. Thus, some of the gifted among women have been induced to hide their light beneath an exterior of levity and frivolity, while others have gained the pardon of the lord of the creation for encroaching on what he claims as his peculiar domain – the intellectual – by falling down and worshipping him, and then devoting their talents to instructing their sex in all the duties of this idolatry . . .

We are aware that it is said, that woman is virtually represented in Parliament, her interests being the same as those of man; but the many laws which have been obliged to be passed to protect them from their nearest male relatives are a sufficient answer. The simple fact of such laws being necessary would be a strong presumption that woman requires to have her interests really represented in the Legislature; but the manifestly unjust nature of the laws which this necessity has produced, convert presumption into proof, by showing most distinctly, that no sentiment, either of justice or gallantry, has been sufficient to ensure anything like impartiality in the laws between the sexes. Those laws, then, are in themselves a convincing proof, first, that woman requires representation, and, second, that she is not represented . . . They are evidently the production of men legislating for their own most obvious interests . . .

Marion Reid, *A plea for woman being a vindication of the importance and extent of her natural sphere of action: with remarks on recent works on the subject*, Edinburgh: W. Tait (1843).

5.7 Female Reform Societies

Those residents of Blackburn who mounted the stage were not only of the lowest class, but *men of very bad moral character*. No inhabitant spoke. For some reason not yet explained the fire engines, belonging to the town were brought with great rapidity near the place of meeting; and the women and some of the timid ran in various directions, apprehending the arrival of magistrates with proper powers to interrupt the debates of the eloquent reformers. Many hats, shoes shawls and handkerchiefs were lost in the confusion that ensued, and it was with some difficultly that the folly of their fears was ascertained, and order restored. With repugnance we mention that one novel and most disgusting scene took place – a Deputation from the Blackburn *Female* Reform Society mounted the stage, to present a cap of liberty and an address to the meeting. The latter was read, and in it the women composing the society, 'pledged themselves to instil into the minds of their children a hatred of (what they pleased to call) civil and religious tyranny!' These women then mixed with the orators, and remained on the hustings during the rest of the day. The public scarcely need be informed, that the females are women well known to be of the most abandoned of their sex.

The Times, 13 July 1819.

5.8 Female Union Society, established at Stockport

Declaration and Rules of the Female Union Society of Stockport, . . .
    1. That the members shall be classed, with 12 members in each class, who shall select a leader or collector from amongst themselves every 14 weeks; also, every female on becoming a member, shall pay weekly to her

collector *one penny* for the purpose of assisting our male friends in obtaining their object.

2. That a Committee of 12 be appointed, 1 out of each section of the General Union, to manage the affairs of the Society, 6 to go out of office every 6 weeks.

3. We collectively and individually pledge ourselves to instil into the minds of our children a thorough knowledge of their natural and inalienable rights, whereby they shall be able to form just and correction notions of those *legalized banditti of plunderers*, who now rob their parents of more than half the produce of their labour; we also pledge ourselves to stimulate our husbands and sons to imitate the ancient Romans in their courage, who fought to a man in defence of their liberty, and our daughters and female friends to imitate the Spartan women, who, when their husbands, sons and other kindred had gone out to fight in defence of their freedom, would rather have heard of the death of any of them, than their deserting *the standard of liberty*, and who rather rejoiced if any of their kindred fell bravely defending the bulwarks of their freedom.

4. We solicit communication with every institution of the kind in Great Britain, as it is by a general correspondence that a national union of sentiment can be formed.

The Times, 21 July 1819.

5.9   Galston female reformers

Glasgow 28 October (from *Glasgow Herald*)
'On Saturday last, a meeting of Radical Reformers was held at Galston ... During the proceedings, the female Reformers from Galston, accompanied by a band of music arrived. When they came within 20 yards of the hustings, a vocal band sung, "*Scots Wha ha'e wi' Wallace bled*", and moving on "solemn and slow", to the music, a deputation of female Reformers mounted the hustings, and one of them placed a splendid cap of liberty on the head of the Chairman, and another presented a flag inscribed "Annual Parliaments, University Suffrage, Election by Ballot"; reverse, "Rise Britons and assert your rights:" and a third presented an address from the Galston Female Reform Society, consisting of 279 members. When the cap of liberty was placed upon the head of the Chairman, the meeting gave three cheers. Speeches of the usual kind were delivered. The people dispersed in an orderly manner.'

The Times, 2 November 1819.

5.10 Women political orators

Ladies and Gentlemen, Before we proceed into the business of the evening, I desire that the gentlemen will withdraw; it is not done with a view to transact anything of a secret nature, for it is commonly said that women can keep no secrets, but merely with a view that if in our debates (for it is something new for women to turn political orators,) we should for want of knowledge make any blunders, we should be laughed at, to prevent which we should prefer being by ourselves [Their male brethren immediately obeyed] and she proceeded on . . .

The Times, 4 August 1819.

5.11 Rules of the West of England Female Union Society

That we assist the male population in recovering their invaded rights, and in obtaining a full, free, and fair representation in Parliament, by means of householders' suffrage, annual parliaments, and election by ballot. That every female, on being enrolled a member of this society, pay down on shilling, and continue to pay one penny weekly so long as she shall remain a member. That the unmeaning distraction of Whig and Tory be not entertained, but that we train up our children in the investigation of measures, and strongly persuade them that no man ought to be entrusted with power for any length of time which should enable him to abuse it. That our representatives should be elected by *private ballot*, as the *only* means of annihilating corruption. That every country, according to the number of electors, should elect their share of representatives.

Eliz. Russell Chairwoman for 1819
Rules of the West of England Female Union Society.

The Times, 26 July 1819.

5.12 Whig tyranny

Whig tyranny is more atrocious than Tory tyranny, there is an apology in education, though not in morals and in politics. Whig tyranny has no apology but its hypocrisy. We have proof enough that the Whigs wish to keep every thing as near as possible to its present state: that is, they wish if possible, to collect the present revenue of fifty millions for the state and ten for the church. There is a very agreeable feeling associated with the fingering of large sums of money; as agreeable to dishonesty as to honesty. Whigs have this feeling as well as the Tories. They are not light-fingered gentry. The siftings of fifty millions through the various public offences is an onerous task and justifies *liberal* takings.

Eliza Sharples, *Isis*, 27 October 1832, quoted in Edmund and Ruth Frow, *Political women 1800–1850*, intro. Julie Swindell, London: Polity Press (1989), p. 50.

5.13   The politics of women Chartists

Sisters and women of England, much is yet in your power, to aid the great and holy cause now so gloriously spreading throughout the land. Aid your husbands, brothers, friends and children. Urge and demand, at their hands, the fulfilment of their duty in the great and holy cause of freedom and eternal justice. Let them know that the union of millions is strength and power, not to be resisted by tyrants. Urge upon them the necessity of throwing in their mite to the general and national fund, in order to give strength and power to those deputed by the people, to fight the great and glorious fight of freedom . . . we respectfully suggest that the shopocracy be left to their fate, and that no persons are so well qualified to bring these very important personages to their senses as the women of England upon whose minds we would impress as a public duty the necessity of expending their money only with the people or shopkeepers friendly to the cause of freedom, justice, Universal Suffrage, &c. In a very few months the common enemy would be made to bite the dust of their empty shops and empty tills. You, sisters, the patriotic women of England, in these transactions are the most fit and proper persons to deal out the blow and most effectually too; . . . Let every shop and shopkeeper be noted in a book kept for the purpose, stating name, residence, trade, and whether Whig or Tory;

also, another book containing the names of those friendly to the cause of the people . . .

We remain, your devoted friends and sisters,
The Members of
The Nottingham Female Political Union
Nottingham, Nov. 26, 1838
Mary Savage
Secretary.

'The Address of the Female Political Association of Nottingham to the Patriotic Women of England', *Northern Star*, 8 December, 1838.

5.14 Newcastle Female Political Union

Fellow-Countrywomen, – We call upon you to join us and help our fathers, husbands, and brothers, to free themselves and us from political, physical, and mental bondage . . .

We have been told that the province of woman is her home, and that the field of politics should be left to men; this we deny; the nature of things renders it impossible, and the conduct of those who give the advice is at variance with the principles they assert . . .

For years we have struggled to maintain our homes in comfort, such as our hearts told us should greet our husbands after their fatiguing labours. Year after year has passed away, and even now our wishes have no prospect of being realised, our husbands are over wrought, our houses half furnished, our families ill-fed, our children uneducated – the fear of want hangs over our heads; the scorn of the rich is pointed towards us; the brand of slavery is on our kindred, and we feel the degradation. We are a despised caste; our oppressors are not content with despising our feelings, but demand the control of our thoughts and wants! – want's bitter bondage binds us to their feet, we are oppressed because we are poor – the joys of life, the gladness of plenty, and the sympathies of nature, are not for us; the solace of our homes, the endearments of our children, and the sympathies of our kindred are denied us – and even in the grave our ashes are laid with disrespect.

'Address of the Female Political Union of Newcastle upon Tyne to their Fellow Countrywomen', *Northern Star*, 2 February 1839, as quoted in D. Thompson (ed.), *Early Chartists*, London: Macmillan, pp. 128–9.

5.15   Women's rights to 'meddle in politics'

I have said that a domestic sphere is most suitable to woman . . . when it becomes no longer a home – when it is changed into a hell, shall not women come forth and enquire the causes of this? seek the remedy? If they do not, they must part with home and with all that is domestic in their character. The evils that threaten home, threaten all that makes home valuable. When virtue is rendered vain, it frequently turns to vice; temper is frequently lost with comfort. Wives and children become afflictions to husbands and parents when they must see them suffer without the power of relieving them, and they will sometimes mistake the effects for their causes, and visit on them the woes which result from their wants . . . 'Women should not meddle with politics!' then they must make up their account to be marred by them. If politics did not meddle with them, this inhibition might be just; but ought not the woman who values her home – that human nest – to be sensitive of everything which threatens its welfare. If she be forced to the workhouse, what kind of a home will she find there? She is no longer a wife – a mother. Her husband and children may be living in the same house, – but she is separated from the former when she most needs his sympathy, and the latter are taken from her when they most need her succour . . .

So far from being excluded from taking a part in politics, women ought to be allowed to vote; not wives – for they and their husbands are one, or ought to be as one – but maids, and widows. They pay rates, cesses, and taxes; they participate in the prosperity or adversity of the state. They have an equal stake in the land they live in. Why should the law exclude them? I do not know that they would make better laws than men make: they could scarcely make worse. They would be more likely to seek the true interests of their children, for the husband who does this, cannot consult a better judge than a good wife. She is certainly the best adviser in domestic happiness, which is the best of life.

English Chartist Circular, 1, 23 June 1841.

5.16   'Address to the women of England'

Do not say you have no business with politics, and that you leave such things for your husbands, fathers and brothers. You have an interest in politics, a deeper interest than you are aware of. If the country is mis-governed, and bad laws instituted, and good laws perverted, it is on you those laws fall heaviest; witness those which regulate the price of food and the monopolies. If the country is well governed, and good laws acted upon, does it not naturally follow that we shall also feel the benefit of them? Besides, if you have husbands, fathers, or brothers who are Chartists, your participating in that which interests them most will please and urge them to further exertions. If you have husbands, fathers, or brothers who are not Chartists, your example will influence them, and induce them to become such.

The principles of the Charter, if carried out, are such as will give man not only his political rights, but will enable him to get a more equitable remuneration for his labour, and that will enable you to live in more comfortable homes – to give your children as much food as they require, and to prevent your leading such wretched lives of poverty and unrequited toil.

Susanna Inge, *Northern Star*, 2 July 1842.

5.17   Female Chartist Association

A meeting of Female Chartists was held on Monday evening in the National Charter Association-hall, Old Bailey, for the purpose of forming a 'Female Chartist Association' . . .

Mr Cohen was for maintaining the 'social rights' of women. 'Political rights,' such as he understood that the meeting aspired to, she would never, in his opinion, attain.

Miss Mary Anne Walker . . . repudiated with indignation the insinua-tion that if women were in Parliament any man, be he husband or be he lover, would dare be so base as to attempt to sway her from the strict line of duty ('Hear, hear,' cries of 'Bravo' from the men, and much applause). She would treat with womanly scorn, as a contemptible scoundrel, the man who would dare to influence her vote. . . .

The Times, 20 October 1842.

5.18 The Chartist meeting – Miss Mary Anne Walker again

Miss M. A. Walker presented herself on the platform and became at once the grand attraction of the audience, in connexion with the prominent place she had filled within the last few days in the public eye, as the founder, or at least leading personage, of the female Chartist Association. Miss Walker was habited in deep mourning, and being tall and of pre-possessing countenance and figure with much grace and dignity in her manner and action, she looked a heroine in the cause which she has taken up with so much enthusiasm. She was received with the plaudits of some, while others, 'from the curiosity to hear a woman speak,' remained 'silent and breathless,' that they might hear.

So soon as the anxious press towards the platform had ceased, Miss Walker observed, she had a few words to say to the meeting. ('Hear, hear') 'Wonders,' she continued 'would never cease.' (Laughter) Who would have thought that Mr Cohen, Miss Susannah Inge, and herself (Miss Mary Anne Walker), would have been so far distinguished as to be made the subjects of a 'leading article' in *The Times*? – *The Times!* Yes, *the Times*, indeed! (Laughter.) Mr Cohen had brought all this upon them by his question – 'Suppose ladies were in the House of Commons for a Parliamentary borough, and that a young fascinating sprig of Tory aristocracy were to try to sway their votes through an influences over their affections, how could they resist?' (Laughter from the gentlemen, and tittering among the ladies.) How ridiculous that was! (A laugh.) She (Miss Walker) would tell Mr Cohen and *The Times* too, that they had got a nice little point in 'the Charter,' which would act as an antidote to that sort of 'influence over their affections.' They would be discharged from their situation of members at the end of twelve months, should they weakly prove 'unworthy of their trust.' And thrown 'on the wide world, out of place,' and 'without a char-acter from their last masters and mistresses.' (Laughter, and much applause from the gentlemen.) . . . she hoped that husbands would bring their wives and daughters to the meetings of the 'Female Chartists,' ('Hear, hear,' from the ladies, and cheers mingled with laughter from the gentlemen.) At those Chartist meetings the wives and daughters would hear good instruction; and she (Miss Walker) would tell *The Times* that they might hear reason and sound political wisdom from the lips of women, and even from the daughter of a working man. ('Hear, hear,' and cheers.) For the advancement of their glorious cause – 'the People's Charter,' 'love and union' should go 'hand in hand.' ('Hear, hear,' from the young men.) She called upon the women, then, to attend these Chartist meetings; and she assured the mothers, that by so attending they would, at least, learn and know where to send their children to school, after which they would no longer send them to the 'national humbugs.' . . . She (Miss Walker) 'came out' alive to the abuses of her country; and she was sure *The Times* would not differ from her when she said, that it was shameful that while Englishwomen were receiving but 5d. the pair for the making of policemen's trousers, a German woman was receiving 100,000*l.* a year wrung in taxes from the earnings of the hardworking men of England. ('Hear, hear,' cheers, and laughter from the men, and sly glances from the ladies.) It would take, she (Miss Mary Anne Walker) would tell *The Times,* 4,000,000 policemen's trousers at 5d. the pair to pay this German woman's pension. (Laughter from the gentlemen, and deep 'sensation' among the ladies.) She would further ask *The Times* if it were not a shame that this enormous pension should be given, while Englishwomen were also receiving but 9d. the dozen for making shirts! ('Hear, hear,' and sensation.) . . . Miss Mary Anne Walker's was decidedly the speech of the evening. Miss Susannah Inge, the other lady Chartist who spoke at the female Chartist Meeting, was also present on this occasion, and looked in all the flush of youth, popularity, and beauty.

The Times, 25 October 1842.

5.19   Women and the Anti-Corn Law League Bazaar

The Bazaar, which for nearly three weeks continued to be the most attractive spectacle ever displayed in London, had finally closed; the decorations are taken down, and the goods removed. As all the accounts are not yet closed, we cannot state the results with perfect accuracy; but we have ascertained that rather more than £20,000 have been obtained for admissions and sales, independent of about £5,000 in money contributed from various localities, and of the unsold goods, which are reserved to stock the Bazaar that will be held at a later period of the year, in the Free-Trade Hall, in Manchester. There were aggregated those ladies who, for seventeen days, had devoted their time, their toil, and, we fear, their health, with unwearied assiduity, to advance the great cause of humanity and justice; ladies who had manifested an intelligence, tact, and spirit of self-sacrifice which cannot be too highly estimated, or too gratefully remembered. They were not conscious of the capabilities they possessed until they found them developed in action by the force of circumstances. Everybody was willing to concede to everybody; and there was no need for administrative functions when all minds were animated by the same feelings, guided by the same principles, and directed to the same object.

From *The League,* quoted in Archibald Prentice, *History of the Anti-Corn Law League,* London: W. F. G. Cash (1853), pp. 335–6.

5.20 Women Anti-Corn Law Leaguers

During the last week a whole host of Lancashire females, comprising Mrs. Cobden, Mrs. Massie and Mrs. M'Kerrow, with about a hundred other spouses and spinsters, have appeared as *debutantes* on the boards of polit-ical agitation. The peculiar walk which their ambition happens to have taken, is that of hot and passionate abettors of the anti-Corn Law League. Mrs. Massie and Mrs. M'Kerrow (who, as the spruce ribs of two Dissenting preachers, are evidently bent upon being upsides with the patriotic Mrs. Cobden, are leading performers in this new Manchester pantomime, just as their husbands were in the old one) have advertised themselves to all England, in the novel character of anti-Corn Law bazaar-ers. These fair agitators, anxious to surmount the unprofitable inefficiency of their forlorn and fusty *Benedicts,* have determined to display their charms as sellers of finery at public stalls for the benefit of the Cobden League. Under such attractive and influential auspices, the forthcoming bazaar, for which all manner of contributions are solicited in order to have a grand display, is expected to replenish the League's exhausted treasury, and sustain it a little longer with the earnings of its female lovers.

. . . Although the ladies themselves, as presumably acquainted with the proprieties of their sex and sphere, are by no means excusable for having consented to lay them aside, their male advisers in this affair are mainly responsible for the unseemly and revolting position into which the poor creatures have been drawn. Charitable bazaars, which present respectable females in the position of extortionate shopwomen, we morally detest in every form. But political bazaars are ten thousand times worse. If men, by the necessities of society, must unhappily be estranged by party differ-ences, for Heaven's sake, let us ward such a curse from the hallowed and bland reciprocities of female life. To make a woman a politician is to make her a monster. Only figure the Cobden divinities, with their fans, parasols, and vinaigrettes, converted into anti-Corn law termagants, scowling defi-ance upon the retiring ladies who prefer their nurseries and prayer books to the pleasures and wages of political libertinism! Presently we shall have the petticoat politicians of Manchester schooling us on the most recondite questions of national policy . . . Nothing can be more heartless on the part of the Leaguers that that they should have sought to escape from their embarrassments by subjecting to a sort of political prostitution those confiding creatures whose virtuous seclusion they are bound upon every manly principle to maintain inviolate.

The Times, 1 January 1842.

5.21   Labour Women as Guardians of the Poor

The work of the Poor Law Guardians is like housekeeping for a very big and difficult family, and we want women's help to run this publicly managed household, just as much as to arrange for their own homes. All sorts of questions arise which a woman knows more about, or can tackle better than a man.

First, there are the children, thousands of whom have no other parents than the State, whilst others, still more unfortunate, have to be protected against their own parents by the public authorities. These children want *mothering*. The old barrack system of herding them together in huge institutions is being gradually replaced by something more human, and we want women with Labour ideals to hasten this improvement and to see that each child has a good start in life – not as a machine, but as a human soul.

Training also should be provided to make the children good wage earners when the boys and girls go out into the world. It makes all the difference whether the Guardians take trouble to fit each one to the work he or she will do best, and with employers who will treat them well, or whether they are content to fit square pegs into round holes, and to take any employer's application, without consideration of wages and conditions. For instance, a Labour Woman is not likely to send all girls indiscriminately into domestic service, whether they have any capacity for household work or not; and when she does send them to private mistresses, she will not risk them in places where they may come to physical or moral ruin.

One of the most difficult classes with whom Guardians have to deal is that of the mother of illegitimate children. Here, above all, a women's committee is necessary, for to bring such women before a Board of men is open to serious objection, whilst a woman friend – as the woman

Guardian should be – will advise the mother how to do the best for herself and her child.

Many of the sweated home industries, which horrify us by their low wages and long hours, are carried on by widows with children dependent on them. A good percentage of these are receiving out-relief from the Guardians, which sometimes only helps them to accept the low wages for their work. The aim of Labour Guardians would be to give these mothers sufficient to keep themselves and their children respectably: and women will understand better than men what is required.

Our system of dealing with vagrants has been shown by the recent Commission to perpetuate the class it seeks to help. Some courageous women have visited the women's wards as inmates, and have told us that their effect is to lower rather than raise the woman who is in temporary difficulties. Here is a field of work for Labour Women who can realise the needs of destitute working women.

Until the Labour Party persuade the Government to give us a system of Old Age Pensions, many old people must come upon the rates as paupers. Just as in the case of children, there is all the difference between treating these old people as machines and as human beings, and the Labour Guardian who stands for the rights of the workers will see that the aged workers have a home and not a barrack for their declining years.

It has always been woman's special mission to look after the sick, and the presence of women on the Boards of Guardians has done much to improve the infirmaries. The Labour Women will insist upon a high standard of nursing, upon good food and plenty of light and air, and will have the infirmaries separate from the workhouse buildings, wherever possible. For the women imbeciles and lunatics a woman Guardian's supervision is most necessary.

There must be many women employed as officials by the Guardians – matrons, domestic servants, sick nurses, etc. Labour women, as Guardians, will stand up for good conditions and 'equal pay for equal work' for the women employed. They should insist, too, upon having women as relieving officers, especially to visit the lying-in cases, to travel to the infirmary or the asylum with women patients, etc. This is almost a new work for women, but one of our Labour League Guardians, Miss Bell, of Leicester, helped to get one appointed by her Board, and no one who has seen the experiment would like to go back to the old days of having men to visit and attend such cases.

It is good to have women on Boards of Guardians, but unless you have the right woman, you may be out of the frying pan into the fire. We do not want women who will look upon the applicants from a 'superior' point of view and treat them as naughty children, or as dirt beneath their feet. Labour women are near in sympathy, and often in personal experience to those they are called upon to help. They will be less likely to be imposed upon by the humbugs, and more likely to bring out the best qualities of independence in those who apply through real misfortune. In a word, they will treat the poor as brothers and sisters, not as 'paupers'.

Therefore work and vote to return labour women as guardians.

Women's Labour League Leaflets, No. 6. n.d.

5.22   Labour women and town councils

Women electors may now serve on Town Councils, and this opens a new opportunity for useful work to the Women's Labour League.

Women are needed badly for our **Municipal Housekeeping.**

Let us use our **women's brains and women's hearts** to help guide the Labour policy on matters where we have knowledge and experience which the men cannot have.

We must ask that the Housing Committee clears away the back courts and alleys, **makes the slum landlords rebuild or cleanse** their dirty dwellings, and **itself builds comfortable, convenient houses** for the workers. We women know the ·waste of precious time and health due to insanitary, crowded surroundings. Let us claim for ourselves and our children **decent homes to live in.**

Then we need to secure the appointment of well trained and properly paid **women sanitary inspectors.** They can visit in the homes and in the women's workrooms and shops, and give help and advice as no man inspector can do.

Every woman should find out **the death rate of the babies** in the poor wards of her town and in the rich wards. If she has a motherly heart, she will not rest till the babies of the poorer workers have as good a chance of life as the babies of the well-to-do. Babies need light, cleanliness, fresh air, good milk.

We can never be sure that our milk is pure so long as it is sold for private.

Let us see how the Midwives' Act is administered and agitate until **every mother is secured careful and skilled attendance** in her hour of need.

Baths and washhouses, asylums, hospitals libraries, parks and playgrounds – all the **ever increasing activities of our Town Councils** need women's support and criticism that they may be carried on efficiently.

We women realise, even more clearly than men, the suffering entailed by low wages and irregular work. We must, therefore demand that the Council should, in each of its departments do its own work directly, and be a **Model Employer**.

Last, but not least, the **education of the children** is under the Town Councils. We women cannot take too active an interest in every stage of this – **from the baby classes right up to the technical schools**, which should be used to fit our boys and girls to do good skilled work, and earn good wages. The **women teachers**, who are paid so much worse than the men, need to be championed by their fellow-women.

The town councillors are now, as the result of the work of our Labour members in Parliament, responsible for providing **meals for necessitous school children**. Very few of them have yet taken up their responsibilities. We women should see that **every candidate** at this election is asked **to give a pledge** that he or she will not allow our future citizens to grow up stunted and stupid because they are not properly fed.

Women citizens!

Women of the Labour Party!

We cannot properly look after our homes and families unless we do something to influence our Town Councils. For these Councils have the power to make our homes healthy, or to let them be hotbeds of disease; to see that our women wage-earners work under good conditions, or to leave them at the mercy of every selfish employer; to educate our children well or ill.

For the sake of our homes, our fellow-workers, our children, let us do our utmost at this election to **uphold the cause of the workers**.

Women's Labour League Leaflets, No. 8.

5.23   Poster of Women's Social and Political Union

Hon. Secretary – Mrs Edith Martyn B.Sc
Hon. Treasurer – Mrs F.W.
  Pethick Lawrence   4 Clement's Inn,
Chief Organiser – Miss Christabel   London, WC
  Pankhurst, LL.B

We demand the Vote on the same terms as it is or may be granted to men

Why Women Want the Vote

BECAUSE
No race or class or sex can have its interest properly safeguarded in the legislature of a country unless it is represented by direct suffrage.

BECAUSE
Politics have invaded the home, and woman must therefore enter politics.

BECAUSE
Politics and economics go hand in hand. And so long as woman has no political status she will be the 'bottom dog' as a wage-earner.

BECAUSE
Grave questions, such as the death rate of infants, the waste of child life, the employment of married women, unemployment, wages and care of the aged, cannot be satisfactorily settled if the women's point of view is left out.

BECAUSE
While men who are voters can get their economic grievances listened to, non-voters are disregarded.

BECAUSE
All the wisest men and women realise that decisions based upon the point of view of men and women together are more valuable than those based upon either singly.

BECAUSE
The possession of citizenship and the meeting together for political discussion stimulates the faculty for combined action, and gives of itself a greater power of economic resistance.

BECAUSE
So long as the majority of the women of the country have no interest in politics, the children grow up ignorant of the meaning of the struggle for freedom, and lessons learnt in one generation by bitter experience have to be relearned by the next in the same school.

BECAUSE
Women are taxed without being represented, and taxation without representation is tyranny.

BECAUSE
Wherever women have become voters, reform has proceeded more rapidly than before, and even at home our municipal government, in which the women have a certain share, is in advance and not behind our Parliamentary attitude on many important questions.

183

BECAUSE
Women have to obey the laws equally with men, and they ought to have a voice in the deciding what those laws shall be.

BECAUSE
Women, like men, need to have some interests outside the home, and will be better comrades to their husbands, better mothers to their children, and better housekeepers of the home, when they get them.

BECAUSE
The Legislature in the past has not made laws which are equal between men and women: and these laws will not be altered till women get the vote.

BECAUSE
All the more important and lucrative positions are barred to them, and opportunities of public service are denied.

From the *'Reformers' Year Book'* (1907).

5.24   Force feeding and brutality

Day after day, morning and evening, the same struggle. Sometimes they used one steel gag on my jaw, sometimes two. 'Don't hurt more than you can help,' the senior sometimes said when his junior prodded with the sharp point of steel. My gums, where they prised them open, were always sore and bleeding, with bits of loose, jagged flesh; and other parts of the mouth got bruised or pinched in the struggle. Sometimes the tube was coughed up three or four times before they finally got it down. Sometimes, but not often – I was generally too much agitated by then – I felt the tube go right down into the stomach; a sickening, terrifying sensation, especially when it reached the breast. My shoulders were bruised, my back ached during the night. I scarcely slept. Often I fainted once or twice after the feeding . . . There were six of them, all much bigger and stronger than I. They flung me on my back on the bed, and held me down firmly by shoulders and wrists, hips, knees and ankles. Then the doctors came stealing in. Someone seized me by the head and thrust a sheet under my chin. My eyes were shut. I set my teeth and tightened my lips over them with all my strength. A man's hands were trying to force open my mouth; my breath was coming so fast that I felt as though I should suffocate. His fingers were striving to pull my lips apart – getting inside. I felt them and a steel instrument pressing round my gums, feeling for gaps in my teeth. I was trying to jerk my head away, trying to wrench it free. Two of them were holding it, two of them dragging at my mouth. I was panting and heaving my breath quicker and quicker, coming now with a low scream which was growing louder. 'Here is a gap', one of them said, 'No, here is a better one. This long gap here!' A steel instrument pressed my gums, cutting into the flesh. I braced myself to resist that terrible pain. 'No, that won't do' – that voice again. 'Give me the pointed one!' A stab of sharp, intolerable agony. I wrenched my head free . . . Again the steel cutting its way in, though I strained my force against it. Then something gradually forced my jaws apart as a screw was turned; the pain was like having the teeth drawn. They were trying to get the tube down my throat, I was struggling madly to stiffen my muscles and close my throat. They got it down, I suppose, though I was unconscious of anything then save a mad revolt of struggling, for they said at last: 'That's all!' and I vomited as the tube came up . . .

I saw Ada Wright knocked down a dozen times in succession. A tall man with a silk hat fought to protect her as she lay on the ground, but a group of policemen thrust him away, seized her again, hurled her into the crowd and felled her again as she turned . . . Two girls with linked arms were being dragged about by two uniformed policemen, One of a group of officers in plain clothes ran up and kicked one of the girls, whilst the others laughed and jeered at her. Again and again we saw the small deputations struggling through the crowd with their little purple bannerettes: 'Asquith has vetoed our Bill.' The police snatched the flags, tore them to shreds, and smashed the sticks, struck the women with fists and knees, knocked them down, some even kicked them, then dragged them up, carried them a few paces and flung them into the crowd of sightseers. For six hours this continued . . . The cry went round: 'Be careful; they are dragging women down the side streets!' We knew this always meant greater ill-usage. I saw Cecilia Haig go out with the rest; a tall, strongly built, reserved woman, comfortably situated, who in ordinary circumstances might have gone through life without ever receiving an insult, much less a blow. She was assaulted with violence and indecency, and died in December, 1911, after a painful illness, arising from her injuries . . . Even some of the old ladies . . . were subjected to ill usage . . .

H. N. Brailsford and Dr Jessie Murray collected evidence from witnesses and sufferers, who testified to deliberate acts of cruelty, such as twisting and wrenching of arms, wrists, and thumbs; gripping the throat and forcing back the head; pinching the arms; striking the face

185

with fists, sticks, helmets; throwing women down and kicking them; rubbing a woman's face against the railings; pinching the breasts; squeezing the ribs.

Sylvia E. Pankhurst, *The Suffragette Movement*, London: Longmans (1931), pp. 443–4, 343.

5.25 Why women should have the vote

Platform and Press constantly declare, and, therefore, the ordinary citizen believes, that the average wife of the average working man can neither sew, cook, nor wash, manage her children, nurse her baby, nor keep her husband from the public-house. Why, then, complicate Government by introducing into the body politic these ignorant and unsatisfactory creatures?

Among the poorer families especially, the mental superiority of the wife to the husband is very marked. The ceaseless fight which these women wage in defence of their homes against all the forces of the industrial system develops in them an alertness and an adaptability to which the men, deadened by laborious and uninspiring toil, can lay no claim. The wives are, indeed, without the smattering of newspaper information which their husbands exchange as political wisdom in the public-houses, but they have a fund of common-sense, an intimate knowledge of the workings of male human nature, and an instinctive righteousness of attitude which make them invaluable raw electoral material.

Anna Martin, *The married working woman: A study*, London: National Union of Women's Suffrage Societies (1911), pp. 2–4.

5.26 Anti-suffragism

... The recruiting field for the militant suffragists is the half million of our excess female population – that half million which had better long ago have gone out to mate with its complement of men beyond the sea ...

... Even in animals – I say *even*, because in these at least one of the sexes has periods of complete quiescence – male and female cannot be safely worked side by side, except when they are incomplete ...

There is also quite a fatuous element in the programmes ... We have this, for instance, in the doctrine that notwithstanding the fact that the conditions of the labour market deny it to her, the woman ought to receive the same wage as a man for the same work.

This doctrine is fatuous, because it leaves out of sight that, even if woman succeeds in doing the same work as man, he has behind him a much larger reserve of strength.

... It will have been observed that there is in these programmes, in addition to the element of mental disorder and to the element of the fatuous, which have been animadverted upon, also a very ugly element of dishonesty. In reality the very kernel of the militant suffrage movement is the element of immorality ... There is no one who does not discern that women in her relations to physical force stands in quite a different position to man. Out of that different relation there must of necessity shape itself a special code of ethics for woman. And to violate that code must be for woman immorality.

Sir A. Wright, *The Times*, 28 March 1912.

5.27 Membership of women's organisations

Membership of Women's Organisations, 1930–60

	1930s	1950s
Labour Party Women's Sections (est. 1918)	250,000	364,000
Mother's Union (est. 1885)	538,000	500,000
National Council for Equal Citizenship (est. 1928)	48 branches	3,000
National Union of Townswomen's Guilds (est. 1928)	54,000	250,000
National Federation of Women's Institutes (est. 1915)	238,000	500,000
Six Point Group (est. 1921)	NA	200
Women's Co-operative Guild (est. 1883)	90,000	48,000
Women's Freedom League (est. 1907)	26 branches	NA

	1930s	1950s
Women's National Liberal Federation (est. 1918)	88,000	400 branches
Women's Unionist Association (est. 1918)	940,000	2.8 million

Note: Figures approximate only
Source: M. Pugh, *Women and the Women's Movement in Britain 1914–1959* (London, 1992); and I. Zweiniger-Bargielowska, 'Explaining the Gender Gap: the Conservative Party and the Women's Vote, 1945–64', in M. Francis and I. Zweiniger-Bargielowska (eds), *The Conservatives and the British Society 1880–1990* (Cardiff, 1996).

From I. Zweiniger-Bargielowska, *Women in twentieth-century Britain,* London: Pearson Education (2001), p. 266

5.28 Demands of the Women's Liberation Movement (c.1960/70s)

Equal pay
Equal education and job opportunities
24-hour nurseries
Free contraception and abortion
An end to discrimination against lesbians and the right of all woman to define their own sexuality
Freedom from violence and sexual coercion
An end to all the laws, assumptions and institutions that perpetuate male dominance and men's aggression towards women

5.29 Centre for battered wives urges tougher penalties

A voluntarily run centre that shelters battered women and their children seeking refuge from brutality by the man of the household is preparing a report for Sir Keith Joseph, Secretary of State for Social Services.

It wants wife beating made a criminal offence and not just a civil one.

In April and May this year 73 women and 157 children sought refuge in the centre. It is a small house due for demolition in Chiswick. Chiswick Women's Aid says it serves a desperate need that no social services department seems able to meet.

The *Nursing Times* says today that the battered women have difficulty in finding help.

The police were not interested, it says. Only the exceptional policeman intruded in a marital dispute, even if the wife was locked out of the house, bruised and bleeding.

Social service departments turned a blind eye or weakly offered marital casework. Social workers sometimes were too terrified to go near the violent husband.

The *Nursing Times* says it was not the occasional rough and tumble or momentary loss of control by men which brought women to the centre. It was out and out brutality, administered by men usually mentally disturbed or alcoholics.

Women came to the centre kicked, bruised and bleeding, with broken noses and broken ribs. Some pregnant women had been repeatedly kicked and beaten and babies, when born, were often retarded, blind or had epileptic fits.

One woman was bound and gagged and beaten in front of her children. Another was beaten and locked in a cupboard all day.

Doctors, the centre found, were unwilling usually to commit themselves on paper to agreeing that a wife had been brutally assaulted, because it meant a day wasted testifying in court. . . . Men who were charming to neighbours at the front gate could be brutal to their wives behind the front door.

Doctors called to examine husbands proclaimed nothing wrong with them. Some women had suffered brutality for more than 12 years and many were too terrified to rebel. . . . The centre, started by a group of women, has usually 20 to 30 women and children sleeping on mattresses. Women had been referred to it from as far away as Edinburgh.

The Times, 14 June 1973.

5.30 Women's Aid

1. To provide temporary refuge on request for battered women and their children.

2. To encourage these women to determine their own futures and to help them achieve this, whether it involves returning home or starting a new life elsewhere.

3. To recognize and care for the educational and emotional needs of the children involved.

4. To offer support and after-care to any women and children who have left the refuge.

5. To educate and inform the public, the police, the courts, the social services and other authorities with respect to the battering of women, mindful of the fact that this is a result of the general position of women in our society.

National Women's Aid Federation, 1974.

5.31 Grunwick women

For the last eight years since Jayaben Desai came with her family from East Africa to Britain she has been watching the activities of trade unions on television.

'All this time I have been watching the strikes and I realized that the workers are the people who give their blood for the management and that they should have good conditions, good pay and should be well fed. The trade unions are the best thing here – they are not so powerful in other countries.

'They are a nice power and we should keep it on,' said Ms Desai, the most vocal of the fifty or so Asian and West Indian women involved in the eleventh-month Grunwick strike . . .

'This dispute is bringing us so many good things,' said Ms Desai. 'Before the mass picketing began in June the issue was not so clear in our community, it was misty before. But now the Asian community sees what we are fighting for.

'And before, the trade unions in this country were feeling that our community was not interested – that was always a gap in our community. But this will bring the distance nearer. We can all see the result – people coming here from all over the country are seeing us as part of the workers now.'

Being seen at all wasn't automatic, however, for the women who make up 60 per cent of the strikers.

'In our community ladies are always obedient,' Ms Desai explained. 'So some had problems at the start. There was some bad feeling. But men know the women are always obedient, and in his heart a man knows he must not disturb a woman.' . . . But what if a husband lays down the law and blocks his wife's independent decisions, like in a Grunwick situation? The woman must make him understand, she replied. Does that mean persuading him? 'No, not persuade. If she feels capable then she should tell him powerfully?' . . .

Ms Desai's foot was run over by a director's Jaguar, two young Asian women were run down at the factory gate by a scab driver, and in the forty-second week, before the mass picketing and its consequent mass arrests began, Ms Desai was arrested on the picketline . . .

Beatrix Campbell & Valerie Charlton, *Spare Rib* 61, August 1977.

Notes

1 E. P. Thompson, 'The moral economy of the English crowd in the eighteenth century', *Past and Present* (1971), no. 50, pp. 115–16.

2 'Chronicle 1776', in *Annual Register* (1776), pp. 124–5, 137–40, as quoted in G. D. H. Cole & A. W. Filson, *British working-class movements: Select documents, 1789–1875*, London: Macmillan (1967), p. 21.

3 '1795, the year of what may be called the revolt of the housewives': Hammond and Hammond, *Village labourer*, London: Longmans (1948), p. 116. 'Initiators of the [food] riots were, very often, the women': Thompson, 'Moral economy of the English crowd', pp. 115–16.

4 John Bohstedt, 'Gender, household and community politics: Women in English riots, 1790–1810', *Past and Present* (1988), no. 120, pp. 88–122.

5 Robert B. Shoemaker, *Gender in English society, 1650–1850*, London: Arnold (1998), p. 234.

6 Bohstedt, 'Gender, household and community politics', p. 114.

7 As quoted in M. I. Thomis and J. Grimmett, *Women in protest*, London: Croom Helm, p. 107.

8 *The Times*, 22 March 1934.

9 See Chapter 7, 'Sexuality'.

10 See Chapter 6, 'Health'.

11 See Chapter 3, 'Education'.

12 See Chapter 6, 'Health'.
13 See Chapter 4, 'Work'.
14 For a useful summary, see I. Zweiniger-Bargielowska, *Women in twentieth-century Britain*, London: Pearson Education (2001).

6
Health

1967   Family Planning Act: enabled local authorities to provide advisory birth control services.

1974   Free contraception.

Health is one area where class difference is very apparent. Women were held to be 'frail' in view of their reproductive functions and were seen as at the mercy of their menstrual cycle which was considered to have detrimental effects not only on physical, but also mental health. (**6.1, 6.2**) Instability, therefore, could be expected during the pre-menstrual period, the menstruation itself and the menopause. (**6.5**) The effects of the menopause were also described in dispiriting detail. (**6.6**) Furthermore girls were not prepared for the onset of menstruation (**6.3, 6.4**) and this lack of knowledge continued well throughout the twentieth century. One woman I once interviewed who had started her periods in the 1950s had been astonished to find that this was to be a monthly occurrence. Menstruation also imposed restrictions such as not swimming (**6.3**), though by the 1890s cycling was deemed to be possible (**6.7**). Middle-class women could expect to be 'ill' for one week in four, but working-class women had no such luxury.

Added to this, pregnancy and childbirth also brought their own concerns. It would seem therefore that a woman was at risk of madness throughout her adult life and this in turn could be used to deny women basic rights such as that of higher education and the vote as claimed by Sir Almroth Wright (**6.21**), though others such as Sir Victor Horsley disputed it. (**6.22**) Women were defined in relation to their biological role, thus they were potential mothers, actual mothers or retired mothers. Their duty was to ensure the continuation of the race, and their intellect was not suitable for anything else.

Male doctors were viewed as scientific authorities on the female nature and what was considered acceptable behaviour. Even by the beginning of the twentieth century the number of women doctors was very small: it had increased from twenty five in 1881 to four hundred and seventy seven in 1911. Furthermore women doctors were still not considered on a par with men. Their main sphere was seen to be looking after women and children.

Obviously the conditions in which people lived directly affected health. Among the working classes, poverty was widespread.[1] (**6.10, 6.11**) Owenites proposed community as the answer to the depressing conditions in which some families lived. (**6.9**)

As far as the working-class woman was concerned, interest tended to centre firstly on the moral aspects of her health and behaviour, and secondly on the needs of the nation. Working-class women's health suffered not merely through repeated pregnancies (**6.12**) but because of the tradition of always putting the husband (breadwinner) first in terms of nutriment.[2] This was looked on as sensible since if the man did not work, then the entire family would suffer. Inadequate nourishment, however, obviously contributed to general ill health, which was further worsened by sweated and home work. General household duties such as doing the laundry (**6.13**) particularly in mining families often meant backbreaking work – concerns of frailty did not hold good for working-class women. A lack of adequate nourishment also made it difficult for women to breastfeed successfully. In the late nineteenth century there was agitation to protect working-class women with a concentration on married women's work, but again, this was public work. Work in the home, which could be just as heavy was ignored. Sexual health was a concern only as far as it affected men. The Contagious Diseases Acts were designed to safeguard the health of the armed forces and police working-class sexuality. The health of the women involved was seen as only incidental to the health of the client. This gave rise to the Social Purity movement at the end of the nineteenth century.

A constant theme running through the centuries was the lack of proper medical care for women. The working classes could not afford medical care and tended to rely on herbal remedies. The one area where women predominated was midwifery which was seen as women's work (and this continued till the Sex Discrimination Act 1975). A dearth of adequately trained midwives, however, contributed to the deaths of children and mothers. (**6.14**) Medical journals, such as *The Lancet*, regularly reported on the detrimental effects of unqualified midwives (**6.15**), though this butchery was not confined to unqualified women: unqualified men referred to as 'disembowelling accouchers' by the *London Medical Gazette* also committed acts of gross negligence often leading to the death or permanent injury of the mother and child.

Most midwives had no formal training and by the mid-nineteenth century, the tide, if anything, was moving against the training of women. By contrast, the status of the male GP was rising and the medical establishment was beginning to accept obstetrics as a part of medicine. Furthermore other ancillary branches of medicine such as chemists and dentists had their own professional organisations: the Pharmaceutical Society (1852), and the Licence in Dental Surgery (LDS) were recognised by the Royal College of Surgeons in 1859 and therefore were increasing in status. There were no midwife societies, and no journals or books published by midwives on the subject since 1797. Midwives were too few and too weak to band together to further their own interests.

By the late 1870s there was increasing concern over the high rates of maternal mortality in childbirth. Lord Derby in 1875 asked government representatives in Paris, Berlin, Brussels, The Hague, St. Petersburg, Stockholm, Vienna and Washington to secure information on the degree of training that midwives in these countries undertook prior to practising. Only the United States 'shared with England the unenviable distinction of caring nothing for the welfare of the community as regards the education of women'.[3]

Despite the Midwives Act of 1902 which sought to 'secure the better training of midwives and to regulate their practice' by ensuring certification and providing penalties for practising illegally (fine of £5 before 1910, £10 thereafter) by 1915, nearly half of the country's midwives remained untrained (those who had experience had been given a licence to practise) and up to 75 per cent of women were delivered by midwives. Middle-class women since the mid-century had been going to doctors who were allowed to use anaesthesia and instruments. However, this did not necessarily improve maternal health since instruments were often used without antiseptics which could result in puerperal fever. The dreadful effects on women's health occasioned by ignorance, poverty, too many pregnancies and the need to work throughout pregnancy were revealed in letters sent to the Women's Co-operative Guild, published by Margaret Llewlwyn Davies in 1915 and entitled *Maternity*. (**6.10, 6.11**)

Concern for infant health however, remained paramount. The Boer War had revealed the poor physical condition of many recruits. Furthermore, the needs of the State to replace the appalling loss of life in World War I helped to drive improvements through better child welfare. To raise awareness a 'Baby Week' took place in July 1917. This opened with an exhibition at Central Hall, Westminster, and was attended by the Queen. The Bishop of London pointed out that, 'while nine soldiers died every hour in 1915, twelve babies died every hour, so that it was more dangerous to be a baby than a soldier. The loss of life in this war had made every baby's life doubly precious'.[4]

In line with this, the Maternity and Child Welfare Act 1918 set up Welfare clinics, while the Midwives Act 1918 was designed to improve the quality of midwives and therefore the health of children and mothers. Local authorities were to be liable to pay or guarantee a midwife's salary. Continuous updating of knowledge was to take place through inspection by an inspector of midwives once a quarter. Should midwives have to bring in doctors, then local authorities would pay for this in the first instance with patients, where able, reimbursing the cost. As far as training was concerned, midwives had to have six months' training, attend twenty cases and pass a written examination before qualifying. This Act was more successful in that by 1920, 80 per cent of practising midwives were trained and by 1954 this had risen to 97 per cent.

Child welfare was also improved by a rise in the number of full time health visitors (**6.20**) in England and Wales, rising from 600 in 1914 to 1,355 in 1918 and there was a further increase in the number of midwives from 37,000 in 1914 to 43,000 in 1918. Since there was a decline in the birth rate this meant more provision for mothers. Better nutrition also contributed.

The needs of the nation were at the forefront of post-war legislation where the emphasis was on the health of the child rather than the mother. Thus in the inter-war years the mortality of mothers increased while those of children decreased. Dr Janet Campbell, the chief woman advisor to the Board of Education, undertook an investigation into the prevention of maternal mortality. (**6.25, 6.26**) As part of her recommendations, Dr Campbell called for longer training for midwives and the exclusion of the unqualified. (**6.23**) The Final Report of the Departmental Committee on Maternal Mortality and Morbidity (1932) showed that poor health among women before childbirth led to complications in childbirth, many preventable deaths and poor health which continued after the birth and led to increasing claims for sickness and disability benefit. As a result, in 1933 the Women's Health Enquiry Committee was formed from representatives of the Women's Co-operative Guild, the Women's National Liberal Federation, the Standing Joint Committee of Industrial Women's Organisations, midwives, the National Council for Equal Citizenship, Women's Public Health Association, Council of Scientific Management in the Home (National Council of Women) and the North Kensington Women's Welfare Centre, with the aim of investigating the general health of women, especially married working-class women. The initial intention was to gather information also from middle-class women and the unmarried but they did not get sufficient response from these two groups. In the end 1,250 women replied to the survey. This revealed that despite the improvement in infant health due to the Maternity and Child Welfare Act, working-class women often still lived with the effects of multiple pregnancies and miscarriages, a lack of adequate treatment due to the need to pay the doctor, constant ill health (though they tended not to complain) (**6.33, 6.34**) a poor diet and unrelenting toil. There had been marginal improvement since the eighteenth century.

Women's health was not helped by the fact that they did not have the same access to medical professionals as men. Prior to the formation of the National Health Service in 1948, a married woman was only entitled to free medical care if she were pregnant or recently delivered. The 1911 Health Insurance Act covered manual workers and those earning less than £160 per annum, and in return for contributions provided unemployment and sickness benefits, the services of a panel doctor and free medicine, but nothing for the man's dependants other than a maternity grant of £1.50. Furthermore no one was very interested in women's health problems once they had passed the menopause (**6.8**) since they had outlived their reproductive purpose. The main change, however, which would improve women's lives was effective birth control but this was to be a long struggle. Most doctors were against it and when Dr. Arthur Allbutt published in 1886 *The Wife's Handbook* which had a chapter on birth control he was struck off. Both Llewelyn Davies and Spring Rice's investigations had demonstrated the effects of too many pregnancies and there was no doubt that women resorted to back street abortionists. In 1930 birth control was sanctioned for those women whose health would suffer if they had another pregnancy but many working-class husbands did not wish to use birth control. The National Birth Control Council was set up in 1930 and this became the Family Planning Association in 1939, however, by 1937, only 95 out of 423 local authorities had birth control clinics. (**6.36**) The big advance came with the contraceptive pill which was licensed in 1961 and became more popular from the mid 1960s.[5] The law on abortion was not reformed until 1967 (**6.38**) and then after a long and bitter campaign.

By the end of the 1970s there was no doubt that women's health had improved and with the advent of the NHS they had at least achieved equal access to health services. Despite visiting the doctor more often, taking more medicine, and having more care duties, women still outlived men. Women's diseases, however, continued to lead to loss of life and attitudes still have a long way to go before women are seen as not at the mercy of their hormones. Furthermore, black women also had to contend with racism when they attempted to make use of the Health Service. (**6.39**)

6.1 Sexual function and insanity

[Dr Hugh Fenton] said that no one who studied women or who was thrown amongst them and had to observe them could possibly overlook the fact that at certain sexual crises they were liable, with very slight determining causes, to have their mental balance overthrown, as, for instance, at puberty, marriage, maternity, and the menopause. When they bore these facts in mind it was impossible to disassociate mental disorders in the female from her sexual functions. This was certainly the case to a much more marked extent than in the male . . .

'Discussion on sexual function and insanity', *The British Gynaecological Journal*, 6, (1890–91), p. 442.

6.2 Women's ill health

. . . man was created independent because destined to govern the family, society and nature; while woman was made dependent, tied to hearth and home by a long chain of never-ending infirmities, as if to point out the destined sphere where her activity could find more happiness, although a paler glory.

E. J. Tilt, *On the preservation of the health of women at the critical periods of life*, London: John Churchill (1851), pp. 70–1.

6.3 Menstruation

I was for all practical purposes a boy until the awful thing happened. I was twelve [in 1909], still at the Dragon School, unsuspecting. I had little or no pubic hair; my breasts were ungrown and did not in fact develop until my mid-teens. And then there was blood on my blue serge knickers. I was quickly pulled out of school and I never went back. I couldn't quite understand why, only it seemed that it was something about me which was shameful and must above all never be mentioned to a school friend. It had been a complete surprise, because I had not taken in my mother's carefully veiled and no doubt physiologically inaccurate information. The process was not at all well known at that time and there were many superstitions about it and little medical help. . . .

Girls of my age were not allowed to swim at these times, which for me sometimes went on for ten days, and were discouraged from many other activities. Tampax did not come in till I was in my thirties, though at least disposables must have arrived with or soon after World War One.

It was very discouraging and I acquiesced in it, . . . but no doubt resentments and determinations built up inside. . . .

Naomi Mitchison, *All change here: Girlhood and marriage*, London: Bodley Head (1975), pp. 11–12.

6.4 Periods

The girl ought to be warned that some day she will find that she has a discharge or blood, or of bloodstained fluid, from the vagina, and that this discharge may be accompanied by feelings of lassitude and heaviness, by discomfort, and perhaps by pain. She must also be told that the amount and the duration of the discharge are uncertain. In these matters each girl and woman is a law unto herself, and equally good health may be maintained whether the monthly discharge (the *period*, as it is generally called) last three or seven days, and whether the number of sanitary towels used daily during the first few days be two – the least demanded by decency and comfort – or three. The total numbers of diapers or sanitary towels that may been needed varies much, but probably any number under eight may be considered to denote scantiness, and any number over twelve profuseness of the discharge . . .

Mary Scharlieb, *The seven ages of woman: A consideration of the successive phases of woman's life*, London: Cassell & Co. (1915), p. 12.

6.5 Menopause I

But although the tendency to mental disorder prevails to the greatest extent during the period of menstruation, – that is, from the age of fifteen to forty five, – yet it must be acknowledged that the natural cessation of this function is with women a most critical period; and indeed the woman herself is not wholly insensible to the important revolution which menstruation produces in the female economy: hence the emphatical expression, 'the turn of life'. Women dread this period, because hitherto occult or latent diseases now manifest themselves; hence tumours and cancer of the breast, various distressing affections, even cancer of the womb itself, pulmonary diseases, indigestion, dropsy, etc., form but a small proportion of the formidable category of ills to which women become liable, and from they often suffer at this period. . . .

Samuel Mason, *The philosophy of female health*, London: H. Hughes (1845), p. 3.

6.6 Menopause II

When menstruation is about to cease, the period is called critical, 'the change, or turn of life, the climactic period;' and many important changes take place in the constitution at this epoch. All the characters of puberty and the peculiarities of women cease, the breasts collapse in most cases, the fullness of habit disappears, the skin shrivels, and appears too large, and loses its colour and softness, and many diseases develop, occasionally and rarely, in the womb, ovaries, and breasts, which had lain dormant for years. The cheeks and neck wither, the eyes recede in their sockets, and the countenance often becomes yellow, leaden-coloured or florid, and the women become corpulent, and lose the mild peculiarities of their sex. When this period has, however, passed, women often enjoy better prospects of health and of long life than the other sex, and become remarkably corpulent.

Dr Michael Ryan, *A manual of midwifery or compendium of gynaecology and paidonosology*, London: 4th edn (1841), p. 73.

6.7 Cycling

Let it at once be said, an organically sound women can cycle with as much impunity as a man. Thank Heaven, we know now that this is not one more of the sexual problems of the day. Sex has nothing to do with it, beyond the adaptation of machine to dress and dress to machine.

With cycles as now perfected there is nothing in the anatomy or the physiology of a woman to prevent their fully and freely enjoyed within the limits of common sense . . .

W. H. Fenton, 'A medical view of cycling for ladies', *Nineteenth Century*, 39, May 1896, p. 797.

6.8 'A certain age'

There appears to be a lack of skill or knowledge in dealing with certain types of ailments. For instance, the Rotherham woman writes that her doctor says 'all women get back ache around 40, so why worry.' A woman of 43 who has had ten children and three miscarriages (four children have died), has had bad haemorrhage for nine years; this has resulted in a weak heart. The doctor puts it down to a 'certain age', and tells her to rest in bed!

Margery Spring Rice, *Working-class wives*, Harmondsworth: Penguin (1939), p. 45.

6.9 Effects of poverty on health

Marriages resulting from sordid motives, and not from pure affection, must produce an inferior offspring. Under the present evil system of society, it is impossible to bring healthy constitutions. The health of mothers was not attended to during pregnancy – they were allowed to live in damp cellars and an impure atmosphere – infants were brought into the world without the wants of their nature being provided for – influences too exciting for their nervous system produced convulsions and death, their lungs were for the first time developed in an impure and poisonous air, and thus were the seeds of sickness and disease interwoven with our very nature. This could not be the case in Community. The sexes would unite from pure affection; they would be surrounded by good moral influences; the common wants of nature would be provided for under all circumstances;

New Moral World, 16 March, 1844, p. 302.

6.10 'I think a lot'

Oh, for the time when the Maternity Scheme becomes law, and the Divorce Reform. No one will welcome it more than I, for the sake of those who have not got true companionship in life . . . I have only had one child and no miscarriage. Perhaps my husband and myself have taken a different view from most people. . . . we both belong to a large family of brothers and sisters, and both had a drunken father, who did not care for their wife and offspring as much as the beast of the field.

My mother, whom I loved with all my heart, brought fifteen little lives into the world; twelve are still living. I remember many a time she has gone without food before and after confinement, and without fire in winter. I have gone round the house many a time to try and find a few rags to sell for food. I have seen my father strike my mother just before confinement, and known her be up again at four days' end to look after us. . . . my mother had no education, and had been brought up to obey her husband. But, poor dear, she left the cares of this world some years ago now, at the age of fifty-nine. My father has always been in business for himself, and used to have plenty of money, but spent it on himself, and is still living at the age of seventy-four. When I got married to the man I loved, and who loves me, he said I should never suffer as our dear mothers had done, and that we would only have what little lives we could make happy, and give a chance in life. My son will be eighteen years of age in June and is still at Technical College, for which he won a scholarship. I get no grant-in-aid, and my husband is only a working man, so I go out to work for two hours every morning to help to keep him, as he is a good lad . . .

(Wages 26s; one child)

Women's Co-operative Guild, *Maternity: Letters from working-women*, London: Bell & Sons (1915), No. 47, p. 74.

6.11   Ill-effects of working while pregnant

I myself had some very hard times, as I had to go out to work in the mill. I was a weaver, and we had a lot of lifting to do. My first baby was born before its time, from me lifting my piece off the loom on to my shoulder, as two of us had them to lift, and then carry them from the shed across the yard to be weighed. If I had been able to take care of myself I should not have had to suffer as I did for seven weeks before that baby was born and for three months after; and then there was the baby suffering as well, as he was a little weak thing for a long time, and cost pounds that could have been saved had I been able to stay at home and look after myself. But I could not do so, as my husband was short of work and ill at the time. So there was another poorly baby. While I was carrying this one he only worked three months out of the nine. I could not get any support at all then. I had to go out to work again at the month-end, and put the baby out to nurse. I had to get up by four in the morning, and get my baby out of bed, wash and dress it, and then leave home by five, as I had half an hour walk to take my baby to my mother's, and then go to my work and stand all day till half-past five at night, and then the walk home again with my baby. I had to do this with three of them. I think you will understand I have had my share; and all my children have had to be brought with instruments. I have had six living children and one miscarriage. I lost two from injury at birth; and when I had the last, the doctor told me he did not know how I had kept one, the times that I had had, and the way they had to use the baby before birth. And now I am suffering myself, all from not being able to take care of myself during pregnancy. My baby that I lost died from haemorrhage when he was eight days old; then the second, when she was four months old, died from an injury to the spine, both done at birth. I think it would have been a good thing for me if all these reforms had been in force, as I should have both been better in health and saved a lot of suffering to myself and my children.

It was from no fault of my husband that I had to suffer; it was from shortness of work. I know I should have been the best of everything if he had been able to get it for me. He had 28s a week and all holidays off. Then there was out of work, many a time playing for six weeks at a time. (Wages 28s; six children, one miscarriage)

Women's Co-operative Guild, *Maternity: Letters from working-women*: London: Bell & Sons (1915), No. 83, p. 107.

6.12   The effects of multiple pregnancies

The key to the condition of the workman and his family, the reason for the possibilities and impossibilities of his existence, is the capacity, the temperament, and, above all, the health of the woman who manages his house; into her hands, sometimes strong and capable, often weak and uncertain, the future of her husband is committed, the burden of family life is thrust... there are many of the working women who carry that burden, in spite of its enormous weight, with a courage and a competence alike marvellous to the onlooker...

The married woman of the working classes has to fulfil single-handed – often on less food, less health, less strength than her more prosperous sisters – the duties that in the houses of the latter are divided among several people, and even then not always accomplished with success...

It is estimated that of the over 600 children under twelve months who die in one year in Middlesbrough one-third die from preventable causes, mostly improper feeding. The cause of death in many of the cases is given as premature birth, and is accounted for partly by the mother being physically worn out and unfit for child-bearing owing to the short intervals between each birth.

> One woman had 6 children in 8 years.
> One woman had 7 children in 10 years.
> One woman had 9 children in 11 years.
> One woman had 11 children in 14 years.
> One woman had 12 children in 15 years.
> One woman had 15 children in 23 years.
> One woman had 17 children in 23 years.

What chance has the welfare, physical and moral, of the children thus rapidly brought into the world by a mother whose strength, owing to imperfect nourishment and unhealthy surroundings, must be steadily declining under this immense strain as time goes on?... if all these children were well and strong, it would still be a strain on the mother, but it is worse than that.

One woman had had seventeen children and twelve had died; another fourteen, of whom eight had died. One woman had had ten stillborn children, in addition to which four more were born alive . . . It is easy to write these words; it is wellnigh impossible for the ordinary reader to call up the true picture of what they really mean. Women among the well-to-do hardly ever have this terrible experience of having one still born child after another. To be going to bring a child into the world; to be constantly ill before its birth, as must be the case if it dies during this time; to have either the awful suspicion that the hope is over, or else to go on to the end; to go through all the necessary agony, to bear a dead child, to have the shock of realizing what has happened; then in a few months begin over again facing the terrible possibility, which in course of time comes to pass, and live through the whole dread story once more. And even when the children are born alive, what must that other woman have gone through who lost twelve out of her seventeen children? . . .

During the time before the birth of the child, which to the mother in easy circumstances is full of happiness and hope albeit of physical discomfort, the life of the working woman is led with increased difficulty and hardship. The woman who is well-to-do makes her health the first consideration; everything in her life turns upon it, allowances are made for her. She rests as much as she chooses, she can relinquish the duties or the disagreeables of her existence as she pleases. If she is unwise in the ordering of her life at this time, and does things that are undesirable, it is for her own pleasure and by her own wish; no one compels her to do them. But the working woman generally goes on with her daily round of toil until the very last minutes before the child is born; she has no one who can take the burden of her life off her if she is tired, cross, depressed, unwell. The moment of childbirth among the prosperous is surrounded in these days in every direction by extremes of antiseptic precaution to ensure healthy conditions, the absence of infection or of poisoning. Gallons of water boiled for several days previously stand ready for use, the room is spotlessly clean and airy, a well-qualified doctor is ready to be summoned, a trained and experienced nurse is in attendance as well. The mother's sufferings are mitigated by chloroform. After her confinement the whole house turns on her comfort and well-being. If she has older children they are in charge of other people. She is fed with the most nourishing and palatable food, she has a sufficiency of quiet and of sleep, at this moment of the highest importance. Again let us ask, if all these precautions are necessary, or even desirable, what are we to think of the conditions of childbirth in the cottages? In some of these, situated actually in the midst of the works, the ground floor consists of a kitchen, behind the kitchen another room, sometimes kept as a parlour, sometimes used as a bedroom; opening out of the kitchen is a sort of closet, also looking on to the front, in which there is just room for a double bed. The confinement often takes place in this room, unventilated in winter, too hot in summer, because it is next to the kitchen, and with the air charged with all the impurities that the works send forth, constantly blowing in. In houses that have not this extra little room on the ground floor the mother is often lying in the front one that serves as kitchen and living-room, though sometimes happily she is in the back room in comparative privacy.

One woman, who had suffered a great deal when her child was born, was lying, when it was only a few hours old, in one of the tiny rooms described, to which penetrated the sounds and smell from the adjoining works, and her husband who had come in from his work tired out and had thrown himself down to rest before going to change, was lying asleep in his black working clothes on the outside of the bed.

Lady Bell, *At the works, a study of a manufacturing town*, London: Edward Arnold (1907), pp. 171, 198–204.

6.13   The strain of the family wash

... washing is undoubtedly a very great strain on the health of many women. With the best possible appliances the washing day in the small homes of the workers is always a considerable trial. The washing of blankets, sheets, and heavy clothing needs a woman who is muscularly strong, and takes a very large amount of time ... For pregnant mothers there is no greater difficulty than that of the family wash, and often they have to sacrifice a great deal of what they need in the way of nourishment in order to pay for it going out at these times ...

A.D. Sanderson, *The working woman's house*, London: The Swarthmore Press (1919), p. 57.

6.14   Mortality of mothers in childbirth

'In the middle of the 17th century,' he [Dr. Arthur W. Edis] said, 'about one in every 40 or 50 women delivered in London died in childbirth or its consequences; but gradually, as medical science has advanced, that mortality has decreased, till now not above 1 in 150 or 200 die.

In the last annual report of the Registrar-General for the year 1876 we find that no less than 4,142 mothers succumbed during that year to the accidents and diseases incidental to childbirth, not including 1,034 who died after child-bearing from various diseases not referred to childbirth. The mortality of mothers in England, notwithstanding the progress of the obstetrical art, was higher in the two years 1874–75 than it has ever been since 1847. In the 30 years from 1847 to 1876, no less than 106,565 mothers died in childbirth; that is, five to every 1,000 children, one to every 200 children born alive. Well may Dr. William Farr append to his report, 'How long is this sacrifice of lives to go on?' This is a deep, dark and continuous stream of mortality. How can it be accounted for? Bear in mind we are not dealing with the data of some mysterious disease that baffles our art and bids defiance to our efforts to restrain it, but with the records of what should be the performance of a mere physiological function at the period when the powers of life are presumably in full working order, and where in the majority of instances the process is under the supervision of a skilled attendant . . .

'The number of live-born children registered in the United Kingdom in 1876 was 1,155,186, of whom about 173,278 belonged to the middle and upper classes, and 981,908 to the lower classes of society. Assuming that 30 per cent of the mothers registered were attended exclusively by medical men, 687,336 will remain among the lower class to be attended by midwives. Let us inquire for a moment what measures, if any, are adopted for the training or instruction of midwives. The Committee of the Society on Infant Mortality says that, in answer to the question, widely circulated, Are the women instructed in midwifery? answers in the negative have been received from all parts of the country, with the exception of Glasgow and Sheffield. From several districts the replies indicate not merely a want of any special education, but gross ignorance and incompetence, and a complete inability to contend with any difficulty that may occur; and yet the Obstetrical Society of London shows in its valuable report that, in the country villages, from 30 to 90 per cent. of the cases of midwifery are attended by midwives. This society has done good work in directing the attention of Government to the necessity of properly educating women to act as midwives to the lower classes.'

The Times, 5 October 1878.

6.15   Midwives I

I FORWARD to THE LANCET the following specimen of midwives' midwifery, not that I imagine such to be of rare occurrence, or hitherto unnoticed, but because that it is but discharging a duty to society to set on record proofs of the lamentable extent to which life and limb are brought into jeopardy by the culpable rashness of ignorant persons . . .

I was called up at a quarter past eleven, p.m., yesterday to go to a midwife engaged at a labour in the immediate neighbourhood of my residence. I found the patient tossing about on the floor in a state of great excitement, afraid that all was not going on well, and calling aloud for the use of instruments, having been in labour since early in the morning, although the midwife had 'worked like a horse.' On a rapid examination I found the head low down in the pelvis; there being time, I consequently lifted the patient on to the bed, in which proceeding I was resolutely opposed by the midwife, who loudly exclaimed against any interference with 'her case.' She boasted that the 'hand had been down, and that she had turned the child.' On the strength of this feat, and of having been twenty-six years a '*medical woman*,' she was determined not to yield, although the friends had sent for me . . . I then found the head on the perineum, a large mass of the umbilical cord protruding, and the expelling pains strong; there was, as might be expected, no pulsation in the cord. Having ascertained the state of affairs, I asked the 'midwife' her opinion as to the nature of the case. 'The hand had come down, and she had turned the child,' was the reply! I took leave to accuse her of ignorance, and pronounced the child to be dead, in all probability through improper treatment. As the woman stuck resolutely to her post, I left the bedside to remonstrate with the husband, and to insist upon the midwife's leaving, and to send for another practitioner to support me, and witness the proceedings. The midwife hereupon named . . . an unqualified practitioner, as a proper person to be called in . . . In the mean time the child was born, and the midwife, as is the wont of the sisterhood, lost no time in hauling away at the placenta, which, by way of enhancing her own cleverness, she declared to be a 'fixture.' It, however, soon came away, though she worked as hard as she could to make it a difficult matter. The job done, she fell down on her knees and thanked the Lord for his mercy, not forgetting to extol her own share of the merit, that she 'had brought her patient through.' She unconcernedly enough overlooked the fact that there were two patients in the case instead of one, the child was of no importance; and besides she said '*the children were always born dead when the cord came down.*' . . .

... I considered the child might have been dead nine or ten hours. I have seen the patient this morning; she feels assured that the child was alive at twelve, p.m. *The midwife broke the membranes at eleven, p.m.* The patient has passed a bad night, and complains of great pain in the abdomen, which is hardly to be wondered at. Were I to turn to the records of my experience while house-surgeon to the Queen Adelaide's Lying-in Hospital, I could easily cite other cases as appalling as the preceding. This one will serve to show the fearful dangers to which *poor women* are exposed in the critical moment of parturition, when left to the tender mercies of midwives and 'their consulting surgeons,' to wit, such as the unqualified practitioner alluded to. And now, without stopping to comment upon the foregoing case, to prove the homicidal ignorance of the midwife, to show that the child might have been saved, or that the woman's life was perilled, all this being a work of supererogation, I would inquire what is the remedy for so fearful a state of things? Are the lives of the labouring classes to be utterly despised? Is there to be no care for the prevention of manslaughter? ... laws are made for the rich and not for the poor.

It may be argued that medical practitioners could not possibly take charge of all the midwifery of the country. There is no proof of that; but ... if women must be employed, let them have an obstetric education, as in France, let our poor countrywomen have some guarantee that they fall into the hands of respectable and competent persons; let us be assured that these persons shall know the difference between the human hand, and a handful of umbilical cord ...

Robert Barnes, 'Midwives' midwifery', *Lancet* 1, 31 August 1844, pp. 699–700.

6.16 Lack of attention for the poor in childbirth

The frequent inefficiency, or the absolute hurtfulness, of the help rendered to vast numbers of poor women in childbirth has long amounted to a public scandal, and has occasioned a mortality, both maternal and infantile, to which attention has again and again been publicly directed by the coroners of many districts. So long ago as in 1878, a Bill dealing with the subject was introduced into the House of Commons. In 1892, a Select Committee of that House reported that, in their opinion, no woman ought to be allowed to call herself a midwife, or to practice as a midwife, except under suitable regulations. A similar committee reported to the same effect in 1893; and, in 1900, a Bill drafted on the lines of their report passed its second reading by a majority of 90, but reached the report stage too late for enactment. The present Bill . . . was read a second time on the 26th February, was referred to the Standing Committee on Law, and was brought up amended on the 14th March.

The Times, 5 July 1902.

6.17 Midwives II

. . . Is it necessary that we should rest satisfied with returning the work to women of the same class after they have received a minimum of training? The majority of those demanding the services of a midwife are not paupers, but the wives of self-respecting artisans and labourers, who, as has been proved in town and country, are thankful to pay an adequate fee for adequate attendance.

We have among us a large proportion of educated gentlewomen, who are anxious, besides incidentally earning their livelihood, to do work that is worth doing. Midwifery, as yet, has never been set before them as a possible profession, and it is held in contempt by the nurses of our hospitals and infirmaries, on account both of the class and standing of those who practise it, and the limited range of its work.

. . . a general hospital with a maternity annexe should be built in one of those thickly-populated outlying districts of London, which so greatly need those institutions . . . It would be known as a national training school for midwives, and in it educated women would receive an 18 months' course of general and monthly nursing, prior to a six months' course of midwifery in hospital and district.

The Times, 17 March 1903.

6.18 Rural Midwives' Association

By the time the Act came into force in 1905 there would, no doubt, be a good supply of candidates qualified and ready to take up work where there was plenty to do, but the rural districts might present some difficulty. It would not be an easy matter all at once to find the right class of women – those who, while sufficiently educated, would yet be humble enough to take the place of the friendly neighbour and give a little assistance in the ordinary household duties of the cottage. The legislation passed was entirely in the interests of the labouring classes, for in present conditions thousands of lives were lost annually from avoidable causes . . . Sir Michael Foster M.P. . . . said that the rural midwives should be so trained as to know when danger was ahead. Beyond this the training need not go. There was a practical danger lest the midwife, when too highly trained, should, through over self-confidence, take upon herself the work which could only be safely accomplished by a qualified practitioner. Her training should be neither too long nor too expensive.

The Times, 17 June, 1903.

6.19   Training and supply of midwives

Surely, Sir, we are justified in pleading that the life and health of thousands of working-class mothers and infants are of vital importance to the nation, and that some of the 'physical degeneracy' of which we hear so much is due to the ruined health of so many of these mothers owing to unskilled attendance in childbirth.

A woman with impaired vitality cannot bear healthy children, nor can a mother whose life since the birth of her first child has been a daily struggle against weariness and pain have strength to bring up a happy or a healthy family; yet the cases in the women's wards in hospitals and the common experience of workers among the poor prove only too clearly that this is the piteous state of things in thousands of homes.

. . . a great problem now faces us in the difficulty of meeting the cost of such training.

Midwifery among the poor is of necessity badly paid; those who practise it are as a rule women of the same class as their patients, and it is impossible to expect that any large number will be able to afford even the *minimum* outlay of £20 to fit themselves for an employment so uncertain and so unremunerative.

Eventually it is to be hoped that the necessary funds may come out of public money available for technical education; but in the meantime help must be given, and largely and speedily, to enable suitable women to take up this work and to fill the gaps already being created by the retirement in every county of great numbers of those who have hitherto practised freely, but who are unwilling to face the light that will in future be thrown upon their methods.

The Times, 31 October 1904.

6.20 Women health officers

The changed attitude towards women public health officers was commented upon by Miss A. Sayle, chairman of the Women Public Health Officers' Association ... In 1910 and earlier, she said, home visits were not infrequently resented, especially where the need for health teaching was greatest – mothers who had 'had 10 and buried nine,' felt strongly that a young, unmarried health visitor could have nothing to teach her about babies. It was because those mothers, their daughters, their friends, and their neighbours had since learnt the value to their children of the practical advice given, both at home and at welfare centres and clinics, that the door was now open wide, even on washing day.

The Times, 21 November 1932.

6.21 Women's health and suitability for politics

For man the physiology and psychology of woman is full of difficulties. He is not a little mystified when he encounters in her periodically recurring phases of hypersensitiveness, unreasonableness, and loss of the sense of proportion. He is frankly perplexed when confronted with a complete alteration of character in a woman who is child-bearing. When he is a witness of the 'tendency of woman to morally warp when nervously ill', and of the terrible physical havoc which the pangs of disappointed love may work, he is appalled. And it leaves on his mind an eerie feeling when he sees serious and long-continued mental disorders developing in connection with the approaching extinction of a woman's reproductive capacity ...

... The woman of the world will even gaily assure you that 'of course half the women in London have to be shut up when they come to the

213

change of life'. . . . No doctor can ever lose sight of the fact that the mind of woman is always threatened with danger from the reverberations of her physical emergencies . . .

Sir A. Wright, *The Times*, 28 March 1912.

6.22   Reply by Sir Victor Horsley

Sir, – Viscount Helmsley in the House of Commons said of Sir A. Wright's letter to you of the 28th March that to him it was 'extraordinary able and interesting.' Surely in this respect Viscount Helmsley occupies a somewhat singular position for everyone I meet agrees with me that Sir A. Wright's statements are most repulsive in the debased picture they present of woman in her relation to man. Since Sir A. Wright has been freely referred to as specially representing a medical view of women's suffrage, I, as a medical practitioner, would be glad if you would allow me to show that the recital of a few facts destroys the fabric of Sir A. Wright's attack.

To the majority of his colleagues who know his views, his perverted ideas of the relations of the two sexes will come as no surprise, but the public need to be warned against the assertions he makes concerning the physical constitution of women, assertions which he boldly advances as if they were physiologically and neurologically true.

We may summarily dismiss his first accusation against women – namely, that before 50 years of age they fail with 'serious and long con-tinued mental disorders,' for we are well aware that our women folk of that age are sane. Indeed Sir Almroth Wright so completely forgets his duty to science that he actually quotes as evidence against the mental physique of women the vulgar words of a woman of the smart set. As regards his next paragraph, on what he calls the 'incomplete woman,' few, if any, of my colleagues will have read it without disgust. Certainly all those who have worked for years in the mixed committees or in the Met-ropolitan Branch Council of the British Medical Association will join in protesting against Sir A. Wright's suggestion that 'when a medical man asks that he should not be the yokefellow of a medical woman' it is because such co-operation can only be obtained 'at the price of continual constraint' on the part of the man.

As Mr McCurdy truly said in the House of Commons every one of us regards the letter as an insult to women, but in this paragraph Sir A. Wright has also insulted his profession and his sex. In truth his statements and allegations are essentially pornographic, for to medical practitioners in consultation, 'modesties and reticencies' have no existence save to a prurient mind. The women medical practitioners have shown the world what is real modesty, and have always stood for a single code of moral conduct which should ennoble the lives of men and women alike.

Sir Almroth Wright complains that the 'incomplete women' wish to convert the world into an 'epicene institution in which men and women shall everywhere work side by side at the selfsame tasks and for the self-same pay.' Why does he attribute to women alone this aspiration for common justice and social reform? The equality of the sexes in work, and the equality of their pay for the selfsame work, is the fundamental principle of his own profession. In the opinion of the British Medical Association (the men members of which outnumber the women by about 60 to 1) the world is an institution in which women are human beings as much as men are, in which they have precisely the same right to work for their living and precisely the same claim to be justly paid for what they do.

... His crowning argument on the work question is his astounding proposition that although a man and a woman do precisely the same amount of work, the man should, all the same, be paid more because he will probably be less tired at the end of the day. In other words, he is to be paid for nothing. Surely this 'argument' of Sir Almroth Wright is notably more 'fatuous' than the opinion of the British Medical Association that equal work deserves equal wage.

Yours faithfully,
VICTOR HORSLEY.

The Times, 1 April 1912.

6.23   Midwives – need of a higher standard

Suggestions in regard to midwifery training and practice..: –

1. There should be an extension of the training for unqualified women from six months to twelve months, and for trained nurses from four months to six. The examination for the certificate of the Central Midwives Board should be taken at the end of this period.

2. The curriculum should be revised and reconstructed ... *(a)* to include clinical and theoretical instruction in the management of labour, both in maternity wards and on the 'district'; and *(b)* to provide that adequate attention is devoted to such matters as maternity nursing, anti-natal care, breast feeding, the care of the newborn infant, the nursing of puerperal fever, opthalmia, neonatorum, etc.

3. Midwifery training schools, whether under the Poor Law or otherwise, should be graded in accordance with the facilities they are able to offer for a complete or partial training...

4. Careful consideration should be given to the establishment of a 'teacher's' certificate in midwifery for midwives desiring to occupy responsible educational positions. The certificate... would ensure that those midwives who possessed it had actually practised as midwives for a specified period, that they had not only received suitable instruction in the theory and practice of their profession, but understood the relation of midwifery to the public health service and the social circumstances of the patients, and that they were themselves competent to teach students.

The Times, 11 September 1923.

6.24 The unmarried mother and her child

Mrs H.A.L. Fisher said the council had originally come into existence owing to many of those who, like herself, were engaged in infant and child welfare work realizing how high was the death-rate and damage-rate of illegitimate children, due to the many handicaps which they had over and above those suffered by ordinary babies. They found it was impossible to help the child without helping the mother, which brought them up against the 'unco'guid,' who thought such help was condoning immorality, and the unduly sentimental, who imagined every unmarried mother an angel to whom a wrong had been done. They endeavoured to bring common sense to bear on the matter, and had done something by linking up the many organizations in this country dealing with the problem, and they had dealt with 800 or 900 individual cases every year.

The Times, 10 July 1924.

6.25 Maternal mortality I

Sir, – Three thousand mothers die every year in Great Britain when their babies are born. So we are told by Sir George Newman and Dr Janet

Campbell in the pamphlet issued by the Ministry of Health in 1924 and entitled 'Maternal Mortality'. In this pamphlet they state that the general death rate has been reduced during the last 20 years by one-third, but that the maternal mortality rate has hardly altered during that period . . . that *avoidable* maternal deaths are a matter of everyday occurrence, and that responsibility can be assigned primarily to the adequacy *or otherwise* of the professional attendance during pregnancy and at the time of birth.

That is to say, that, except in those cases where the baby was an only child, and fortunate enough to die with its mother, there are 3,000 families of tiny helpless children left every year without their natural protector, and that, had England cared enough, most of these tragedies might have been averted.

The Council for the Promotion of the Higher Training of Midwives, as well as some other people who feel deeply on the subject, have been working to improve one branch of this professional attendance for just this period of 20 years. In consequence of their efforts the British Hospital for Mothers and Babies has been called into existence, the object of its foundation being expressed in its sub-title, the 'National Training School for District Midwives.'

The Times, 18 March 1925.

6.26 Maternal Mortality II

. . . the position it [the final report of the Departmental Committee on Maternal Mortality] showed was that half of the deaths investigated ought and could have been saved. They needed better education of medical students in obstetrics, more effective supervision of pregnancy, more effective midwifery for every mother in childbirth, and the co-ordination of maternity services. It was intended to secure their fulfilment, not by novel and costly administration schemes, but by using and developing the vast machinery which was already in being for securing those ends . . . The system was not yet complete or perfect, but there could be no question that the public facilities provided for women in childbirth were vastly better than those which existed at no distant time previously. The young women of the country had to be educated. They must grow healthy girls and young women and enlightened mothers. (A voice: 'And fathers.') He [Sir Hilton Young] accepted that home thrust and apologised for not

rounding the picture. (Laughter.) He realized how much the fathers of the
nation needed enlightening.

The Times, 16 November 1932.

6.27 Housework for young people

He [Sir Arnold Wilson M.P.] would like to see in the upper-middle and
middle class girls who would be willing once in a way, instead of talking
about things, to sit down for a fortnight and learn how to look after two
children and one man and how to cook and wash and do all the other
things which, in his experience, not a single secondary school in England
taught them the beginning of how to do. He deplored the fat-headed
incompetence of a very large number of young well-to-do people, male
and female, who, having had a most expensive education, were the most
helpless members of the community. They could not even boil an egg or
make a stitch, and yet they were to be seen on a public platform laying
down the law on what was good for the working class.

The Times, 30 December 1936.

6.28 The man in the home

Up to the present, he [Dr James Fenton, medical officer of health for
Kensington] said, health workers had been concentrating on the education of mothers in mothercraft. The father, who was a factor they could
not afford to ignore, was apt to be forgotten. Some thought that to teach
fathercraft was to make men effeminate, weak, and uninteresting sort of
fellows. Women wanted a strong, manly man, but they wanted a man to
have an understanding of women's problems sufficient to make them sympathize with them when necessary. The man must be taught that his wages
were no more his than they were his wife's. He had no more right to keep
10s. a week for pocket money than she had. The balance left over when
all essentials had been paid for should be equally divided between the man
and the woman. (Cheers)

Another lesson they must teach was that a man's work was no more laborious than that of a woman, and it was probably much less monotonous. He was no more entitled to a spare evening than his wife was. It was the duty of working-class fathers to look after the children in the home while the mother went out shopping or out for an evening. A free evening in the week made a woman a hundred per cent better wife and mother. (Laughter) Fathercraft made men more manly, stronger, firmer and better husbands. In no sense did it make them effeminate. Good fathers were not born, but made – and made by themselves.

Dr. Fenton said that many marriages were wrecked by the little things in life which mounted up and up until the crash came, with disastrous effects for the parents and the children. Husbands must be taught that dinners had a habit of going all wrong just when a wife wanted them to go all right. The last thing a man should say in these circumstances was, 'I shall never forget my mother's pastry!' (Laughter) It would be more to the point if he suggested that his wife should take lessons in cookery. There she would meet other young brides and be able to talk over their common problems. If a wife wanted silk stockings it was no good saying that woollen stockings would last twice as long. It was futile to try to reason with a woman on a matter of clothing. No man could possibly convince her that what she wanted was not the best thing for her to have.

The Times, 30 December 1932.

6.29   Maternity benefit

Sir, – Clause 34 of the National Insurance Bill states: – 'Where a woman who, having before marriage been an insured person, marries and is supported by her husband, she shall, unless she continues to be employed within the meaning of this part of this Act, be suspended from receiving any benefits under this part of the Act until the death of her husband.' The maternity benefit, it is stated in Clause 16, 'shall be treated as a benefit for her husband.' In the event of any serious illness subsequent to her confinement no sickness disablement or medical benefits are available.

These enactments appear, by penalizing unemployed – i.e. unpaid – married women who up to the time of marriage have paid their contributions under the Bill, to be a strong encouragement to them to continue in paid employment after marriage, a condition which is known by wide experience to be undesirable in the interests of the children. The employed married woman and the unmarried woman who are insured persons and entitled to maternity benefit are eligible for sickness disablement and medical benefits at a period beginning not less than four weeks after confinement. I quite see that Mr Lloyd George, knowing of the greater mortality amongst the children of employed married women and unmarried women, and desirous of doing something to prevent infant mortality, has made the benefits to mothers in paid employment and to the unmarried mothers greater than to the married mothers whose arduous home work is unpaid. My sympathy with the unmarried mother is great, for I know from experience how often she is an exploited and inexperienced girl; but I do strongly protest against a 'national' Bill which encourages married mothers to remain in paid employment and offers greater benefits to them and to unmarried mothers than it does to the wife of the working man who does his best to provide a home for his wife.

Yours truly,
MAY THORNE

The Times, 14 July 1911.

6.30   Maternity benefits

The committee of the Women's Co-operative Guild has sent to the local insurance committees and to approved societies a circular relating to the administration of maternity benefits.

The Act states that this benefit shall be given in 'cash or otherwise', and the committee urge that these alternatives should not be used to differentiate between individuals and classes of persons, nor lead to inquiries into character. If it were left to any committee or official to decide whether in individual cases the benefit should be given in 'cash or otherwise', any person receiving the benefit in kind, they say, would be publicly exposed as unfit to handle a sum of 30s. The committee also express the hope that no differentiation will be made between married and unmarried mothers in the administration of the benefit. They deprecate the giving of the benefit in vouchers or tickets for goods as being connected with the idea of charity or relief, whereas the fund is largely provided by the persons concerned. Should the direct payment of doctor or midwife out of the grant be decided upon, the amount allocated for that purpose, the committee consider, should not exceed the present minimum medical fee in any district, and should always leave a substantial sum to be given in cash.

They hope that any other form of allocation would only be made at the request of the woman herself, who might specify whether she would prefer allocation to a maternity home, milk from a municipal depot, nursing, help in the home, or some other purpose. A certain amount of cash to be spent by the mother herself on immediate home requirements will always be necessary, and the present 30s benefit, it is suggested, is not too much for this purpose, but constructive State-aided schemes for improving the conditions of maternity are also recommended. The committee therefore suggest that the action of health committees as regards milk depots, baby clinics and health visitors should be made known among insured persons and that insurance committees should use every means to co-operate with and help forward municipal efforts.

The Times, 4 October 1912.

6.31   Effects of pregnancy on health

At the commencement of all my pregnancies I suffered terribly from toothache, and for this reason I think all married child-bearing women should have their teeth attended to, for days and nights of suffering of this kind must have a bad effect on both the mother and child. I also at times suffered torments from cramp in the legs and vomiting, particularly during the first three months. I hardly think the cramp can be avoided but if prospective mothers would consult their doctors about the inability to retain food, I fancy that might be remedied. At the commencement of my second pregnancy I was very ill indeed. I could retain no food, not even water, and I was constipated for thirteen days, and I suffered from jaundice. This had its effect on the baby, for he was quite yellow at birth, and the midwife having lodgers to attend to, left him unwashed for an hour after birth. She never troubled to get his lung inflated, and he was two days without crying. I had no doctor. I was awfully poor, so that I had to wash the baby's clothes in my bedroom at the fortnight's end; but had I had any knowledge like I possess now, I should have insisted at the very least on the woman seeing my child's lungs were properly filled. When we are poor, though, we cannot say what must be done; we have to suffer and keep quiet. The boy was always weakly, and could not walk when my third baby was born. He had fits from twelve to fourteen, but except for a rather 'loose' frame, seems otherwise quite healthy now.

Maternity: Letters from working-women, No. 11, p. 31.

6.32   Day nurseries

... through insufficient attention given to babies in the first two or three years of their lives, thousands reach school age suffering from some often preventable disease or defect ...

One reason for this very serious state of affairs is obvious. In a large number of factory areas married women are the economic mainstay of their homes, either because the husband is unemployed, because his wages are too small to maintain his family, or because he does not give the wife enough money week by week. To enable herself to go out to work, the woman puts her child or children in the care of a 'minder,' usually some elderly woman who agrees to take a number of children for so much a day. Even when the 'minder' is well disposed towards the children – though this is not always the case by any means – the babies often receive unsuitable or insufficient food, no regular periods of rest, and are left to play in dirty backyards or on the floor.

The remedy for this state of affairs is the day nursery, where children of working mothers can spend the whole day in clean, airy, happy surroundings under the supervision of a fully trained matron and her staff. At present there are just over 100 of these nurseries in England, and there is absolutely no comparison between the children who attend them and the thousands of other children who are put out to be minded. Yet this number of nurseries is a mere drop in the ocean. The demand for nurseries is such that every town of any size could make full use of three or four ...

If we are to raise up a healthy generation from our working class mothers all over the country, the need for providing a large number of new day nurseries is both urgent and vital.

The Times, 3 August 1939.

6.33   'One room and a kitchen'

... Mrs. MacN. of Glasgow, lives in one room and kitchen. She says it has no drawbacks. 'I take everything as it comes, and the only difficulty is when the baby is restless.' Her husband is an unemployed carter and she gets £2 unemployment money and 10/- from one boy (aged 16) who is working. Out of this £2 10s. 0d. she pays 9/- rent. She is 37 and has had 14 pregnancies, which include four children who have died and two miscarriages; there are therefore eight living children; five boys and two girls living at home; the eldest girl of 18 is married and 'living in her own home'. She is 'never ill unless with children, and that passed off comfortably'. She gets up at 6 and goes to bed at 10. Her leisure consists of '15 minutes round the block with baby till he goes to sleep; 15 minutes for messages at 2p.m. Club gymnasium on Tuesdays, 45 minutes, and sewing class on Thursday, one hour or so' . . . The visitor who saw her says 'This woman has absolutely no complaints about accommodation, health or lack of funds. She plans her time very methodically and manages to feed herself and her family sufficiently well to maintain health.' The Scots are truly a wonderful people.

Margery Spring Rice, *Working-class wives*, Harmondsworth: Penguin (1939), p. 34.

6.34   Lack of leisure

'I believe myself that one of the biggest difficulties our mothers have is our husbands do not realise we ever need any leisure time. My life for many years consisted of being penned in a kitchen 9 feet square, every fourteen months a baby, as I had five babies in five years at first until what with the struggle to live and no leisure I used to feel that I was just a machine, until I had my first breakdown, and as dark as it was and as hard as it was it gave me the freedom and the privilege of having an hour's fresh air. . . . So many of our men think we should not go out until the children are grown up. We don't want to be neglecting the home but we do feel we like a little look around the shops, or if we go to the Clinic we can just have a few minutes. . . . It isn't the men are unkind. It is the old idea that we should always be at home.'

Margery Spring Rice, *Working-class wives*, Harmondsworth: Penguin (1939), p. 95.

6.35 Abortion

Offences Against The Person Act: August 6, 1861

58. Administering Drugs or Using Instruments to procure Abortion
Every woman being with child, who with intent to procure her own Miscarriage, shall unlawfully administer to herself any Poison or other noxious thing, or shall unlawfully use any Instrument or other means whatsoever with the like intent, and whosoever, with intent to procure the Miscarriage of any woman, whether she be or be not with child, shall unlawfully administer to her or cause to be taken by her any Poison or other noxious thing, or shall unlawfully use any Instrument or other means whatsoever with the like intent, shall be guilty of Felony, and being convicted thereof shall be liable, at the discretion of the Court, to be kept in Penal Servitude for life or for any term not less than three years, – or to be imprisoned for any term not exceeding two years, with or without Hard Labour, and with or without Solitary Confinement.

59. Procuring Drugs, etc., to cause Abortion
Whosoever shall unlawfully supply or procure any Poison or other noxious thing, or any Instrument or thing whatsoever, knowing that the same is intended to be unlawfully used or employed with Intent to procure the Miscarriage of any Woman, whether she be or be not with child, shall be guilty of a Misdemeanor, and being convicted thereof shall be liable, at the Discretion of the Court, to be kept in Penal Servitude for the term of three years, or to be imprisoned for any term not exceeding two years, with or without Hard Labour.

6.36 Birth control

... A few women in London, Rotherham and Devon speak of having been to Birth Control Clinics, but there are dozens of women in obvious need of such advice either for procuring proper intervals between births, or to have no more children, who, although they have been told by their doctor that it is necessary, are not instructed by him in scientific methods and do not go to a Birth Control Clinic, even if there is one in reach ... Birmingham for instance many of these cases occur ... Mrs. H. is 35 and has had eight children (one of whom died). She has bad varicose veins, which she puts down to repeated pregnancies, and anaemia, which has become acute in the last four years, due 'mostly to poverty and malnutrition'. For this she gets 'an occasional iron tonic from the family Doctor'. He has also advised her to 'eat more fruit and vegetables and to have less children'. This advice at the best seems a little belated! . . . Birmingham has several Birth Control Clinics.

Margery Spring Rice, *Working-class wives*, Harmondsworth: Penguin (1939), Virago (1981), ed., pp. 44–5.

6.37   Back street abortion

. . . this was in 1958, when I had a young doctor who was quite good. He gave me some tablets and said, 'If you're not pregnant this will bring on your period.' I took them. Nothing happened. I went back and he said, 'Well, it's obvious that you are pregnant. There's nothing I can do, but there are one or two people around . . .'

. . . He mentioned somebody's name. . . . I'd heard she used knitting needles. 'No, she doesn't,' the doctor said, 'that just gossip. She uses a syringe and she's quite good. Once it happens, once it comes off, you can tell me and I'll come in. I don't mind cleaning up, you know.'

You went to the woman he suggested?

Agnes: Yes. No one knew I was going. If anything had gone wrong she could have just dumped me and nobody would have known. She was about seventy years old. She had all these Catholic pictures on the walls; big old-fashioned pictures of Our Lord with the lamb and the crook, pictures of the Lady of Lourdes, and rosaries and palm crosses draped everywhere.

She said, 'Well, it's expensive dear.' So I said, 'Look, all I've got is £30.' 'All right,' she said, 'I'll do it.' Later I discovered that she did it for other people for £5.

Her house was none too clean and a bit musty smelling. You sat in a funny, dirty-looking armchair and put your leg over the arm so that she could get into your vagina with the syringe.

Afterwards I waited twelve hours (it comes off within twelve to twenty-four hours after being syringed) but nothing happened. Altogether I went back to her about seven times.

How pregnant were you?

Agnes: Oh, I ended up about three and half months pregnant. I knew she wasn't really trying so I finally said 'Look, if you can possibly try and do it I'll see you all right again. I haven't got any money but I'll get some by the end of the week.' Then, as I walked home, so this soapy water started to come away from me. This has never happened before so I thought, well, at least it's penetrated the womb. Before it has just acted like a douche.

Anyway, the next day I woke up with a slight show. I went to work and started to feel a bit queasy. I came home and it came off that night. I didn't have as much pain with that one as I did with the one when I was six and a half weeks pregnant, funnily enough. I had pain for only about two or three hours before the thing came away. Then I thought, well I'll go to bed, but I was frightened to lie down because I felt I'd die if I did. So I propped myself up all night and with the slightest movement of my body I felt all this blood coming away from me. It was, you know, quite frightening.

Spare Rib 50 (1976).

6.38 Abortion law

The Bill [The Medical Termination of Pregnancy] set out for the first time firm grounds on which it might be lawful for a termination of pregnancy to be carried out. It also introduced safeguards.

I have with me (he [David Steel] (Roxburgh, Selkirk and Peebles, L. said) a seven-week old embryo. Members who know little of the subject should have a look at this. It is only half an inch long. To talk of this in terms of crying, wriggling, or anything like that is quite misleading and overemotionalizing. This is what we are weighing against the life and welfare of the mother and her family.

The main case for the Bill rested on the ground that it was hoped the scourge of criminal abortion would be substantially removed, though he did not say it would be entirely wiped out.

Even before the Bill had been passed there had been a change of climate and practice. He had been told by gynaecologists that more patients were being seen by general practitioners, and more were being referred to specialists.

. . . Mr Peter Mahon (Preston, South, Lab.) said that the choice in the debate was between life sanctified by God or legalized infanticide.

The Bill would be a ticket for the 80 per cent abortion seekers, the married women whose supreme concern was the strain that an additional birth would impose. If they were determined enough they would find grounds for abortion as often as they wished. An intolerable strain would be placed on the conscience of many doctors.

The Times, 15 July 1967.

6.39   Racism in the Health Service

In the case of Black women, however, the extent of racism and the degree of tension to which it gives rise is not only based on 'feelings' about the racist attitudes of some health workers. In the course of my research I have come across many instances which suggest ill-treatment of Black women in the National Health Service.

For example, a Muslim woman was left in a hospital for two days without food. The ward staff knew she was not eating hospital food but assumed that relatives were bringing her own religiously acceptable food. But nobody actually checked if this was the case. As it happened, her husband was at sea and she had no visitors for those two days in hospital, and nobody told her that she could ask for Muslim food.

In another instance a pregnant woman who was diabetic was admitted for stabilisation with insulin. But she did not like hospital food and therefore requested her husband to bring her food from home. The nursing staff, however, would not let her eat her own food because it was not 'a diabetic diet', but they continued giving her insulin. For two days she lived on crackers and bread and when the dietician was informed it took her three days to find an interpreter which in all meant five days without proper food. All it needed was to substitute hospital food with the food that the patient preferred to eat. In any case the very process of stabilisation should be based on the food that the patient is given to live on after leaving the hospital.

In the above examples the temptation is to explain the experience of these women as arising from cultural differences in food and in language. What must be stressed here is that cultural differences in themselves are not the real problem. The problem arises when white culture is imposed on other groups, and the groups' own cultures are treated as deviant or even bizarre. It is the response by those in power to the difference in culture that is crucial in the experience of some Black women. It would be misleading, however, to see even this racist response to cultural differences as determining the overall experience of Black women in the National Health Service. Many Black women are British-born and their experiences cannot be explained in terms of cultural differences.

Spare Rib 138, January 1984.

Notes

1 For further examples, see Chapter 2, 'Marriage'.
2 See Chapter 2, 'Marriage'.
3 *The Times*, 5 October 1878.
4 *Daily Telegraph,* 12 July 1917, quoted in J. M. Winter, 'The impact of the First World War on civilian health in Britain', *Econ, H.R.,* 30, 3 (1977), p. 498.
5 See Chapter 7, 'Sexuality'.

7

Sexuality

Timeline

1826 Richard Carlile, *Every Woman's book or What is love?*
1864 Contagious Diseases Act.
1866 Contagious Diseases Act.
1869 Contagious Diseases Act.
1885 Criminal Law Amendment Act: age of consent raised to sixteen.
1886 Repeal of the Contagious Diseases Act.
1898 Living on the earnings of a prostitute an offence.
1912 Criminal Law Amendment Act: brothel owners subject to £100 fine or twelve months' jail.
1918 Marie Stopes, *Married Love.*
1918 Marie Stopes, *Wise Parenthood.*
1921 First birth control clinic.
1928 Radclyffe Hall published *The Well of Loneliness*, about a lesbian relationship. Within weeks, the book is declared obscene and withdrawn from sale.
1960 Penguin Books prosecuted for publishing D. H. Lawrence's *Lady Chatterley's Lover.* Not guilty verdict.
1961 Contraceptive pill introduced
1967 Abortion Act.
1968 Pope Paul VI condemns artificial contraception.
1974 Free contraception available on National Health Service.
1975 English Prostitutes Collective founded.

As previous chapters have demonstrated, women were expected to be modest, reserved, passive and chaste, though there were some like Richard Carlile who advocated the benefits of sexual intercourse. (**7.1**) Women's sexuality generally was seen as problematic: women were either Madonnas or whores and this coloured attitudes and policies towards prostitution. While there was some understanding that poverty could be a reason why women turned to prostitution (7.2) the main inclination was to blame women for leading men astray. (7.3) Prostitution was the seamy side of Victorian respectability and while large numbers of men indulged in it, there was also the fear that it was undermining the health of the nation and particularly the fighting forces. With this in mind, a Royal Commission was set up to investigate the health of the armed forces after the Crimean War (1854–6). This revealed high rates of VD in the Army: 394 per 1,000 were hospitalised for these conditions – seven times as many as in the Navy. As a result, the Contagious Diseases Acts of 1864, 1866 and 1869 were passed. These were designed to protect the health of the armed forces – women were seen as the problem. Women in garrison towns and ports were to be subjected to compulsory physical examinations if suspected of being a common prostitute and if found to be diseased had to spend six or nine months incarcerated in a 'lock' hospital, till they were deemed 'cured'. Since there was no real cure at this time, and men were not subject to treatment, it simply meant that prostitutes were returned to infect more men. There was no concern about the health of the prostitutes: no inspection was to take place of the clients.

The nature of the whole process (7.6) horrified many. The examination by a speculum was considered 'instrumental rape', while the effect of legislation to preserve men's health by putting restrictions on women, meant that the Acts came to be seen as a symbol of female oppression. Women were being imprisoned for medical reasons. This was at the forefront of women's campaigns against the Contagious Diseases Acts led by Josephine Butler and the Ladies National Association. (7.4) The campaign focused on the double standard of morality (7.5) and the effects this had on all working-class women, not just prostitutes. Innocent women could be stigmatised as common prostitutes simply by being seen talking to a soldier. The effects of these Acts were to ensure that the prostitute could not dip in and out of the profession as had often happened previously when times were bad.

For middle-class women to campaign on such an issue required much courage. (7.4) Standing up in public was difficult enough but discussing such an intimate topic was breaking all the taboos.

Furthermore, Butler had no hesitation in displaying the speculum used in internal examinations. As a result largely of women's efforts, the Acts were suspended in 1883 and repealed in 1886. A by-product of this campaign was the increasing interest in prostitution. The 'Social Purity Movement' (named so by its opponents) initially concerned with repealing Contagious Diseases Acts, emphasised the effects on women of infection by their husbands. (7.18) This was responsible for much of women's 'problems'. They argued for a common single higher moral standard. The Social Purity Movement consisted of many organisations such as the National Vigilance Society, the Alliance of Honour, the Moral Reform Union and the White Cross League. It also campaigned for a raising of the age of consent (thirteen since 1875). In 1885 the Criminal Law Amendment Act set the age at sixteen. Feminists emphasised that men were responsible for prostitution, therefore the answer was chastity in men, not regulation of prostitutes. Similarly they pointed out that women were often accosted on public transport and the streets but men were never prosecuted for this. The militant suffragette, Christabel Pankhurst, argued in *The Great Scourge and How to End it* (1913) for a political solution: 'chastity for men, guaranteed and confirmed by the greater independence which the Vote will give to women'. Prostitution would only be abolished once the sexes enjoyed economic and political equality though other feminists such as Teresa Billington Grieg did not like her emphasis on men's 'bestiality'.

In the third quarter of the nineteenth century, the movement that was later to be known as 'Sexology' developed. Sexologists classed the characteristics of the new woman – particularly her independence – as those of the lesbian. (7.14) They were concerned about frigidity (7.11) in women and some such as Ellis believed that women even cried rape to cover up their own sexuality. (7.9) Spinsters were viewed as dangerous since they were not in a subordinate position because they were not under the control of a man. Spinsters were also seen as important in the women's movement since as a result of women's growing economic position they could, in contrast to their situation in the eighteenth century, survive without marriage. (7.12) Edward Carpenter stated that both household drudgery and the fact that women were men's property suppressed women's sexual feelings. Feminist historians such as Jeffreys and Jackson, however, are critical of sexology for what they see as its work in reinforcing tradition male views of sexuality and undermining feminist campaigns to deal with male abuse of women and children.[1] Jackson argued that,

> 'the art of love' was a strategy for teaching women to accept male violence as inevitable, male sexual demands as normal, to experience submission as pleasure, to 'consent' to conquest – in other words to 'enjoy' precisely that form of male sexuality and heterosexual sex which feminists had struggled long and hard to challenge… While it appeared to offer sexual liberation to women, in effect it offered to men a means of reconstituting male power and the structure of hetero-relations.[2]

This co-existed with the Women's Movement since it contributed to the debate on the nature of the 'Woman Question'. Feminists began to discuss sexological topics. At the 'Men and Women's Club' founded by Karl Pearson in 1885, questions of the nature of sexual, romantic and passionate relationships were debated, though the topics were always set by Pearson and other men. Similar discussions took place in the new Socialist societies where the ideology of sex and gender was of interest given that Socialism was to cover transformation of all aspects of life.

Prominent among such groups was F. W. Stella Browne (a Canadian socialist and feminist) who in *The Freewoman* boldly asserted women's rights to a sex life. Sexual experience was 'the right of every human being'.[3] Similarly. Dora Marsden also stressed the importance of sexual passion. The *Freewoman,* edited by Marsden, however, was not popular with mainstream feminists. It is important to note that although Browne (**7.17**) and Dora Russell believed that sex did not have to take place within marriage, this was not a general belief even within feminist circles: Kathryn Oliver championed abstinence. (**7.16**) In contrast Marie Stopes, *Married Love* (1918) directed specifically at married couples, urged that both partners should achieve sexual satisfaction and campaigned vigorously against sex outside marriage. As Kingsley Kent argues, enjoying sex with a husband was now what constituted being 'a good wife'. As a eugenicist, Stopes, however, was concerned with middle-class women and advocated birth control since she feared the undermining of the race through over population by the working classes. She advocated birth control both from her desire to bring sexual satisfaction and from the eugeneticist agenda. As a result she opened Britain's first birth control clinic at Holloway in 1921.

The interest in 'free love', however, meant that effective contraception was necessary. As mentioned in Chapter 6, 'Health', increased attention was paid to birth control with detailed descriptions (7.7) and justifications of the various methods available, though this information still did not reach all women. (7.20) Feminists such as Stella Browne were prepared to advocate abortion as an 'absolute right' for all women. As noted in an earlier chapter, however, many women, especially those of the working classes, still lacked sexual knowledge and this was not really to change till the advent of the contraceptive pill, though the idea that woman was an 'undeveloped man' still held sway with some sections of society. (7.8)

During the twentieth century, then, the social construction of the female role moved away from the image of the 'angel in the house'. Women's sexuality was reinterpreted by the media and medical science which produced cultural definitions of the 'normal woman' and in contrast, sexual 'inversion,' abnormality, and spinsterhood. By the late forties and early fifties, however, some women such as Dr Helena Wright were advocating not only that married sex could be pleasurable, but also that it should be so with both partners working to achieve this. Wright was also important in that she championed the importance of the clitoris as opposed to the vagina as the single 'region of primary female orgasm'.[4] In advance of the second wave of feminism of the late sixties and early seventies Wright counselled women to explore their sex organs. (7.21) Sex, however, was still to remain the preserve of the married. Young women continued to be seen as the guardians of society's morals. Thus they were cautioned against petting lest they got carried away.[5]

The 1950s and 1960s saw a greater interest in writing about sex. Gorer undertook two surveys (*Exploring English character*, 1957 and *Sex and marriage in England today*, 1971), the second of which contrasted attitudes in the fifties with those of the sixties and Schofield investigated the sexual behaviour of young people (*The sexual behaviour of young people*, 1965). Care must obviously be taken with such surveys. Some respondents may exaggerate their sex lives while others may be unwilling to tell the truth. As with all oral interviewing, there is always the tendency for the interviewee to tell the interviewer what he/she thinks the other wants to hear. The interviewer must also avoid any moral judgements.

Nevertheless, bearing such provisos in mind, Gorer found that a change had occurred in what respondents considered the best qualities required in a husband/wife. Instead of emphasising 'moral and economical qualities' by 1969 what was wanted was 'understanding, love and affection'. And while it certainly seemed that Britain was not in the middle of a permanent revolution, yet there was a move towards greater sexual intimacy among the unmarried. Schofield's study of 1873 young people (934 boys and 939 girls) aged between fifteen and nineteen, found that 12 per cent of girls had had intercourse, but of those who were engaged, the figure rose to 37 per cent.

As far as contraception was concerned, the unmarried still tended not to use birth control regularly, with Schofield finding that many boys still preferred to bury their heads in the sand over the possibility of their girlfriends becoming pregnant.[6] Furthermore both Gorer and Schofield found that the double standard still held sway, with 'a sizeable minority' still believing in it.[7] Nor did the Pill appear to be promoting adultery among the married: ninety two per cent believed that fidelity was as important as it ever had been, even though the Pill 'provides absolute safety'.[8]

By the end of the 1970s, both the introduction of the pill and the Women's Liberation Movement had ensured that female sexuality was seen to be a right for all women, pre-marital sex was becoming more common, though lesbians still faced much discrimination. Attitudes to prostitution, however, had changed little, the emphasis was still on the prostitute and not the client as the cause of the 'problem'. (7.23)

7.1 The effect of the lack of sex on health

It was a fact that can hardly have escaped the notice of anyone, that women who have never had sexual commerce begin to droop when about twenty-five years of age, that they become pale and languid, that general weakness and irritability, a sort of restless, nervous fidgettyness takes possession of them, and an absorbing process goes on, their forms degenerate, their features sink, and the peculiar character of the old maid becomes apparent . . .

Richard Carlile, *Every woman's book or what is love?*, London (1828), pp. 35–6.

7.2   Causes of prostitution

To use his [Captain Millar's] own words, 'That the want of employment is frequently a cause of prostitution is obvious from the fact, that whenever the least depression of trade takes place in any of the manufacturing towns, a number of girls come to Edinburgh, where they abandon themselves to a licentious course of conduct. Some of them feel so much pleasure in dissipation and idleness, that they do not manifest any great inclination to leave it; but in general they do so as soon as they hear that there is a prospect of again being employed in the vocation to which they had formerly been accustomed'. And I learn from police authorities here that the statement is quite correct. I also know, from a conversation with Mr Troup, the superintendent of the Glasgow Lock Hospital (and who has been 20 years in charge of that institution), that such is his opinion. He thinks that at least one-half of the inmates were driven to their sad course of life from the want of honest employment and the means of subsistence. Well then may Dr Tait ask (p. 112), 'Are the guardians of the poor no way accountable for this lamentable evil? Is not the smallness of the sum which is allowed (he might have said, in most instances, the total want of provision) the cause of it? Is it not as desirable to cultivate morality as economy? And is it not much more agreeable to the dictates of humanity that such helpless individuals should be put beyond the necessity of adopting any such immoral practices for their support?' Dr Tait also specifies 'ignorance or defective education and want of religious instruction' as among the causes of prostitution; and are not the wealthier classes to blame in this respect, as well as in others, for the prevalence of this fearful vice? Averse as every moral man must be – and no immoral man is competent to the task – to enter on such a subject, I trust that no false delicacy will prevent some of our able philanthropists from getting it thoroughly probed, and the evil, if not entirely removed, at all events materially lessened.

Sanitary inquiry of the labouring population: Scotland, HL xxviii, 1842, p. 193.

7.3   Causes of prostitution

The demand for prostitution arises, then, from ill-regulated and uncontrolled desire, and may be referred to the following heads:

The natural instinct of man.

His sinful nature.

The artificial state of society rendering early marriages difficult if not impossible.

The unwillingness of many, who can afford marriage, to submit to its restraint, and incur its obligations.

To a man's calling preventing him from marrying, or debarring him when married from conjugal intercourse.

The unrestrained want and lawless demand, call for the infamous supply; but want and demand are insufficient of themselves to create supply; they are strong provoking causes, but not creative. We must go a step further to discover the sources of supply. It is derived from the vice of women, which is occasioned by

Natural desire.

Natural sinfulness.

The preferment of indolent ease to labour.

Vicious inclinations strengthened and ingrained by early neglect, or evil training, bad associates, and an indecent mode of life.

Necessity, imbued by the inability to obtain a living by honest means consequent on a fall from virtue.

Extreme poverty.

To this blacklist may be added love of drink, love of dress, love of amusement, while the fall from virtue may result either from a woman's love being bestowed on an unworthy object, who fulfils his professions of attachment by deliberately accomplishing her ruin, or from the woman's calling peculiarly exposing her to temptation.

William Acton, *Prostitution considered in its moral, social and sanitary aspects in London and other large cities and garrison towns with proposals for the mitigation and prevention of its attendant evils*, London: John Churchill & Sons (1870), p. 165.

7.4 Campaigning against the Contagious Diseases Acts

Public meeting of women at York.

A public meeting was held on Tuesday afternoon, the 13th ult., in the Merchants Hall, Fossgate, to advocate the repeal of the Contagious Diseases Acts.

Mrs Henry Richardson was called upon to preside over the meeting, which was attended by many ladies of influence, and by a large number of the wives of respectable workingmen . . . Nothing but a strong sense of duty and an earnest desire to help an oppressed and grievously wronged portion of the common sisterhood could have induced her to occupy the position she now did; but she believed that no one who feels rightly on the subject of the Contagious Diseases Acts could forbear lending a helping hand, and if needs be even raising her voice in public against them, until the solemn cry for repeal is heard through the land; for when these Acts were passed the gravest wrong ever done to woman was inflicted upon her. They must not let the matter rest; their rulers and members of Parliament must have no respite from their appeal, memorials and petitions, until these Acts were swept away, and, sooner or later, though it would be a work of time, they would succeed; in the words of 'The Ladies Protest', they undertook the work under a deep sense of duty. They had not lightly entered upon it, and they should not lightly abandon it, because they believed that in its attainment were involved not only the personal rights of the sex, but also the morality of the nation . . .

Miss Wolstenholme of Congleton, then rose to move the first resolution, 'That this meeting considers the Contagious Diseases Acts immoral, unjust, an outrage on all womanhood, a direct violation of the British constitution as regards the liberty of women; and that the working of these Acts is accompanied by great and unjustifiable cruelty. The meeting, therefore, solemnly pledges itself to seek by every legitimate means the destruction of such legislation throughout the British dominion.' Miss Wolstenholme . . . spoke with indignation of the system of introducing police spies into the subject towns to watch all the women. They dog the steps of poor women and girls who may be out late in the evening, and have been known to entrap them, by themselves making the first advances. The fallacy of the so-called voluntary submission was spoken of; the poor girls are terrified by threats into signing the hateful paper, the true meaning of which they are often quite ignorant. She urged upon all present to use their utmost endeavours to induce their husbands and brothers to make this an election question, and to refuse their votes to any man who supported legislation so terribly unjust to women.

Mrs John Casson then read an address, in which she pleaded that the subject under the consideration of the meeting is essentially a woman's question; it is the rights and liberties of women only that are assailed by these Acts; and therefore all women capable of forming a judgment should do so on this subject . . .

The resolutions were passed unanimously.

The Shield, 7 January 1871, www.attackingthedevil.co.uk/miscellanea/acts.php.

7.5   The double standard

... there are certain expressions that have become almost proverbial and till lately have passed unchallenged in conversation and in literature, plainly revealing the double standard of morality which society has accepted. One of these expressions is, 'He is only sowing his wild oats;' another is, that 'a reformed profligate makes a good husband.' The latter is a sentiment so gross that I would not repeat it, if it were not necessary to do so – as a proof of the extent of the aberration of human judgment in this matter.

Here we are at once brought into contact with the false and misleading idea that the essence of right and wrong is in some way dependent on sex. We never hear it carelessly or complacently asserted of a young wom[a]n that 'she is only sowing her wild oats.' ... It is a fact, that numbers even of moral and religious people have permitted themselves to accept and condone in man what is fiercely condemned in woman.

And do you see the logical necessity involved in this? It is that a large section of female society has to be told off – set aside, so to speak, to minister to the irregularities of the excusable man. That section is doomed to death, hurled to despair; while another section of womanhood is kept strictly and almost forcibly guarded in domestic purity. Thus even good and moral men have so judged in regard to the vice of sexual immorality as to concede in social opinion all that the male profligate can desire. This perverse social and public opinion is no small incentive to immorality. It encourages the pernicious belief that men may be profligate when young without serious detriment to their character in after-life. This is not a belief that is borne out by facts.

Marriage does not transform a man's nature, nor uproot habits that have grown with his years: the licentious imagination continues its secret blight, though the outward conduct may be restrained. The man continues to be what he was, selfish and unrestrained, though he may be outwardly moral in deference to the opinion of that 'society' which having previously excused his vices, now expects him to be moral. And what of that other being, his partner – his wife – into whose presence he brings the secret consciousness, it may be the hideous morbid fruits, of his former impurity? Can any man, with any pretension to true manliness, contemplate calmly the shame – the cruelty – of the fact that such marriages are not exceptional, especially in the upper classes?

The consequences of sins of impurity far out-last the sin itself, both in individuals and in communities. Worldly and impure men have thought, and still think, they can separate women, as I have said, into two classes – the protected and refined ladies who are not only to be good, but who are, if possible, to know nothing except what is good; and those poor outcast daughters of the people whom they purchase with money, and with whom they think they may consort in evil whenever it pleases them to do so, before returning to their own separated and protected homes.

The double standard of morality owes its continued existence very greatly to the want of a common sentiment concerning morality on the part of men and women, especially in the more refined classes of society ... Even those men who are personally pure and blameless become persuaded by the force of familiarity with male profligacy around them, that this sin in man is venial and excusable. They interpret the ignorance and silence of women as indulgent acquiescence and support ...

Obviously, then, the essence of the great work which we propose to ourselves, is to Christianize public opinion, until both in theory and practice, it shall recognize the fundamental truth that the essence of right and wrong is in no way dependent upon sex, and shall demand of men precisely the same chastity as it demands of women.

J. Butler, *Social purity* (Address given at Cambridge, May 1879) London: Morgan & Scott, pp. 8–12.

7.6 Provision at the London Lock Hospital

In a little room at the end of the ward water is laid on, and copper basins are hung by a chain to the wall; these basins are kept for the women to wash their faces. This arrangement is specially made to prevent any possible contagion. Fixed to the floor is a bidet, across which the female sits. There is here an admirable device for facilitating the cleansing of the private parts; by which means, a brass syringe, with a long pewter ball, and holding, say six ounces, she injects the lotion, and the waste fluid runs away on opening a plug fixed in the bottom of the bidet. The only improvement I could suggest was that each patient be furnished with two small napkins to dry the organs after injection. The patient always uses an injection before presenting herself to the surgeon, in order that the organs may be in a proper condition for examination, and I must say the cleanliness shown does great credit to the nurses who manage the wards.

The inspections are conducted in the following manner:- The women are introduced one at a time from the wards by one nurse into a special room, containing a properly-raised bed, with feet, similar to the one in use on the Continent. The patient ascends the steps placed by the side of the bed, lays down, places her feet in the slippers arranged for the purpose, and the house surgeon separates the labia to see if there are any sores. If no suspicion of these exists, and if the female is suffering from discharge, the speculum is at once employed. In this institution several sizes are used, and they are silvered and covered with India-rubber. The head nurse after each examination washes the speculum in a solution of permanganate of potash, then wipes it carefully, oils it ready for the next examination, so that the surgeon loses no time, and the examinations are conducted with great rapidity. In the course of one hour and three-quarters I assisted in the thorough examination of 58 women with the speculum.

William Acton, *Prostitution considered in its moral, social and sanitary aspect in London and other large cities and garrison towns with proposals for the mitigation and prevention of its attendant evils*, London: John Churchill & Sons (1870), p. 85.

7.7 Contraception

Seeing, then, that the ova are discharged at the menstrual period, and that conception depends on the fertilisation of the ova by the male, it is obvious that conception will most readily take place immediately before or after menstruation. . . .

The preventive check advocated by Dr Knowlton consists in the use of the ordinary syringe immediately after intercourse, a solution of sulphate of zinc or of alum being used instead of water. It is probable that this check is an effective one, a most melancholy proof of its effectiveness being given by Dr J. C. Barr, who, giving evidence before the Commission on the working of the Contagious Diseases Act, stated: 'Every woman who leaves the hospital is instructed in the best mode of preventing disease. These are cleanliness, injections of alum, and sulphate of zinc.' Professor Sheldon Amos, dealing with the same painful subject, refers to this evidence, and quotes Dr Barr, as saying again: 'My custom is to instruct them to keep themselves clean, to use injections and lotions.' These women are not meant to bear children, they are to be kept 'fit for use' by Her Majesty's soldiers. Apart altogether from this sad, but governmentally authorised, use of this check, there are many obvious disadvantages connected with it as a matter of taste and feeling.

The check which appears to us to be preferable, as grating on no feeling of affection or of delicacy, is that recommended by Carlile many years ago in his 'Every Woman's Book.' . . .

. . . To prevent impregnation, pass to the end of the vagina a piece of fine sponge, which should be dipped in water before being used, and which need not be removed until the morning. Dr Marion Sims, who in cases of retroversion of the uterus constantly used mechanical support to maintain the uterus in its normal position, and so make pregnancy possible, gives much useful information on the various kinds of pessaries. He sometimes used a 'small wad of cotton, not more than an inch in diameter,' which was 'secured with a string for its removal;' this was worn during the day and removed at night. He says that the woman using a pessary should be able 'to remove and replace it with the same facility that she would put on and pull off an old slipper.' There is, in fact, no kind of difficulty in the use of this check, and it has the great advantage of unobtrusiveness.

There is a preventive check attempted by many poor women which is most detrimental to health, and should therefore never be employed, namely the too-long persistence in nursing one baby, in the hope of thereby preventing the conception of another. *Nursing does not prevent conception.*

Another class of checks is distinctly criminal, i.e., the procuring of abortion. Various drugs are taken by women with this intent, and too often their use results in death, or in dangerous sickness . . .

Annie Besant, *The law of population: Its consequences and its bearing upon human conduct and morals*, London: Freethought Publishing Co. (1884), pp. 34–5.

7.8 Woman an undeveloped man

Herbert Spencer regards woman as to some extent an undeveloped man, believing that her general development has been arrested by the special activity of her sexual system, in her the procreative functions playing a more important part than in the man . . .

MENTAL RESEMBLANCES BETWEEN THE WOMAN AND THE CHILD

We have now to inquire how far the mind of the woman resembles that of the child . . . The man scarcely attains his full mental power before his

241

twenty-eighth year, the woman is mature at her eighteenth. But there is a reason for this; it is because there is little to mature in her. Wherefore women remain throughout life children, seeing only the nearest, cleaving to the present, mistaking the appearances of things for the things themselves, and placing trifles before the most weighty concerns . . . Only the man blinded by sexual passion could call the stunted, narrow-shouldered, wide-hipped, short-legged sex the beautiful one . . .'

After the climacteric we should expect the woman to approach the man in her nervous proclivities, for it is well known that disease, atrophy, or removal of the ovaries causes the female to assume many of the characteristics of the male. And such is the case. Not only does the woman approximate the masculine type in certain physical characters, but in her nervous constitution also. She becomes more active, less a creature of feeling, more intellectual. Nevertheless, she happily retains many of her feminine characteristics. The events of her procreative life, the bearing and rearing of children, years of sympathy and affection for them, leave an impress which persists to the end. In only rare cases is all womanhood thrown off, as by one famous character, who acknowledged the fact in the words: *'autrefois, quand j'etais femme.'* . . .

The Sexual Instinct in Unmarried Women – We may take it for granted that in practically all men desire comes with puberty, and continues in a greater or less degree so long as the testes remain active . . . Wherefore we may regard puberty as the normal period in the man for the first appearance of the sexual instinct. Is the like true of the human female? It is very difficult, though very desirous, to get at the truth in this matter, inasmuch as unappeased sexual craving, conscious or unconscious, is so frequently invoked by the physician to account for disordered nervous function in the unmarried woman. Of fifty-two unmarried women from whom information was obtained as to the condition of the sexual instinct before marriage, it was said to be present in twelve and absent in forty. This probably does not represent the correct proportion, for in the latter number are included thirteen special cases in which the sexual instinct never appeared; nevertheless, there is not the slightest doubt that a large proportion of women do not experience the desire in the woman were absolutely essential to congress, and if each intercourse made physiological demands upon her as great as those made upon the man – then monogamy would assuredly be fatal to woman's health; she would needs suffer from sexual excess. On the other hand, if the woman were incapable of sexual connection beyond the limits originally imposed – i.e., after conception – then probably the institution of monogamy had never been.

. . . A large number of women never marry; some from choice, many from necessity. How far, it may be asked, is spinsterhood inimical to health? The exercise of a complex generative system, which would otherwise remain quiescent, must obviously affect the entire woman, and probably, on the whole; in a beneficial way; furthermore, the awakening of the maternal instinct, and the numerous duties connected with the care of children, give the woman a purpose in life which is otherwise often lacking. To this extent the unmarried woman probably suffers ...

H. Campbell, *Differences in the nervous organisation of man and woman physiological and pathological*, London: H. K. Lewis (1891) pp. 155, 161, 175, 200.

7.9   Sexology

With reference to Lawson Tait's observation that violent assaults on women, while they do occur, are very much rarer than the frequency with which such charges are made would lead us to believe, it may be remarked that many medicolegal authorities are of the same opinion (See, *e.g.*, G. Vivian Poore's *Treatise on Medical Jurisprudence*, 1901, p. 325. This writer also remarks: 'I hold very strongly that a woman may rape a man as much as a man may rape a woman.') There can be little doubt that the plea of force is very frequently seized on by women as the easiest available weapon of defense when her connection with a man has been revealed. She has been so permeated by the current notion that no 'respectable' woman can possibly have any sexual impulses of her own to gratify that, in order to screen what she feels to be regarded as an utterly shameful and wicked, as well as foolish, act, she declares it never took place by her own will at all.

H. Ellis, *Studies in the psychology of sex*, London (1905, 1942 edn) Part II, p. 226.

7.10   'Inverts'

When they [female inverts] still retain female garments, these usually show some traits of masculine simplicity, and there is nearly always a disdain for the petty feminine articles of the toilet. Even when this is not obvious, there are all sorts of instinctive gestures and habits which may suggest to female acquaintances the remark that such a person 'ought to have been a man.' The brusque, energetic movements, the attitude of the arms, the direct speech, the inflexions of the voice, the masculine straightforwardness and sense of honour, and especially the attitude towards men, free from any suggestion either of shyness or audacity, will often suggest the underlying psychic abnormality to a keen observer.

In the habits not only is there frequently a pronounced taste for smoking cigarettes, often found in quite feminine women, but also a decided taste and toleration for cigars. There is also a dislike and sometimes incapacity for needle-work and other domestic operations, while there is often some capacity for athletics.

H. Ellis, *Studies in the psychology of sex*, London: Heinemann (1905), 1942 edn, Part II, p. 250.

7.11   Sexual impulse

There is, however, much uncertainty as to what precisely is meant by sexual frigidity or anesthesia. All the old medical authors carefully distinguish between the heat of sexual desire and the actual presence of pleasure in coitus; many modern writers also properly separate *libido* from *voluptas*, since it is quite possible to experience sexual desires and not to be able to obtain their gratification during sexual intercourse, and it is possible to hold ... that women naturally have stronger sexual impulses than men, but are more liable than men to experience sexual anesthesia ... it is very much more difficult ... to obtain quite precise and definite data concerning the absence of either *voluptas* or *libido* in a woman. Even if we accept the statement of the woman who asserts that she has either or both, the statement of their absence is by no means equally conclusive and final ... Some of the most marked characteristics of the sexual impulse in women, moreover, – its association with modesty, its comparatively late development, its seeming passivity, its need of stimulation, – all combine to render difficult the final pronouncement that a woman is sexually frigid ... The fact that a woman is cold with one man or even with a succession of men by no means shows that she is not apt to experience sexual emotions; it merely shows that these men have not been able to arouse them ... the female throughout nature not only requires much

244

loving, but is usually fastidious in the choice of a lover. In the human species this natural fact is often disguised and perverted. Women are not always free to choose the man whom they would prefer as a lover, nor even free to find out whether the man they prefer sexually fits them; they are, moreover, very often extremely ignorant of the whole question of sex, and the victims of the prejudice and false conventions they have been taught. On the one hand, they are driven into an unnatural primness and austerity; on the other hand, they rebound to an equally unnatural facility or even promiscuity. Thus it happens that the men who find that a large number of women are not so facile as they themselves are, and as they have found a large number of women to be, rush to the conclusion that women tend to be 'sexually anesthetic.' . . . it is very doubtful whether we can assert that a woman is ever absolutely without the aptitude for sexual satisfaction. She may unquestionably be without any conscious desire for actual coitus . . . All we can assert with some degree of positiveness in some cases is that she has not manifested sexual gratification, more particularly as shown by the occurrence of the orgasm, but that is very far indeed from warranting us to assert that she never will experience such gratification or still less that she is organically incapable of experiencing it.

H. Ellis, *Studies in the psychology of sex*, London: Heinemann (1905), 1942 edn, Part II, pp. 204–5.

7.12 Nobler womanhood

The whole evil of commercial prostitution arises out of the domination of Man in matters of sex. Better indeed were a Saturnalia of *free* men and women than the spectacle which as it is our great cities present at night. Here in Sex, the woman's instincts are, as a rule, so clean, so direct, so well-rooted in the needs of the race, that except for man's domination they would scarcely have suffered this perversion. Sex in man is an unorganised passion, an individual need or impetus; but in woman it may more properly be termed a constructive instinct, with the larger signification that that involves. Even more than man should woman be 'free' to work out the problem of her sex-relations as may commend itself best to her – hampered as little as possible by legal, conventional, or economic considerations, and relying chiefly on her own native sense and tact in the matter. Once thus free – free from the mere cash-nexus to a husband, from the money-slavery of the streets, from the nameless terrors of social opinion, and from the threats of the choice of perpetual virginity or perpetual bondage would she not indeed choose her career (whether that of wife and mother, or that of free companion, or one of single blessedness) far better for herself than it is chosen for her to-day – regarding really in some degree the needs of society, and the welfare of children, and the sincerity and durability of her relations to her lovers, and less the petty motives of profit and fear?

The point is that the whole conception of a nobler Womanhood for the future has to proceed candidly from this basis of her complete freedom as to the disposal of her sex, and from the healthy conviction that, with whatever individual aberrations, she will on the whole use that freedom rationally and well. And surely this – in view too of some decent education of the young, on sexual matters – is not too great a demand to make on our faith in women. If it is, then indeed we are undone – for short of this we can only retain them in servitude, and society in its form of the hell on earth which it largely is to-day . . .

Edward Carpenter, *Love's coming-of-age* (1906),
www.sacred-texts.com/lgbt/lca/ pp. 61–3.

7.13 'The new morality'

For, to most of us – the great common mass – the Open Gateway through which we may lose – and find – ourselves in an 'O Altitudo' must be the gateway of sexual passion. This will have to be for us the holy ground, for walking whereon we make due preparation . . . Sex-love is, or ought to be, the most highly wrought experience that the conscious universe has yet produced. Men and women are likely to get out of it, results in proportion to that which they put into it. A great many people put into it nothing, and they are disappointed when they get out of it – nothing. A Dante put a soul into it, and brought out of it a new heaven. Most women have put their most secret hopes into it, and they have brought out of it a new sense. We shall put more into it, and not less, and, in proportion as we value our hopes, we shall defend it against the conventions of the stupid and the slow of understanding.

Dora Marsden, *The Freewoman*, 28 December 1911.

7.14   The new woman

The Modern Woman with her clubs, her debates, her politics, her freedom of action and costume, is forming a public opinion of her own at an amazing rate; and seems to be preparing to 'spank' and even thump the Middleclass Man in real earnest! What exactly evolution may be preparing for us, we do not know, but apparently some lively sparring matches between the sexes. Of course all will not be smooth sailing. The women of the new movement are naturally largely drawn from those in whom the maternal instinct is not especially strong; also from those in whom the sexual instinct is not preponderant. Such women do not altogether represent their sex; some are rather mannish in temperament; some are 'homogenic,' that is, inclined to attachments to their own, rather than to the opposite, sex; some are ultra-rationalizing and braincultured; to many, children are more or less a bore; to others, man's sex-passion is a mere impertinence, which they do not understand, and whose place they consequently misjudge. It would not do to say that the majority of the new movement are thus out of line, but there is no doubt that a large number are; and the course of their progress will be correspondingly curvilinear.

Perhaps the deficiency in maternal instinct would seem the most serious imputation. But then, who knows (as we have said) what evolution is preparing?

Sometimes it seems possible that a new sex is on the make – like the feminine neuters of Ants and Bees – not adapted for childbearing, but with a marvellous and perfect instinct of social service, indispensable for the maintenance of the common life. Certainly most of those who are freeing themselves – often with serious struggles – from the 'lady' chrysalis are fired with an ardent social enthusiasm; and if they may personally differ in some respects from the average of their sex, it is certain that their efforts will result in a tremendous improvement in the general position of their more commonplace sisters.

Edward Carpenter, *Love's coming-of-age* (1906), pp. 66–8.

7.15   'The individualism of motherhood and the "normal" woman'

To the Editor of the Freewoman
. . . The letter of Helen Winter, which appears in the issue of March 7th, seems to strike the highest note that can be struck. I think the writer

has grasped the whole of that vast question – the individualism of motherhood . . .

What Helen Winter feels, and is honest enough to say, is that she wants to bear children for her own ends, and she seeks no aids from anyone.

Here is the real spirit of independence, of freedom, that a woman with a large and open mind really aspires after. It is what we all want, I am sure – not to be dependent on anyone but ourselves. Oh, for such glorious freedom! I speak feelingly on this subject, as I have never in my own life been independent, and, moreover, have been always in more or less adverse cirumstances, where one is at war with one's surroundings, from a limited, narrowly defined home life to that most miserable of all conditions – an unhappy marriage, wherein I still exist.

I have often wondered whether any of your correspondents, with many of whom I feel so entirely sympathetic, could find a remedy for my own case? I am a clergyman's wife, which, I suppose, makes difficulties even more complicated; one is afraid of damaging other people, giving unnecessary pain and trouble in so many ways, as one is constantly driven up against the brick walls of narrow thought and convention. Strength to break away, one could have; but – and here is the difficulty – I have a child. Again, I am absolutely dependent on my husband; also, I am neither very young nor very strong, so how could I support myself?

Your correspondent, C. Gasquoine Hartley, touches this subject in the last paragraph of her article, 'The Dangerous Age'; but she only states the fact, and offers no remedy – women must be free, free to love and work. Yes; but how? I should like to say something about the other correspondent, 'Normal' Woman. I cannot help thinking that we are still held back, to a great extent, by false modesty from acknowledging that we are in reality much the same as men in regards to physical desires. I do not agree that the sexual appetite in women is weaker than in men; it is different, that is all . . . It is, I suppose, quite true of most women that they do not want to satisfy a physical desire without, at the same time, satisfying spiritual ones; therefore I suppose one might say most women would only give themselves for love. But there are women who dissociate the spiritual from the bodily appetite, and satisfy the latter without the former just as man can. There are some, in fact, to whom it is a necessity of health so to do.

It seems to me a contradiction of terms and absolutely wrong in every way to say that two people who have one mind and one spirit may not also be one flesh because they are not married, while, if they are married, the husband may insist on his 'rights,' no matter what her feelings of repugnance or distaste may be.

If there is one thing in which there ought to be freedom for women, it is in this matter, as there are hardly two feminine natures alike, and nowhere so great as in this, sexual temperament.

A would-be freewoman.

The Freewoman, 28 December 1911.

7.16 'Asceticism and passion'

... I do hope with all the earnestness of which I am capable that the new 'morality,' which would permit for women the same degrading laxity in sex matters which is indulged in by most of the lower animals, including man, will be choked and crushed before it grows any stronger.

How can we possibly be Freewomen if, like the majority of men, we become the slaves of our lower appetites? This is surely a strange method of advancement and emancipation, and I am not at all prepared to travel this road myself, thanking the new 'moralists' all the same. I am neither a prude nor a Puritan, but I am an apostle of the practice of self-restraint in sex matters.

What is it that raises us above the brute level but the exercise of self-restraint?

'What proof,' E.M. Watson asks, 'is there that the abstinence of many single women is injurious to them?' What proof, indeed? I am an unmarried woman, nearly thirty years of age, and have always practised abstinence; and though I am not a powerful person, I enjoy the best of health, and have never troubled a doctor since I was six months old. My married women friends, on the contrary, have always some complaint or something wrong.

Who has not seen the girl married at twenty almost immediately degenerate into a nervous, haggard wreck? I deny absolutely that abstinence has any bad effect on my health.

Wishing the Freewoman all success,
Kathlyn Oliver.

The Freewoman, 15 February 1912.

7.17 'The chastity of continence?'

... E.M. Watson asks: 'What proof is there that the abstinence of many single women is injurious to them?' And Kathlyn Oliver, for whose clear and courageous statement on a most important subject one must feel grateful, says: 'I deny absolutely that abstinence has any bad effect on my health.' ... and one must admit that there are many women whose constitution and temperament are what Professor Forel calls 'sexually anaesthetic,' without thereby suffering any lack of mental or motor energy, or of capacity for affection, or even the maternal instinct. Let women so constituted by all means abstain from what affords them no pleasure; but do not, therefore, let them make their temperamental coldness into a rigid standard for others.

There is probably a far greater range of variation sexually among women than among men, and the sister or friend of the cold-blooded woman may be capable of intense sexual emotion. I have known specimens of all varieties intimately, and I can assure E.M. Watson and Kathlyn Oliver that the health, the happiness, the social usefulness, and the mental capacity of many women have been seriously impaired and sometimes totally ruined by the unnatural conditions of their lives. That there is a psychological side to the question as well as a physiological, I should be the last to deny, nor do I deny that many women have been made ill and wretched by the unrestrained indulgence of married life with ignorant or brutal husbands. There is surely a middle path between total abstinence and excess; the abuse of a natural pleasure does not make it entirely injurious and to be deprecated.

May I remind your correspondents that sex is only beginning to be scientifically studied in its various aspects? Also that what is needed, above all things, is a spirit of mutual tolerance, comprehension, and help among women and between men and women. For this reason I deplore the reference in Miss Oliver's letter to 'the lower animals, including man.' The lower animals, by the way, are sexually active only at certain times of the year, unless their normal habits have been broken up by domestication . . .

Sexual abstinence implies absolute abstention from all forms of what Havelock Ellis terms 'auto-erotism,' thus including imaginative and psychic excitation in its various forms. How many single women have entirely refrained from these practices? I imagine that, if reliable statistics were obtainable, they would very much astonish our friends . . . they constitute sexual indulgence just as truly as do normal sexual relations; and I believe that, without having recourse to their aid, many

women would find abstinence from normal sexual relations impossible
...

A new subscriber (Stella Brown), *The Freewoman*, 22 February 1912.

7.18   Results of men's sexual licence

It did not need the doctors' manifesto to warn the more instructed amongst women that prostitution and the diseases caused by it are a menace to themselves and their children. But vast numbers of women are still without this knowledge. Innocent wives are infected by their husbands. They suffer torments; their health is ruined; their power to become mothers is destroyed, or else they become the mothers of diseased, crippled, blind, or insane children. But they are not told the reason of all this. Their doctor and their husband keep them in ignorance, so that they cannot even protect themselves from future danger.

Healthy girls enter into marriage without the smallest idea of the risk they are incurring. Nobody tells them, as Dr. John W. Barrett tells us in his article in the Bedrock, the scientific review, that 'we know, from very careful insurance medical records, that the great majority of men put themselves in the way of infection before marriage' ...

It is therefore hardly too much to say that out of every four men there is only one who can marry without risk to his bride. Such facts are terrible indeed, and the sooner they are grasped the better for the individual and for the race.

Even after marriage, danger arises over and over again unless the husband abstains from immoral acts ...

We repeat, then, that for women to establish their freedom and equality with men, apart from any question of maternity and sex, is a necessary step towards the abolition of prostitution. It is largely because men have been too much persuaded of women's unlikeness to themselves, that they have wanted to put and keep them in subjection and exploit them for purposes of vice. For the abolition of prostitution, it is necessary that men shall hold women in honour, not only as mothers, but as human beings, who are like and equal unto themselves ...

And here we may, perhaps, deal with the statement made by some men, that women suffer who are not mated with men, and that what they are pleased to term 'the unsatisfied desires' of women are a problem. Now, in the old days when marriage was the only career open to women, those who did not marry regarded themselves, and were regarded, as failures – just as a lawyer might who never got a brief, as a doctor might who never got a customer. But nowadays the unmarried women have a life full of joy and interest. They are not mothers of children of their flesh, but they can serve humanity, they can do work that is useful or beautiful. Therefore their life is complete. If they find a man worthy of them, a man fit physically and morally to be their husband, then they are ready to marry, but they will not let desire, apart from love and reason, dominate their life or dictate their action . . .

Christabel Pankhurst, *The great scourge and how to end it*, Lincoln's Inn House (1913), reprinted in Sheila Jeffreys (ed.) *The sexuality debates*, London: Routledge & Kegan Paul (1987), pp. 315, 331, 337–8.

7.19 Will women become sexually unattractive if they work?

What if, the increased culture and mental activity of women necessary for her entrance into the new fields of labour, however desirable in other ways for herself and the race, should result in a diminution, or in an absolute abolition of the sexual attraction and affection, which in all ages of the past has bound, the two halves of humanity together? What if, though the stern and unlovely manual labours of the past have never affected her attractiveness for the male of her own society, nor his for her; yet the performance by woman of intellectual labours, or complex and interesting manual labour, and her increased intelligence and width, should render the male objectionable to her, and the woman undesirable to the male; so that the very race itself might become extinct through the dearth of sexual affection? What, and if, the woman ceases to value the son she bears, and to feel desire for and tenderness to the man who begets him; and the man to value and desire the woman and her offspring? Would not such a result exceed, or at least equal in its evil to humanity, anything which could result from the degeneration and parasitism of woman? . . . If the race is to decay and become extinct on earth, might it not as well be through the parasitism and decay of woman, as through the decay of the sexual instinct? . . .

On the other hand, if it be supposed that the possession of wealth or the means of earning it makes the human female objectionable to the male, all history and all daily experience negates it! . . .

... The female doctor or lawyer earning a thousand a year will always, and to-day certainly does, find more suitors than had she remained a governess or cook, labouring as hard, earning thirty pounds.

The study of all races in all ages, proves that the greater the freedom of woman in any society, the higher the sexual value put upon her by the males of that society.

So axiomatic is the statement that the value of the female to the male varies as her freedom, that, given an account of any human society in which the individual female is highly valued, it will be perfectly safe to infer the comparative social freedom of woman; and, given a statement as to the high degree of freedom of woman in a society, it will be safe to infer the great sexual value of the individual woman to man.

Finally, if the suggestion, that men and women will cease to be attractive to one another if women enter modern fields of labour, be based on the fact that her doing so may increase her intelligence and enlarge her intellectual horizon, it must be replied that the whole trend of human history absolutely negates the supposition. There is absolutely no ground for the assumption that increased intelligence and intellectual power diminishes sexual emotion in the human creature of either sex. The ignorant savage, whether in ancient or modern societies, who violates and then clubs a female into submission, may be dominated, and is, by sex emotions of a certain class; but not less dominated have been the most cultured, powerful, and highly differentiated male intelligences that the race has produced. A Mill, a Shelley, a Goethe, a Schiller, a Pericles, have not been more noted for vast intellectual powers, than for the depth and intensity of their sexual emotions.

O. Schreiner, *Women and labour*, London: T. Fisher, Unwin (1911), pp. 225–34.

7.20 A woman's right to choose

It [the essay] starts with the (as yet still rather unpopular) assumption that women are really human beings, and that freedom of choice and deliberate intention are necessary for them in their sexual relations and their maternity, if they are to make anything of their status and opportunities in certain communities to-day, and if they are to breed a race of greater powers and finer standards of value.

The maternal death-rate and its associated trail of disease and disability have spectacular force and wide appeal as arguments for the legalisation of abortion. They stir many sympathisers whom their logical implications and the entire case for freedom would – at least initially – alarm or repel. The same is true of those much rarer – but still not infrequent – and peculiarly pitiful cases where a young girl or a woman is made pregnant by rape or criminal assault, or through incest as the result of over-crowding or parental negligence or abuse. Such suffering is an indictment of the whole social system that tolerates its infliction and is the ultimate expression of the view of women as vessels – of 'honour' and 'dishonour' as the case may be – for men's use and as automatic breeding machines. But these cases do not include the whole of the demand for women's right to abortion. That is based – as I see it – on justice rather than on pity; on the dignity of knowledge rather than the pathos of ignorance.

An absolute right

The woman's right to abortion is an absolute right, as I see it, up to the viability of her child. It does not depend upon certainty of death for her if the child is carried to term, though such a certainty or probability is, of course, a double claim to this relief. It does not depend on damage or permanent injury to her physical or mental health, whether certain or probable, if her child is born at term. It does not depend on the number of her previous confinements: the suggestion, put forward by some vigorous and veteran agitators for abortion law reform, that the woman should first supply a quota of at least two children, seems to me to disregard the individual needs, nature, and conditions of women. Neither does the right to refuse an unwanted child depend on economic conditions, though these supply an almost universal argument in this era of unemployment. Neither does the right we claim depend on having obtained the sanction of the Law and the Church to live with some special man, to bear his name, and share his home and means. Abortion legal for married women only would be the final climax of the illogical absurdity of our respectability complex; but it is certain to be advocated in some quarters, and it is a perfect example of the narrowest Trade Union spirit. After all, is not contraception for married women only the slogan of much organized feminist respectability?

The right to abortion does not depend on crimes which the conventions of romantic tradition deem worse than death, and which laws justifiably treat as second only to murder. (It is an interesting question how far the reprobation of rape is a defence of women's dignity and personality and how far it is subconscious 'compensation,' communal jealousy, and property defence.) These crimes are barbarous and tragic; but the victim, even the girl in her early teens, is legally compelled to carry and bring to birth the results of sexual violence, whose begetter is punished with the full rigour of the law. Cannot chivalry here be tempered with reason, justice, and common sense?

Abortion must be the key to a new world for women, not a bulwark for things as they are, economically nor biologically. Abortion should not be either a perquisite of the legal wife only, nor merely a last remedy against illegitimacy. It should be available for any woman, without insolent inquisitions, nor ruinous financial charges, nor tangles of red tape. For our bodies are our own.

Stella Browne, *The right to abortion*, Allen & Unwin (1935), pp. 13, 28, 29, 31.

7.21   How to find the clitoris

In the author's opinion it is important that every woman who is about to be married should not only know that her clitoris exists and why, but that she should find out exactly where it is and what it looks like. Women in general take an endless interest in their faces, study them in the mirror and know all their details by heart; but their usual attitude to their far more important sexual equipment is one of fear and ludicrously complete ignorance. It is easy to get a clear description from the many books now available, and then to arrange a good light and take a mirror and identify all the parts described. To find the clitoris, the thighs must be separated widely enough for comfortable vision, then if two fingers hold apart the larger lips, the mucous membrane-covered hood will be seen immediately inside the front end of the space between the larger lips. The hood can be gently drawn backwards by the finger tips and inside will be seen a small, smooth rounded body (sometimes it is very small and only just visible), which glistens in a good light. This is the clitoris.

Helena Wright, *More about the sex factor in marriage*, London: Williams & Northgate (1954 edn), p. 59.

7.22   Views of an 18-year-old girl student working for the 'A' Levels

If a husband finds his wife having an affair with another man, what should he do? Review the situation; decide whose fault it is. If his, they should be reconciled; if the wife's fault, he must decide if it's likely to be repeated or not and separate if he feels she's going to be often unfaithful and he couldn't live with her.

If a wife finds her husband having an affair with another woman, what do you think she should do? Her thinking will be complicated if she has children. She should talk it out with her husband, because often husbands are only trying to get lost youth back by having an affair.

How do you feel about a married man who has an affair with a woman he does not really love? Man's natural inclination; I accept it regretfully.

How do you feel about a married woman who has an affair with a man she does not really love? Sorry for her; obviously something lacking in her married life, if she's not a nymphomaniac.

Should a young man's sexual experience before marriage be restricted to one person or person he loves, or just anyone he feels attracted to?' A young man doesn't want to be emotionally involved with many girls, only physically; he won't feel 'in love' very often.

Should a young woman's sexual experience before marriage be restricted to one person or person she loves, or just anyone she feels attracted to? She will most probably convince herself she is in love at the time.

How old were you when you first had full intercourse? Sixteen.

About how often do you have intercourse? Twice a week if I like the boy. It depends on exams! . . .

On balance, do you think the invention of the pill for birth control a good or bad thing? A good thing; much safer; compared to Durex much more aesthetic.

Now that the pill provides absolute safety, do you think faithfulness is or is not as important as ever in marriage? Just as important; it makes no difference; it means that often people who were faithful before were only faithful out of fear of pregnancy.

Which birth-control method do you use? The pill.

G. Gorer, *Sex and marriage in England today*, Nelson, 1971 pp. 225–7.

7.23 'We're not criminals': Prostitutes organise

'If the law was changed we could work together and be safe from attacks, Blokes think, "She's only an old pro, I can do what I like to her," ' Susan was talking about the dangers of being a prostitute. She has been working with the group since it began: 'I've been thinking about changing the law for years. We're not criminals but the law is always after us. We're picked up all the time, day after day. And now they're thinking of putting the fines up to £100. My friends say "We're on the streets to feed the kids; I can't pay that, they'll have to send me to prison." ' . . .

'The mere charge means you're a "common prostitute", which means you have three previous offences against you.' Eileen points out that prostitutes are the only people who have previous convictions used against them in court. (NB Men accused of rape *don't*).

'We can't do anything right. If you walk down the road with a boyfriend he's accused of poncing. If you walk down the road alone you're picked up.' Susan has a friend whose husband left her with four children; she's been fined £35 for soliciting. 'Sometimes,' says Louise, 'the law actually forces women on to the streets. That woman is on social security. She has to earn the money for the fine or go to prison.' . . .

PROS is opposed to any form of licensing system. 'When we were working on our programme, all the pros were against any regulation and against licensed brothels.' Eileen explains that 'they want to control their own lives and work without being intimidated by anyone' . . .

They are all critical of feminists who haven't taken up the issue of the prostitution laws. Eileen and Louise agreed: 'We want women's liberation to think about the whole thing and discuss it, but not just *use* it. They have used the word 'prostitute' in a really nasty way – about housewives, to sum up their idea of the exploited situation of women. But we need allies to lobby and to publicize our programme. And we need practical help, centres to meet in and money to run the campaign.'

Spare Rib 56, March 1977.

Notes

1 Sheila Jeffreys, *The spinster and her enemies: Feminism and sexuality 1880–1930*, North Melbourne: Spinefex (1997).

2 Margaret Jackson, *The real facts of life: Feminism and the politics of sexuality c.1850–1940*, London: Taylor and Francis (1994), p. 119.
3 *Freewoman*, 22 February, 21 March 1912, quoted in S. Bruley, *Women in Britain since 1900*, Basingstoke: Macmillan (1999), p. 14.
4 Helena Wright, *More about the sex factor in marriage*, London: Williams & Northgate (1954, 5th edn), p. 49.
5 G. D. Shultz, *It's time you knew*, London: Darwen Finlayson (1956), p. 50.
6 G. Gorer, *Sex and marriage in England today*, London: Nelson (1971), p. 74.
7 Gorer, *Sex and marriage*, p. 156. M. Schofield, *The sexual behaviour of young people*, London: Longmans (1965), p. 248.
8 Gorer, *Sex and marriage*, p. 302.

Further reading

Women and the law

Holcombe, L., *Wives and property reform of the Married Women's Property Law in nineteenth-century England*, Toronto: University of Toronto Press (1983).

Shanley, M. L., *Feminism, marriage and the law in Victorian England*, Princeton: Princeton University Press (1989).

Stave, S., *Married women's separate property in England, 1660–1833*, Cambridge, Massachusetts: Harvard University Press (1990).

Marriage, motherhood, the cult of domesticity and the family

Davidoff, L., Doolittle, M., Fink, J. & Holden, K., *The family story blood contract and intimacy 1830–1960*, London: Longman (1999).

Gillis, John R., *For better, for worse: British marriages 1600 to the present*, New York and Oxford: Oxford University Press (1985).

Land., H, 'Eleanor Rathbone and the economy of the Family', in Smith, H. (ed.), *British feminism in the twentieth-century* (1990).

Jalland, Patricia, *Women, marriage, and politics, 1860–1914*, Oxford: Clarendon Press (1986); Oxford and New York: Oxford University Press (1988).

Lewis, Jane, (ed.), Labour and love: women's experience of home and family, 1850–1940, Oxford: Blackwell (1986).

Lewis, Jane, *Women in Britain since 1945: Women, family and the state in the post-war Years*, Oxford: Blackwell (1992).

MacFarlane, Alan, *Marriage and love in England: Modes of reproduction 1300–1840*, Oxford and New York: Blackwell (1986).

259

Macnicol, John, *The movement for family allowances, 1918–45*, London: Heinemann (1980).

Perkin, Joan, *Women and marriage in nineteenth-century England*, London: Routledge, and Chicago: Lyceum Books (1989).

Rathbone, Eleanor, *The disinherited family*, London: Arnold (1924).

Roberts, Elizabeth, *A Woman's place: An oral history of working-class women, 1890–1940*, Oxford: Blackwell (1985).

Roberts, Elizabeth, *Women and families: An oral history 1940–1970*, Oxford: Blackwell (1995).

Spensky, Martine, 'Producers of legitimacy: Homes for unmarried mothers in the 1950s', in Smart, Carol (ed.) *Regulating womanhood: Historical essays on marriage motherhood and sexuality*, London: Routledge (1992).

Spring Rice, Margery (ed.), *Working-class wives: their health and conditions*, Harmondsworth: Penguin Books (1939).

Education

Bennett, D., *Emily Davies and the liberation of women*, London: Andre Deutsch (1990).

Copelman, Dina, M., *London's women teachers: Gender, class, and feminism, 1870–1930*, London and New York: Routledge (1996).

Dyhouse, Carol, *No distinction of sex? Women in British universities 1870–1939*, London: University College London (UCL) Press (1995).

Hunt, Felicity (ed.), *Lessons for life: The schooling of girls and women 1850–1950*, Oxford and New York: Blackwell (1987).

Jordan, Ellen, 'Making good wives and mothers'? The transformation of middle-class girls' education in nineteenth-century Britain', *History of Education Quarterly*, 31(4) (1991), pp. 439–62.

Kamm, Josephine, *Hope deferred: Girls' education in English history*, London: Methuen (1965).

Montgomery, Fiona, *Edge Hill University College: A history 1885–1997*, London: Phillimore (1997).

Moore, L., 'Educating for the women's sphere: Domestic training versus intellectual discipline', in Gordon, E. & Breitenbach, E. (eds), *Out of bounds: Women in Scottish society 1800–1945*, Edinburgh: Edinburgh University Press (1992).

Oram, Alison, *Women teachers and feminist politics, 1900–1939*, Manchester and New York: Manchester University Press (1996).

Purvis, June, *Hard Lessons: The lives and education of working-class women in nineteenth-century England,* Cambridge: Polity Press, and Minneapolis: University of Minnesota Press (1989).

Purvis, June, *A history of women's education in England*, Milton Keynes, Buckinghamshire, and Philadelphia: Open University Press (1991).

Spender, Dale (ed.), *The education papers: Women's quest for equality in Britain, 1850–1912*, London and New York: Routledge & Kegan Paul (1987).

Work

Beddoe, Deirdre, *Back to home and duty: Women between the wars 1918–1939*, London: Pandora (1989).

Braybon, Gail & Summerfield, Penny, *Out of the cage: Women's experiences in two World Wars*, London: Pandora (1987).

Glucksmann, Miriam, *Women assemble: Women workers and the new industries in interwar Britain,* London: Routledge (1990).

Hill, Bridget, *Servants: English domestics in the eighteenth century*, Oxford: Clarendon (1996).

Honeyman, Katrina, *Women, gender and industrialisation in England, 1700–1870*, Basingstoke: Macmillan (2000).

Hudson, Pat & Lee, W. R. (eds), *Women's work and the family economy in historical perspective*, Manchester: Manchester University Press (1990).

Purvis, J. (ed.), *Women's history: Britain 1850–1945*, Bristol: UCL Press (1995).

Rose, Sonya, *Limited livelihoods: Gender and class in nineteenth-century England*, London: Routledge (1992).

Sharpe, Pamela, *Adapting to capitalism: Working women in the English economy, 1700–1850*, Basingstoke: Macmillan (1996).

Snell, Keith, *Annals of the labouring poor: Social change and agrarian England 1660–1900*, Cambridge: Cambridge University Press (1985).

Wightman, Claire, *More than munitions: Women, work and the engineering industries 1900–1950*, London: Longman (1999).

Politics

Chalus, Elaine & Montgomery, Fiona, 'Women and politics' in Barker, H. & Chalus, E. (eds), *British women's history*, London: Routledge (2005).

Graves, Pamela, M., *Labour women: Women in British working-class politics 1918–1939*, Cambridge: Cambridge University Press (1994).

Harrison, Brian, *Separate spheres: The opposition to women's suffrage in Britain*, London: Croom Helm (1978).

Harrison, Brian, *Prudent revolutionaries: Portraits of British feminists between the wars*, Oxford: Clarendon Press (1991).

Holton, Sandra Stanley, *Feminism and democracy: Women's suffrage and reform politics in Britain, 1900–1918*, Cambridge: Cambridge University Press (1986).

Joannou, M. & Purvis, J. (eds), *The Women's Suffrage Movement: New feminist perspectives*, Manchester: Manchester University Press (1998).

Law, Cheryl, *Suffrage and power: The Women's Movement, 1918–1928*, London: I. B. Taurus (1999).

Pugh, Martin, *The march of the women: A revisionist analysis of the campaign for women's suffrage, 1866–1914*, Oxford: Oxford University Press (2000).

Health

Brookes, B., *Abortion in England 1900–1967*, London: Croom Helm (1988).

Donnison, J., *Midwives and medical men: A history of interprofessional rivalries and women's rights*, London: Heinemann (1977).

Garcia J., Kilpatrick, R. & Richards, M. (eds), *The politics of maternity care: Services for childbearing women in twentieth-century Britain*, Oxford: Clarendon (1990).

Harrison, Brian, 'Women's health and the Women's Movement in Britain 1840–1940', in C. Webster (ed.), *Biology, medicine and society 1840–1940*, Cambridge: Cambridge University Press (1981).

Jalland, Pat & Hooper, John, *Women from birth to death 1830–1914*, Brighton: Harvester Press (1986).

Koven, S. & Michel, S. (eds), *Mothers of a new world: Maternalist politics and the origins of welfare states*, London: Routledge (1993).

McLaren, A., *A history of contraception*, Oxford: Blackwell (1990).

Oakley, A., *The captured womb*, Oxford: Basil Blackwell (1984).

Roberts, M. M. & Mizuta, T. (eds), *The mothers: controversies of motherhood*, London: Routledge/Thoemmes (1994).

Showalter, E., *The female malady: women, madness and English culture 1830–1980*, London: Virago (1987).

Sexuality

Bland, L., *Banishing the beast: Feminism, sex and morality*, London: Taurus Parke (2001).

Collins, Marcus, *Modern love: An intimate history of men and women in twentieth-century Britain*, London: Atlantic (2003).

Cook, Hera, *The long sexual revolution: English women, sex and contraception, 1800–1975*, Oxford: Oxford University Press (2004).

Hall, Lesley, *Sex, gender and social change in Britain since 1880*, London: Macmillan (2000).

Jackson, L., *Child sexual abuse in Victorian England*, London: Routledge (2000).

Mason, Michael, *The making of Victorian sexuality*, Oxford: Oxford University Press (1994).

Mort, Frank, *Dangerous sexualities: Medico-moral politics in England since 1830*, London: Routledge and Kegan Paul (1987).

Porter, R. & Hall, L., *The facts of life: The creation of sexual knowledge in Britain, 1650–1950*, New Haven and London: Yale University Press (1995).

Showalter, Elaine, *Sexual anarchy: Gender and culture at the Fin de Siècle*, London: Virago (1992).

Walkowitz, J., *Prostitution and Victorian Society*, Cambridge: Cambridge University Press (1980).

Walkowitz, Judith, *City of dreadful delight: Narratives of sexual danger in late-Victorian London*, London: Virago (1992).

Weeks, J., *Sex, politics and society: The regulation of sexuality since 1800*, London: Longman (1989).

Index